# Religion and Contemporary Management

# Religion and Contemporary Management

## Moses as a Model for Effective Leadership

Arthur J. Wolak

ANTHEM PRESS

Anthem Press
An imprint of Wimbledon Publishing Company
*www.anthempress.com*

This edition first published in UK and USA 2016
by ANTHEM PRESS
75–76 Blackfriars Road, London SE1 8HA, UK
or PO Box 9779, London SW19 7ZG, UK
and
244 Madison Ave #116, New York, NY 10016, USA

*British Library Cataloguing-in-Publication Data*
A catalogue record for this book is available from the British Library.

*Library of Congress Cataloging-in-Publication Data*
Names: Wolak, Arthur J., author.
Title: Religion and contemporary management : Moses as a model for
effective leadership / Arthur J. Wolak.
Description: New York : Anthem Press, 2016. |
Includes bibliographical references and index.
Identifiers: LCCN 2016036847 | ISBN 9781783085996 (hardback : alk. paper)
Subjects: LCSH: Moses (Biblical leader) | Leadership in the Bible. |
Leadership. | Management.
Classification: LCC BS580.M6 W65 2016 | DDC 222/.1092–dc23
LC record available at https://lccn.loc.gov/2016036847

ISBN-13: 978-1-78308-599-6 (Hbk)
ISBN-10: 1-78308-599-1 (Hbk)

This title is also available as an e-book.

To my mother, Elizabeth Wolak, and in memory of my father, Dr. Edward Wolak, who always encouraged a traditional focus on study as a result of Jewish culture, tradition and education in their native Poland; to my wife, Anna, and my brother, Richard; and to my children, Jacob, Joshua and Julia, who may one day read this book among the broader corpus of biblical and rabbinic sources and become effective leaders in any endeavor they choose to pursue.

*"Never again did there arise in Israel a prophet like Moses—whom the Lord singled out, face to face."*

—*Deuteronomy 34:10*

*"When the righteous become great the people rejoice, but when the wicked dominate the people groan."*

—*Proverbs 29:2*

# CONTENTS

*Foreword*                                                    ix
    Ruth Sandberg

*Foreword*                                                    xi
    Larry Pate

*Acknowledgments*                                             xv

*About the Author*                                           xvii

Introduction                                                  1

1.   Ancient Leadership for Present Times        5

2.   Defining Leadership                         13

3.   Leaders and Managers                        27

4.   Heroism, Charisma and Their Limitations     37

5.   Empathic Leadership                         49

6.   Humility—the Antithesis of Arrogance        63

7.   Moses' Essential Leadership Skills          89

8.   Assessing Moses' Leadership Style           119

*Glossary*                                                   129

*Bibliography*                                               137

*Index*                                                      143

# FOREWORD

At first blush, the ancient biblical figure of Moses does not appear to have anything in common with today's political or financial leaders. What Dr. Arthur Wolak has accomplished in his work is to show us that, in fact, Moses has a great deal to teach contemporary leaders. Dr. Wolak also succeeds in connecting the most current work on effective leadership with the figure of Moses, as well as in demonstrating that all the leadership skills most desired today have their roots in the text of the Hebrew Bible as personified by Moses.

Dr. Wolak carefully and thoroughly outlines an amazing array of leadership characteristics described in the Hebrew Bible that are associated with Moses. After reading this work, one is confronted with the following list of leadership traits: humility, empathy, power sharing, vision, tenacity, heroism, self-reflection, patience, charisma, wisdom, compassion and perseverance. In addition, Moses is also shown to exhibit the ability to engender trust, to inspire others, to resolve conflicts, to push people beyond their boundaries, to delegate and to speak truth to power.

This list of qualifications at first glance seems an impossible one for any single human being to possess and more appropriate perhaps for a messianic figure. What Moses shows us, however, is that one human being can reach many, if not most, of these leadership traits, if he or she is willing to take on the lifelong discipline of continual character development and moral growth necessary to foster these traits. What Dr. Wolak has done is to show us that the best leaders are those who strive constantly for *self*-development first before expecting this from others.

Dr. Wolak also demonstrates the ways in which Moses intuitively moves between the roles of leader and manager, and how he succeeds in many different forms of leadership—transactional, transformational and visionary. At the same time, this work focuses on the important theme of the many human imperfections associated with Moses. As great a leader as he is, Moses is just a human being with humanity's inherent flaws. His anger can get out of control; he is not an eloquent orator due to a speech impediment; he has moments of self-doubt and fear. Yet these very weaknesses are what contribute to his great leadership. By having a humble ego, Moses is not interested in power for its own sake or in self-aggrandizement, but is instead a leader who has compassion for those he is leading and an eagerness to share power with those who serve him. Dr. Wolak points out that the dangers of the charismatic cult leader, to whom so many people have been susceptible in the modern world, are not found in Moses, who is its very antithesis.

Dr. Wolak's most important contribution is his insistence that the biblical and rabbinic traditions of Judaism have an important place in Western society, and that the leadership concepts that are assumed to be contemporary discoveries are in fact part of an ancient culture that has much to teach the modern world.

Ruth Sandberg, PhD<br>
Leonard and Ethel Landau Professor of Rabbinics<br>
Gratz College

# FOREWORD

*"As a tree is known by its fruit, so man by his works."*

—The Talmud

When Arthur asked me to write a foreword to his book *Religion and Contemporary Management: Moses as a Model for Effective Leadership*, I was honored and a little surprised. Although I have spent the past 30 years studying and teaching the various facets of leadership and spent several years teaching at a Jesuit university, Loyola Marymount University, I'm not exactly a religious scholar. My focus has been on the modern history of leadership rather than ancient practices.

As I contemplated further, though, I began to ask myself, "Are things really that different?" For thousands of years, there have been effective leaders and corrupt ones. Whether a leader is in politics, business or religion, the dynamics are the same. People are the same. The blazing scandals at Enron, WorldCom, Tyco, Volkswagen and too many other companies illustrate that the age-old battle between right and wrong still rages on.[1]

In the wake of these scandals, we don't need more standards-based guidelines or accounting-based rules to cover every possible situation. Instead, we need leaders of character and integrity. We need leaders who don't put their own egos and greed ahead of the welfare of the company and its employees. We need principled leaders who make ethically based decisions while considering how both other people and the environment will be affected by their actions.[2] Frankly, we need more leaders like Moses.

---

[1] M. R. Bandsuch, L. E. Pate and J. Thies, "Rebuilding Stakeholder Trust in Business: An Examination of Principle-Centered Leadership and Organizational Transparency in Corporate Governance," *Business and Society Review* 113, no. 1 (2008): 99–127.

[2] L. E. Pate, W. E. Lindsey, T. R. Nielson and M. Hawks, "Innovations in Graduate Business Education: The Challenge of Developing Principle-Centered Leaders," in *Advances in Business Education and Training: The Power of Technology for Learning, Vol. 1*, ed. N. Barsky, M. Clements, J. Ravn and K. Smith (Dordrecht, The Netherlands: Kluwer Academic Press, 2008), 129–42. See the following: W. Lindsey and L. Pate, "Integrating Principle-Centered Leadership into the Business Curriculum: Lessons from the LMU Experience," *Journal of Executive Education* 5, no. 1 (2006): 17–29.

Although people and their characters haven't changed much, the demands of leadership have increased. Perhaps today more than ever, people have extraordinarily high expectations of leaders. Leaders are expected to be decisive, strong, commanding, ethical, honest, fair, balanced, thoughtful and just about any other redeeming quality you can think of.

In addition to these personal qualities, leaders are also expected to have a skill set that is above and beyond that of the people they lead. If the people are negotiators, the leader is expected to be the *best* negotiator. If the people are athletes, the leader is expected to have knowledge and understanding in every aspect of the sport. If the people are in academics, the leader is expected to be an expert in the field in addition to leading. Is it really fair to expect all those qualities to be present in one person? Is there some underlying trait that can be considered the foundation of effective leadership?

In *Religion and Contemporary Management: Moses as a Model for Effective Leadership*, Arthur makes the case that humility and empathy are at the core of effective leadership. And for those of us who have worked with humble, empathetic leaders and with those who are not, we know firsthand that the differences between them are great.

For those who work with a person who is a poor leader, every day is a struggle. At any given time, feelings of frustration, anger, helplessness and disillusionment are present. For those who work with a humble, empathetic leader, though, the experience is much different. At any given time, feelings of inspiration, passion, commitment, excitement, connection and accomplishment are present. One leader brings his or her people down. The other lifts them up.[3]

The latter kinds of leaders are often called "servant leaders." In an article on servant leader attributes, Robert Russell and A. Gregory Stone identified several characteristics of servant leaders.[4] These include listening, empathy, healing, awareness, persuasion, conceptualization, foresight, stewardship, commitment to the growth of people, building community, encouragement and teaching.

As you will read in the following pages, Moses embodied each of these qualities. Yet, you will also learn that Moses doesn't fit the most essential criterion for "servant leadership," which is that he or she is a servant first and a

---

[3] L. E. Pate and T. L. Shoblom, "The ACES Decision-Making Technique as a Reframing Tool for Increasing Empathy," in *Organizing through Empathy*, ed. K. Pavlovich and K. Krahnke (New York, NY: Routledge, 2014), 130–44.

[4] R. Russell and A. Stone, "A Review of Servant Leadership Attributes: Developing a Practical Model," *Leadership & Organization Development Journal* 23, no. 3 (2002): 145–57.

leader second. Moses was a leader who served his people, not a servant who led. It's a subtle distinction, and is one that Arthur clarifies well.

A leader influences followers in two ways—directly and indirectly. Leadership researcher Steve Kerr states that a *direct effect* occurs when a subordinate is influenced by the leader's behavior in and of itself.[5] An *indirect effect* occurs when the subordinate is influenced by the implications of the leader's behavior for some future consequence, such as rewards. Put another way, the leader can influence others both by how he or she behaves directly and by inspiring others and making them feel connected to some greater implication.

Leadership uses influence, and with influence comes power. It's what a leader decides to *do* with this power that determines whether or not he or she will be an effective leader. With power, a leader has two options. They can use it to overpower subordinates or to empower them. It depends on their intent. And, this is where the concept of empathy comes into leadership.

Lamm, Meltzoff and Decety conducted research using functional magnetic resonance imaging to look at the neural underpinnings of empathy. They noted that "when strong emotional response tendencies exist, these tendencies have to be overcome by executive functions." They further noted that "regulation of one's egocentric perspective is crucial for understanding others."[6]

In other words, an effective leader must recognize when his or her followers are in a situation that can bring out strong emotions, and must use his or her thinking to lead the followers to what is best for everyone—not just for the leader. Clearly, leading slaves to freedom is an example of that kind of leadership.

For any reader who aspires to change the landscape of modern society, whether in business, politics, religion or any other area where leaders have power, *Religion and Contemporary Management: Moses as a Model for Effective Leadership* is a valuable resource. It's time to free ourselves from the corruption that seems so rampant these days and to follow in the footsteps of Moses.

Larry Pate, PhD
*Chief Learning Officer, Decision Systems International*
*Adjunct Professor, California State University, Long Beach*

---

[5] S. Kerr and J. M. Jermier, "Substitutes for Leadership: Their Meaning and Measurement," *Organizational Behavior and Human Performance* 22, no. 3 (1978): 375–403.

[6] C. Lamm, A. N. Meltzoff and J. Decety, "How Do We Empathize with Someone Who Is Not Like Us? A Functional Magnetic Resonance Imaging Study," *Journal of Cognitive Neuroscience* 22, no. 2 (2010): 362–76.

# ACKNOWLEDGMENTS

While the process of researching and writing a book is often a solitary endeavor that entails countless hours to reach flawless perfection—a virtually unattainable goal for anyone but always the objective to which an author should aspire—this work could not reach publication without the assistance of special individuals who provided moral support or advice along the way.

I would like to thank my wife, Anna, our two sons, Jacob and Joshua, and our daughter, Julia, for their patience and understanding, giving me time to work on this manuscript when they would have preferred me to be engaged in less solitary activities. I would like to express my gratitude to my mother, Elizabeth, and brother, Richard, for their encouragement in the early years when undergraduate and graduate studies preoccupied much of my time, but would later culminate in the writing of numerous publications, including this book that came out of a deeply profound intellectual interest from my graduate work in business, management, history and religious studies. If there ever was an interdisciplinary topic more deserving of book-length treatment, I cannot think of a better one than Moses and leadership because the two—though otherwise seemingly reflective of completely separate fields of inquiry—are inseparable when analyzing the context of Moses, as the pages of this book show.

I would like to express my gratitude to Rabbi Dr. Ruth Sandberg, Leonard and Ethel Landau Professor of Rabbinics at Gratz College, who provided insightful suggestions on the earliest drafts of this work, and from whom I had the pleasure of acquiring a profound interest and respect for the study of the primary religious texts, including those that reveal the character of Moses and the cultures and general atmosphere in which he grew up and ultimately thrived. I would also like to thank Ruth for her thoughtful foreword to this volume.

Likewise, I wish to thank business professor Dr. Larry Pate, currently of California State University, Long Beach, for his kind and thought-provoking foreword. I became familiar with Larry's vast knowledge of leadership and management topics as a doctoral student, when I was appointed copy editor of the academic business journal for which he was then editor-in-chief. I assisted him in the review of countless academic papers submitted for publication consideration and learned a great deal from this experience.

Thanks must go to my editor, Kiran Bolla, and the publication committee and production team at Anthem Press for believing in the value of this book and helping to bring this unique interdisciplinary business title to a broad audience of interested readers.

The front cover image, *The Children of Israel Crossing the Red Sea* (oil on canvas, circa 1855), by the French painter Frédéric Schopin (1804–1880), is courtesy of ©Bristol Culture (Bristol Museums, Galleries and Archives, UK).

# ABOUT THE AUTHOR

Dr. Arthur J. Wolak is president of CMI Chat Media Inc. Having earned a BA in Psychology from the University of British Columbia, followed by an MA in History and an MBA, he went on to receive a PhD from Macquarie University's Graduate School of Management, in Sydney, Australia. He also earned an MA in Jewish Studies and a Graduate Certificate in Jewish-Christian Studies from Gratz College. He has published articles in the *International Journal of Organizational Analysis, Australasian Canadian Studies Journal, Reviews in Australian Studies* and *Jewish Bible Quarterly*, among other academic journals, newspapers and magazines. He is the author of *The Development of Managerial Culture: A Comparative Study of Australia and Canada* (2015). Arthur lives in Vancouver, Canada, with his wife, Anna, and their three children, Jacob, Joshua and Julia.

# INTRODUCTION

Just as leadership is essential for effective management, successful management depends on effective leadership. While each role is important to the proper functioning of any organization, a leader of an enterprise or organization—or any leader in a position of authority to whom others look for guidance—has a broader focus that benefits from particular attributes that managers, and those who report to them, should be able to respond to favorably in order to achieve the common goal of organizational success. The particular qualities a leader should possess are a matter for debate because it can be rationally argued that cultural differences play an important role in how leaders function. This is a reasonable assertion and has been shown in studies to be an important consideration because cultures often differ, even if only subtly, among those that would otherwise be deemed closely aligned.[1]

In my years of academic study of management and leadership along with my experience working under leaders, and holding leadership roles myself, I have recognized the impact of cultural differences.[2] But I have also come to view effective leaders as possessing a particular skill set that separates them from less effective leaders. This skill set includes, but ultimately transcends, such management techniques as the delegation of responsibilities to others and the empowerment of people, and also includes the influence of personal attributes. Charisma can be a powerful quality, but it is not a defining feature of an effective leader. Wisdom matters. Personal values matter. A sense of

---

[1] Seminal works in the field of cultural differences include Geert Hofstede, *Cultures and Organizations: Intercultural Cooperation and Its Importance for Survival* (London, UK: McGraw-Hill, 1991); Geert Hofstede, *Culture's Consequences: Comparing Values, Behaviors, Institutions, and Organizations across Nations*, 2nd ed. (Thousand Oaks, CA: Sage, 2001); and Fons Trompenaars and Charles Hampden-Turner, *Riding the Waves of Culture: Understanding Cultural Diversity in Global Business* (New York, NY: McGraw-Hill, 1998). For a comparison and analysis of research studies on nations deemed culturally close yet revealing of subtle differences, see Arthur Wolak, "Australian and Canadian Managerial Values: A Review," *International Journal of Organizational Analysis* 17, no. 2 (2009): 139–59.

[2] See, for example, Arthur J. Wolak, *The Development of Managerial Culture: A Comparative Study of Australia and Canada* (New York, NY and London, UK: Palgrave Macmillan, 2015); and Arthur J. Wolak, "Australia's 'Irish Factor' as a Source of Cultural Difference from Canada," *Australasian-Canadian Studies Journal* 25, no. 1 (2007): 85–116.

humility is important to assert the message that the organization is not about extolling the virtues of the leader but rather emphasizing the leader's purpose in garnering support for the organization and inspiring the rank and file to feel a similar sense of meaning in the pursuit of achieving the organization's purpose.

Hence, I firmly believe it is possible to identify features of successful leaders that transcend the reality of cultural differences, serving as an almost timeless model for those who aspire to various leadership positions. Naturally, context matters where particular attributes stand out as more significant and effective than others. Management scholars Rob Goffee and Gareth Jones assert,

> The exercise of leadership is contextual. Always. This undermines the notion of a universal leadership formula. Effective leaders understand that there are no universals, no guaranteed ways of ensuring your leadership impact. On the contrary, they practice and hone their context-reading skills and realistically appraise their ability to rewrite that context.[3]

Since context is indeed essential, I maintain that certain leadership features are an *almost* timeless model for leaders to prove their effectiveness. Context will always dictate when certain qualities need to be emphasized over others. Nonetheless, even Goffee and Jones recognize particular core attributes that make for more effective leaders.

In their earlier *Harvard Business Review* article, Goffee and Jones asked—in the title of their work—a direct question of leaders and prospective leaders: "Why should anyone be led by you?" (later expanded into book form under the same title). Their central premise argues the case for "authentic leadership," which, they assert, can be found in leaders who share four unexpected qualities. First, the best leaders tend to reveal their general weaknesses, even if only selectively, because this enables employees to feel they can approach their leaders, building up trust and commitment in the organization's workforce. Second, inspirational leaders are intuitive sensors in varied situations that they use to measure proper timing of actions. Third, employees are managed with a measure of "tough empathy" by giving employees what they require rather than what they desire to achieve particular tasks and meet organizational goals. They assert that leaders must empathize fervently yet realistically with their employees in order to show genuine care for the work employees do for the organization while still being direct with

---

[3] Rob Goffee and Gareth Jones, *Why Should Anyone Be Led by You? What It Takes to Be an Authentic Leader* (Boston, MA: Harvard Business Review Press, 2015), 83.

members of the workforce. Last, effective leaders make the most of employee differences to benefit from their unique talents—a form of delegation or even power sharing—and therefore establish social distance or separateness from their colleagues, because, Goffee and Jones maintain, it motivates employees to perform better.[1]

It is a commonly accepted view that among leaders' various abilities is the articulation of a vision toward which everyone within an organization works to achieve. Leaders certainly need both vision and vitality, but to inspire the rank and file of any organization, leaders need more qualities than just these. On their own, therefore, they remain insufficient. Not only must leaders possess and express personal capabilities through words and deeds but also share their human characteristics that enable people to feel that they are valued as intrinsic elements in the achievement of the visions of leaders and their organization. A leader must be humble rather than arrogant. A leader must show empathy through having strength of conviction and caring for others. These are characteristics one sees in successful leaders that either come naturally or can be developed through productive introspection, an apprenticeship under those who possess such qualities, or from practical leadership training programs.

From my years of academic study in religion, especially the Hebrew Bible and related literature, I strongly believe that Moses provides an exceptionally clear and useful case study in effective leadership. Moses might be criticized for various actions he took, or for personality flaws or even his speech impediment[5]—all of which the Bible relates—but through the pages of the Bible one still sees an example of an incredibly effective leader who galvanized the support of the masses whom he led toward a goal that demanded strong convictions and personal qualities that transcended any limitations he might have otherwise possessed.

What is interesting about Goffee and Jones' four essential qualities of leadership is that, whether or not they were aware of this biblical example, Moses reflects the very same abilities they hold as essential for effective inspirational leaders—and then some. The biblical texts, upon careful analysis, are unambiguous on the importance of humility, authenticity, empathy and sharing power (such as through delegation) with those who have particular skills that serve to help reach organizational goals. Beyond his many other important leadership skills and characteristics, therefore, Moses, as argued herein,

---

[1] Robert Goffee and Gareth Jones, "Why Should Anyone Be Led by You?" *Harvard Business Review* 78, no. 5 (2000): 62–70.

[5] Exod. 4:10. Moses describes himself as "slow of speech and slow of tongue."

serves as a preeminent example of an immensely successful empathic leader. Hence, the biblical figure of Moses presents an ancient case study in effective leadership that reveals qualities that could benefit any contemporary leader.

\* \* \*

This book serves to show Moses' leadership talents by focusing on the biblical texts (quoting from the Jewish Publication Society's 1985 translation of the Hebrew Scriptures unless otherwise noted) that report how Moses grew into his leadership role, as well as other important texts that discuss Moses, particularly sources from the vast Talmudic and Midrashic literature. Each of these texts from the Jewish tradition is particularly insightful because Moses was pivotal to the development of Judaism, and therefore the ancient rabbis probed every angle of Moses that is ultimately of benefit to anyone who wants to become an effective leader regardless of one's personal ethnic, religious or cultural background.

One need not be Jewish, Christian, Muslim nor a member of any Western (or Eastern) religious tradition to successfully learn from the example of Moses. One can view Moses through the lens of a particular religion, even if not one's own, and still learn from the experience. Thus, studying about Moses' life and his rise to leadership in the pages of the Torah (the first five books of the Hebrew Bible), in other sections of the Tanakh (Torah, Prophets and Writings), and in the opinions and stories related in the Talmud and Midrash, the reader derives a portrait of leadership that helps in discerning characteristics deemed desirable for any individual holding a leadership position.

This volume also pays careful attention to the essential ideas reflected in the contemporary leadership field to illustrate the intertwining of Moses, the biblical leader, and the present-day leader of virtually any enterprise, organization or unit therein. Through consideration of biblical and postbiblical religious texts and modern-day leadership theories, key elements of effective leadership can be seen in the leadership model of Moses that, while ancient in origin, offers useful applications for the contemporary era.

# Chapter 1

# ANCIENT LEADERSHIP FOR PRESENT TIMES

Leadership has become one of the key buzzwords in contemporary business, politics and organizations of every type, including the nonprofit, educational and public administration sectors. While modern leadership theorists suggest various models, traits and approaches to leadership behavior that purport novelty, as Ecclesiastes famously reports, "There is nothing new beneath the sun!"[1] The truth is that, while current leadership and management vocabulary might differ from the Torah, many of the notions advocated by contemporary leadership theorists appear to emulate major behaviors, traits, functions, experiences and actions ascribed to Moses in the first five books of the Hebrew Bible.

Few might think of Moses as a *leader*, or even a *manager*, in the contemporary sense, but Moses—among the most significant leaders to emerge in Western civilization—is arguably the quintessential example of leadership from whom much can be learned by people entering, and occupying, leadership positions.

Moses, asserts Rabbi Joseph Telushkin, is "the preeminent figure of the Hebrew Bible"[2] about whom we have considerable biographical details because we are told how he met his wife, Tzipporah,[3] and we know the names of his two sons, Gershom and Eliezer,[4] as well as of his father, Amram; his mother, Jochebed; his brother, Aaron; and his sister, Miriam. We even know the story of a certain amount of animosity that his older siblings, Miriam and Aaron, felt toward him at one point in the desert wanderings.[5] Such ill will has even led some biblical scholars to mark this point as the beginning of the

---

[1] Eccl. 1:9.
[2] Joseph Telushkin, *Hillel: If Not Now, When?* (New York, NY: Schocken, 2010), xvi.
[3] Exod. 2:16–21.
[4] Gershom is mentioned by name in Exod. 2:22 and 18:3. Eliezer is mentioned by name in Exod. 18:4. Both are mentioned in 1 Chron. 23:15. Outside of Midrash, this is all that is revealed about the sons of Moses beyond their offspring in the Book of Chronicles.
[5] Telushkin, *Hillel*, xvii.

end of Moses' leadership.[6] Beyond familial jealousy, however, what we know best about Moses are his leadership qualities, tactics, even errors of judgment, which are amply described in the pages of the Bible.

Indeed, Moses' life and career as a leader are outlined in detail in the Torah, or the Five Books of Moses as the first books of the Hebrew Bible are widely known. He rises to prominence in the second book, Exodus, but his presence is very much evident in the subsequent books of the Torah—Leviticus, Numbers and Deuteronomy—and referenced in later books of the Tanakh, such as in the Book of Joshua, which refers back to particular incidents connected to Moses and his leadership of the Israelites.[7] Moses is also the source of a seemingly endless amount of ancient and modern commentary, not to mention contemporary popular works spanning such diverse fields as religion, history, political science and psychoanalysis.

On the whole, one can easily conclude that Moses was a leader *par excellence*. Yet, while he typically triumphed, he also made mistakes—or, rather, may not always have made the right decision if we are permitted to make such retroactive judgments from an analysis of the biblical text. In his role as leader over a vast number of people, however, he possessed a *vision*, inspired and motivated his followers to ultimately accept it, abided by a *mission statement*, and *empowered* others through *delegation* to become leaders themselves. Each of these terms associated with modern leadership is evident in Moses' personal leadership style, an approach that countless generations have emulated until this very day.

Like other key biblical figures, Moses proves a very important role model because he is an example of leadership that reveals both achievements and failings. In other words, he led but was flawed. He faced human dilemmas as all people do. "Unlike the founders of other religions or great leaders in other traditions," notes Jewish writer, philosopher and Nobel Laureate Elie Wiesel, "Moses is depicted as human, both great and fallible. While every other religion tends to transform its founder into a semi-god, Judaism does everything to humanize Moses."[8] This helps us remember that Moses was neither a divine being nor a saint. He was human, and, as such, he was not perfect. As a human being, he committed sin, to various degrees of identification and

---

[6] See Num. 12:1–16; and Yitzchak Etshalom, *Between the Lines of the Bible, Exodus: A Study from the New School of Orthodox Torah Commentary* (New York, NY: Orthodox Union Press, 2012), 50.

[7] Jonathan Kirsch suggests Moses "is used in the Book of Joshua to symbolize the Divine sanction of Joshua's leadership in the conquest of Canaan," for example, Josh. 3:7. Jonathan Kirsch, *Moses: A Life* (New York, NY: Ballantine Books, 1998), 360.

[8] Elie Wiesel, *Messengers of God: Biblical Portraits and Legends* (New York, NY: Touchstone, 1994), 182.

seriousness. Yet, the wise words of Ecclesiastes apply: "For there is not one good man on earth who does what is best and doesn't err."[9]

Moses must certainly have been good or else why would the pages of the Bible relate how God specifically chose him to become the leader of the Israelites? However, God later chose Saul to become the first king even though this selection did not appear to work out very well, and yet it could be argued that Saul started out with good intentions only to subsequently change for the worse. As the Bible relates, when Saul disobeyed God's command to destroy all of the Amalekites and even their animals, yet Saul chose to spare the lives of King Agag of Amalek and the most valuable animals in the Amalekites' possession—including sheep, oxen and lambs[10]—God complained to Samuel, "I regret that I made Saul king, for he has turned away from Me and has not carried out My commands."[11] Hence, in contrast, based on what we read in the Bible about Moses' behavior, we can easily view Moses as "good" even according to our own human standards of goodness. What the reader of the Torah implicitly understands is that Moses was human, as reflected in the famous words of eighteenth-century English writer Alexander Pope: "To err is human, to forgive, divine."[12]

A human being can only hope—and pray in accordance with religious tradition—that, after expressing sincere remorse, one's sins, or errors of judgment, can be forgiven. But they were not always forgiven by God in the case of Moses, as when Moses twice struck the rock with his rod in order to give a complaining flock of Israelites water to drink, making a mistake in the process that led God to punish Moses by preventing his ultimate entrance into the Promised Land.[13]

In the Jewish tradition, a major theme of the Jewish High Holiday liturgy culminating in Yom Kippur is seeking Divine forgiveness for one's sins against God. Throughout the year, a prayer of forgiveness is also included in the sixth

---

[9] Eccl. 7:20.

[10] See 1 Sam. 15:3–11.

[11] 1 Sam. 15:11.

[12] Alexander Pope, *An Essay on Criticism*, part 2, line 325. Online: http://www.gutenberg.org/dirs/etext05/esycr10h.htm (accessed January 11, 2013).

[13] Num. 20:11–12. According to Numbers 20:12, both Moses and Aaron were told they would not enter the Promised Land: "Because you did not trust Me enough to affirm My sanctity in the sight of the Israelite people, therefore you shall not lead this congregation into the land that I have given them." The view that God forgives does not seem to have held for Moses (and his siblings) perhaps because Moses, as the greatest prophet in the Jewish tradition, was understandably held to a higher standard by God. After all, Moses was the leader God had chosen to bring the Israelites out of Egypt and lead them toward the Promised Land. When a present-day CEO errs significantly, it is not unusual for the board of directors to fire and replace the CEO. This could be an ancient example for a contemporary trend.

blessing of the Weekday Amidah—the "standing prayer," also known as the *Shemoneh Esrei* (eighteen benedictions, though there are traditionally nineteen) or, simply, *Ha'Tefillah* (the prayer) due to the centrality of this prayer rubric to the traditional Jewish weekday prayer services. Rabbi Hayim Donin notes that "the prophets of Israel assure us that God will forgive us in the wake of sincere repentance (Is. 55:7)," a blessing emphasizing "that God has set no limit to His pardoning grace."[14]

God directed Moses to "order the rock to yield its water."[15] Moses' failure to do so amounted to "public disobedience of God's instructions, which in itself is punishable."[16] Biblical scholar Jacob Milgrom argues that Moses may have resorted to Egyptian magic out of desperation, and this very act of idolatry was truly unforgivable in the eyes of God, even though "Moses offers no incantations, recites no formulas, intones no esoteric names; instead, he makes a common place gesture—strikes with his rod, pours water, throws up soot (Exod. 4:9; 9:8), puts his hand in his skirt, or raises his arm high (Exod. 4:6–7; 17:11)—all the while remaining silent." Indeed, Milgrom provides at least ten reasons given by the medieval Jewish commentators for Moses' punishment because, as Milgrom notes, "the punishment is clear; but what is the crime?"[17] Ultimately, we can only speculate about this.

However, given the complaints Moses heard from the people when he presented God's commandments, Wiesel even suggests, "Who knows? Perhaps God's decision not to let him enter the promised land was meant as a reward rather than as punishment?"[18] Whatever the case, it remains clear that Moses' influence was profound since we can learn from his errors of judgment just as we can marvel at his effective leadership skills.

*   *   *

Sir Winston Churchill—the preeminent twentieth-century British political leader—wrote about Moses—the preeminent Israelite and biblical leader. Historian and official Churchill biographer Sir Martin Gilbert observed that "Churchill had long been fascinated by Jewish history, by the Jewish involvement with the events of the time, and above all by the Jews' monotheism and

---

14  Rabbi Hayim Halevy Donin, *To Pray as a Jew: A Guide to the Prayer Book and Synagogue Service* (New York, NY: HarperCollins, 1980), 84.

15  Num. 20:8.

16  Nili S. Fox, commentary to Num. 20:10, *The Jewish Study Bible*, ed. Adele Berlin and Marc Zvi Brettler (New York, NY: Oxford University Press, 2004), 323.

17  Jacob Milgrom, "Excursus 50: Magic, Monotheism, and the Sin of Moses (20:1–13)," *The JPS Torah Commentary: Numbers*, 448–56 (Philadelphia, PA: Jewish Publication Society, 1989), 453.

18  Wiesel, *Messengers of God*, 199.

ethics. These seemed to him a central factor in the evolution and mainte-
nance of modern civilization."[19]

On November 8, 1931, Churchill published an article entitled "Moses" in
the *Sunday Chronicle*—part of a series called "Great Bible Stories Retold
by the World's Best Writers"—in which he argued against those who pro-
claimed that the Jewish leader was just myth and never existed. Quoting
from Churchill's article, Gilbert relates, "We believe that the most scientific
view, the most up-to-date and rationalistic conception, will find its fullest
satisfaction in taking the Bible story literally, and in identifying one of the
greatest of human beings with the most decisive leap-forward ever discernible in the human story."[20]

Churchill stressed that the Bible is an important historical document,
inspired by God, and that Moses was, as the Bible describes, a preeminent
leader. As Gilbert notes, Churchill wrote that Moses

> was the greatest of the prophets, who spoke in person to the God of Israel;
> he was the national hero who led the Chosen people out of the land
> of bondage, through the perils of the wilderness, and brought them to
> the very threshold of the Promised Land; he was the supreme lawgiver,
> who received from God that remarkable code upon which the religious,
> moral, and social life of the nation was so securely fastened. Tradition
> lastly ascribed to him the authorship of the whole Pentateuch [Torah],
> and the mystery that surrounded his death added to his prestige.[21]

Churchill argued vigorously that Moses was not simply an allegorical figure but a real person and that his existence and leadership represented true
historical events. Indeed, while the acceptance of Moses as a leader or even
as a living, breathing human being ultimately rests on faith in the words of
the Hebrew Bible because of lack of tangible evidence of Moses that some
skeptics demand for belief in his existence, this is ultimately irrelevant to the
leadership question because much can be learned from the experiences of
Moses that the Bible carefully describes, which one can argue was either *the*
source—or, at the very least, *a* source—of inspiration for many contemporary notions of leadership.

Jewish-communal leadership authority Hal Lewis notes that the contemporary "organized Jewish community rarely takes a comprehensive approach"
to leadership qualities and their cultivation. Even on those occurrences when

[19]  Martin Gilbert, *Churchill and the Jews: A Lifelong Friendship* (New York, NY: Henry Holt, 2007), 95.

[20]  Quoted in Gilbert, *Churchill and the Jews*, 95.

[21]  Quoted in ibid., 95–96.

organizations and groups offer courses or instructional programs claiming to be "leadership development," they are most typically episodic and/or very elitist. In their methodologies, they are likely to focus either on developing management skills—for example, budgeting, agenda planning and public relations—or general Jewish literacy—that is, holidays, history and religious practices. Lewis is right to emphasize that, while "each of these areas may be important to the success of Jewish organizational life, none can legitimately be called leadership development."[22]

Regarding Lewis' observation of the lack of effective leadership training he found in Jewish organizations—something not exclusive to them but evident in diverse religious and nonreligious organizations—there is evidence for this assertion. Considering one such Jewish publication intended for communal or organizational leaders, the manual claims to be "intended as a guide toward more effective leadership [...] designed for use by leaders of many different kinds of groups," including volunteer and professional associations, nonprofit organizations and fraternal, social and civic organizations.[23] Yet this book, *Leadership Logic: A Manual of Organizational Know-How*—featuring the word "leadership" in its title—only spends three pages actually discussing the functions, responsibilities, duties, attitudes, development, rewards, benefits and pitfalls of leadership.[24] The rest of the book—100 pages' worth—focuses on managerial tasks of very little relevance to effective leadership or the leader's role. This also supports the view that there exists today some confusion over the different roles that separate leaders from managers. The two are not synonymous even though some skills associated with one can be useful for the other.

Moses' example of leadership, therefore, deserves careful consideration for its significant application to contemporary leadership, including its desirable traits, values and actions, because what leadership theorists advocate today largely emulates what the Bible describes concerning Moses and his leadership experience. Thus, Moses' influence on contemporary leadership trends appears pervasive in Western culture, even if contemporary leadership theorists do not explicitly cite the Torah as a source for leadership ideas advanced in our time. Yet, as Lewis notes, "Judaism offers a definitive view as to what it means to be an effective leader [...] honed over centuries that is at the same time profoundly idealistic and abundantly pragmatic."[25] Hence, leadership traits and skills gleaned from Moses are by no means limited to adherents of

---

[22] Hal M. Lewis, *From Sanctuary to Boardroom: A Jewish Approach to Leadership* (Lanham, MD: Rowman & Littlefield, 2006), 81.

[23] Federation of Jewish Women's Organizations of Maryland, *Leadership Logic: A Manual of Organizational Know-How*, rev. ed. (Baltimore, MD: Ottenheimer Publishers, 2000), 3.

[24] Federation of Jewish Women's Organizations of Maryland, *Leadership Logic*, 11–14.

[25] Lewis, *From Sanctuary to Boardroom*, 147.

Judaism but can be emulated by anyone who would like to become a better leader from examining this most worthy of examples.

From a Jewish perspective, Moses certainly represents an inspiring model for this leadership approach. From Moses, we can even apply a popular Yiddish term to his character that comes through his leadership style. Through his example, Moses proved to be a mensch, a state of being and positive reflection of his character and values that undoubtedly fueled his leadership qualities.

# Chapter 2

# DEFINING LEADERSHIP

Winston Churchill stressed in his 1931 article that Moses is among the preeminent figures in the Hebrew Bible. Throughout the history of Western civilization, Moses not only maintains a prominent position in the monotheistic tradition—particularly respected by adherents of Judaism, Christianity and Islam—but also stands as a figure of influence in secular life through his example as a leader of the ancient Israelites.[1]

According to Jewish tradition, Moses is considered to be the greatest prophet. So significant is Moses to Judaism that, in his *Thirteen Principles of Faith*, the great Jewish philosopher, physician and rabbi Moses ben Maimon—popularly known as Maimonides, or by the Hebrew acronym Rambam—includes as the seventh fundamental principle that Moses was the greatest prophet who ever lived and that no other prophet could comprehend God better than Moses.[2] A thousand years earlier, the ancient rabbis said, in the very first verse of Mishnah *Pirkei Avot* (a Mishnaic tractate known as "Sayings of the Fathers" or "Sages"), that Moses received the Torah from Sinai and passed it on to Joshua, who passed it on to the Elders, who passed it on to the Prophets, and that the Prophets passed it on to the Men of the Great Assembly.[3]

"This introductory sentence describes the chain of tradition leading up to the sayings in *Avot*," observes William Berkson, who notes that "*Avot* was put in nearly final form around 200 CE by one of the last and greatest sages in the book, Yehuda [Judah] HaNasi," who made *Avot* a significant part of his "compendium of post-biblical legal rulings known as the Mishnah, meaning 'recitation' or 'repetition'." Berkson notes, the later "Talmud, meaning 'study,' is a collection of extensive commentaries on the Mishnah, known as Gemara, 'completion' together with those portions of the Mishnah that have been commented upon."[4] Hence, the laws of the Torah were described as

---

[1] For example, see Bruce Feiler, *America's Prophet: Moses and the American Story* (New York, NY: William Morrow, 2009).

[2] Isadore Twersky, ed. *A Maimonides Reader* (Springfield, NJ: Berman House, 1972), 419–20.

[3] *Pirkei Avot* 1:1.

[4] William Berkson, *Pirkei Avot: Timeless Wisdom for Modern Life* (Philadelphia, PA: Jewish Publication Society, 2010), 3, 10.

transmitted to the Jewish people from Divine instruction to Moses at Sinai, and passed down through the generations. Moses was pivotal in this chain that transmitted the Torah down to the rabbis, which underscored their authority in subsequent Jewish tradition.

Judah HaNasi, the leading rabbi of his day, had redacted the Mishnah, a document that traditionally remains the repository of the Oral Law. Hence, the Mishnah proved to be an extremely influential intellectual product of the ancient rabbis, who asserted that the Oral Law had been given along with the Written Law at Sinai, only put into writing to prevent its loss after the destruction of the Second Temple in Jerusalem in 70 CE. Thus, in this way, the Mishnah is linked to Moses, who is said to have first received the Torah at Sinai.[5]

Rabbinic tradition holds that these Men of the Great Assembly (known in Hebrew as *Anshei Knesset Ha'Gedolah*) mentioned in *Pirkei Avot* 1:1, who received the Torah from Moses through the listed intermediaries, were the leaders of the Jewish people during the time they functioned. They represented a bridge between the end of the era of the biblical prophets and the Hellenistic period. From them these transmissions of Written and Oral Torah were debated and discussed in rabbinic literature, and their teachings spread throughout the Jewish world. Over time, many of their ideas were transmitted through various channels to Western society generally.

Moses' stature in the Jewish tradition is, arguably, unrivaled, despite personal faults that only confirm he was human and not Divine. As the Torah states, "Never again did there arise in Israel a prophet like Moses—whom the Lord singled out, face to face, for the various signs and portents that the Lord sent him to display in the land of Egypt, against Pharaoh and all his courtiers and his whole country, and for all the great might and awesome power that Moses displayed before all Israel."[6]

Christianity similarly regards Moses as a great leader of the Israelites and retains him within the canon of the Christian tradition—though not to the same significance that Jews give Moses as leader and lawgiver—namely, the first five books of the Bible, which Judaism refers to by various names, particularly the Hebrew word "Torah,"[7] but which includes the broader teachings reflected in the books of the Jewish canon, the Tanakh (that is, the acronym

---

[5] Leonard Kravitz and Kerry M. Olitzky, eds. and trans., *Pirke Avot: A Modern Commentary on Jewish Ethics* (New York, NY: UAHC Press, 1993), 1.

[6] Deut. 34:10-12.

[7] The Torah refers to the first five books of the Hebrew Bible in the strictest sense of the term, but in the broader sense Torah refers to all of the teachings reflected in the books of the Jewish canon, the Tanakh—*Torah* (Genesis through Deuteronomy), *Neviim* (Prophets) and *Ketuvim* (Writings).

for Torah, Prophets and Writings), Chumash (derived from the Hebrew word for "five"), or Pentateuch (Greek for "five books"). Yet, as Moses' biographer Jonathan Kirsch notes, "Moses is unmistakably diminished in the New Testament—when his ghostly figure appears at the transfiguration of Jesus, he is presented along with Elijah as no more than a bystander (Matt. 17:3)—and ultimately he is wholly discarded."[8]

This lack of emphasis on Moses in Christianity was likely due to Moses' close association with Jews, Judaism and its many laws. Still, as popular writer and Torah commentator Rabbi Harold Kushner notes, "The teachings of Jesus and Paul in the New Testament would be unintelligible unless read against the background of the Torah, the Five Books of Moses."[9] If for no other reason than this, therefore, Moses has always been regarded as a prophet in the early church and remains such among the many branches of contemporary Christianity.

Islam also speaks reverentially about Moses. The Koran asserts that Moses "was devoted, and he was a Messenger, a Prophet,"[10] implicitly acknowledging that Moses brought scripture and law to his people. In Huston Smith's classic work, *The World's Religions*, the American historian of comparative religion relates an Islamic hadith that credits the reason Muslims have five daily prayer worship times (rather than fifty) to the influence of Moses. According to this Islamic tradition, Smith notes, "one of the crucial events in Muhammad's life, [...] was his renowned Night Journey to Heaven," where he is described as having encountered Moses, who advised Muhammad to negotiate with God to reduce the Divine instruction "to pray fifty times each day" because this would be oppressive to Muhammad's followers. Muhammad went back and forth four more times, reducing the number "successfully to thirty, twenty, ten and then five," which still seemed excessive to Moses, who recommended that Muhammad try again "to make things lighter for [Muhammad's] people." Ultimately, Islamic tradition holds, Muhammad declined to further negotiate for fewer prayer times, stating that he was satisfied, and submitted to praying five times per day.[11]

In contrast, Judaism's tradition has been three daily worship services, attributed to the early time of the Second Temple (ca. 485 BCE) from the collected wisdom of Ezra the Scribe, and the 120 Men of the Great Assembly—the

[8] Jonathan Kirsch, *Moses: A Life* (New York, NY: Ballantine Books, 1998), 360.

[9] Harold S. Kushner, *Overcoming Life's Disappointments: Learning from Moses How to Cope with Frustration* (New York, NY: Anchor Books, 2007), 5.

[10] Koran 19:51. *The Koran: Interpreted*, trans. Arthur J. Arberry (Oxford, UK: Oxford University Press, 1983), 306.

[11] Houston Smith, *The World's Religions: Our Great Wisdom Traditions* (New York, NY: HarperCollins, 1991), 245.

spiritual and intellectual descendants of Moses through the chain outlined in *Pirkei Avot* 1:1. "Thrice-daily prayer seems to have been an old Israelite tradition among the pious," notes Hayim Donin, because "reference to it is found in Psalms (55:18) and in the book of Daniel (6:11)," a practice encouraged by the aggadic interpretations—found in the Babylonian Talmud, Tractate *Berakhot* 26b—of the biblical verses associated with the three Genesis patriarchs, Abraham (Gen. 19:27, inspiring the morning service), Isaac (Gen. 24:63, the afternoon service) and Jacob (Gen. 28:11, the evening service).[12]

According to the Jerusalem Talmud, *Berakhot* 4:1, observes Donin, the Jewish "tradition of praying three times a day" is associated "with the daily changes in nature and the desire to pay homage to God as the power that makes them happen."[13] Hence, not only is Moses' familiarity with the Patriarchs presumed through his connection to God and the Torah but it also appears that Moses' leadership abilities were acknowledged in Islam as evident in Huston Smith's description of the hadith account of Moses' counseling Muhammad to negotiate fewer worship services during the latter's "Night Journey to Heaven."

Although fervent secularists may dispute whether or not Moses existed, often citing the absence of his resting place[14]—or if he did exist, who he actually was—there still is no denying Moses' influence on Jewish identity, group leadership, and Western civilization as a whole. After all, as Kirsch contends, "the search for the historical Moses is less important—and ultimately less interesting—than the quest for the moral and spiritual values that we might extract from his biblical life story."[15] The same applies to his role as leader.

Even Sigmund Freud, the father of psychoanalysis—though not known for strong personal religious sentiments—always proudly identified himself as a Jew.[16] Freud penned a book—his very last—on Moses called *Moses and Monotheism*, containing Freud's musings on religion, the Jewish people and the significance of Moses in the Jewish collective memory. Freud's argument concerning Moses' origins fails to support his conclusions, namely, that Moses was an Egyptian rather than a "Jew." This latter term, in itself, was a misnomer in the strictest sense as "Jew" implies descent from the tribe of Judah, whereas Moses is described in the Torah, notes Kirsch, "as a member of the tribe of Levi." However, by describing Moses as a Jew, Freud

---

[12] Rabbi Hayim Halevy Donin, *To Pray as a Jew: A Guide to the Prayer Book and Synagogue Service* (New York, NY: HarperCollins, 1980), 10.

[13] Donin, *To Pray as a Jew*, 10–11.

[14] The Torah concedes that "no one knows [Moses'] burial place to this day" (Deut. 34:6).

[15] Kirsch, *Moses*, 358.

[16] David Bakan, *Sigmund Freud and the Jewish Mystical Tradition* (Mineola, NY: Dover, 2004), 46–47.

acknowledged the Jewish people's recognition of Moses as Judaism's greatest prophet.[17]

That Freud's book was never praised for its biblical scholarship has long been noted.[18] However, Michael Berenbaum argues that, "By suggesting that Moses was really an Egyptian, Freud [intentionally] directed responsibility for the law away from the Jews in an effort to alleviate anti-Semitism."[19] The "burden"—as some view it—of Torah law is intimately associated with Moses, as God's Torah was given to Moses at Sinai to be observed. As Berenbaum notes, "Freud suggested that the Jews could end their identification with the superego by terminating their role as the conscience of mankind." Yet, Berenbaum asserts that "Freud's reasoning is incompatible with the traditional Jewish appreciation of law."[20]

Indeed, aside from psychoanalysis, Moses retains a very important position in the transmission of law and thereby wielded a major influence on history. James MacGregor Burns, American historian, political scientist, and leadership scholar, asserts that Freud "dwelt on Moses as a 'Great Man' acting in the network of determining historical causes."[21] In other words, Moses proved an important authority in history through his leadership role, which rests on his tribal origins and leader of the Israelites—Jews—given that Moses' innate qualities and acquired skills helped bring them out of slavery from Egypt.

\* \* \*

A notion of leadership hovering subtly in the background of the Moses story should be addressed so it can be quickly discarded: leadership ought not be viewed in patriarchal terms. After all, there have been effective female leaders since biblical times. The Tanakh depicts many strong female leaders, including Miriam, sister of Moses, whom the prophet Micah raises in stature by citing God as having included her among three leaders sent to Egypt to help bring out the Israelites, namely the siblings Miriam, Aaron and Moses.[22] There are many other female leaders named in the Tanakh. In fact, as Ziony Zevit observes, four women are identified as prophets, including Miriam (Exod. 15:20), Deborah (Judg. 4:4), Huldah (2 Kings 22:14) and Noadiah

[17] Kirsch, *Moses*, 68.
[18] Bakan, *Sigmund Freud and the Jewish Mystical Tradition*, 138.
[19] Michael Berenbaum, *Elie Wiesel: God, The Holocaust, and the Children of Israel* (West Orange, NJ: Behrman House, 1994), 99.
[20] Berenbaum, *Elie Wiesel*, 99.
[21] James MacGregor Burns, *Leadership* (New York, NY: Harper, 1979), 241.
[22] Micah 6:4.

(Neh. 6:14).[23] One can easily trace other female leaders from biblical times through the present, whether Queen Elizabeth I and II, Queen Victoria or Catherine the Great, to name only a few. In other words, leadership is not limited to the male gender, though Moses is asserted as a preeminent biblical model that does not depend on gender for a leader's effectiveness.

Considering biblical female figures, Miriam certainly revealed leadership traits. As the Bible relates, Miriam appears smart, courageous and bold from a very young age by how she stood guard for Moses, her baby brother, linking her mother with the Pharaoh's daughter, Moses' adoptive parent,[24] and, much later in time, is referred to as a prophet who "took a timbrel in her hand" and danced with all of the women after their successful escape and liberation from the Pharaoh.[25] Evangeline Anderson asserts that the use of the *masculine, plural* of the Hebrew word for "them" in the verse from Exodus 15:21—"And Miriam chanted for them"—means that "Miriam was not just a leader of the women's wing of Israel but of the *whole people*," with the caveat that her reputation as a leader was undermined by her personal desire for power and her jealousy of Moses, for which she was punished by God.[26]

Deborah is another prime example of a strong female leader. According to the Book of Judges, "Deborah [...] was a prophetess; she led Israel."[27] Under Deborah's leadership, Sisera, commander of the Canaanite army, was killed by Yael, also female, who accomplished the deed with a tent peg she hammered into the side of Sisera's head.[28] In the post-Talmudic Midrash, *Tanna de Bei Eliyahu* 10, the question of gender does not even arise as a requirement for leadership:

> If it be asked how Deborah inferred that the Lord had commanded her to lead Israel against Sisera, the answer lies in the words of Torah that *The judges shall inquire diligently* (Deut. 19:18). Since Deborah was a judge in Israel, she took the passage immediately following to be the Lord's command to undertake the battle against Sisera: *When thou goest forth to battle [...] and seest horses, and chariots, and people more than thou, thou shalt not be afraid of them* (Deut. 20:1).[29]

---

[23] Ziony Zevit, commentary to 2 Kings 22:14, *The Jewish Study Bible*, ed. Adele Berlin and Marc Zvi Brettler (New York, NY: Oxford University Press, 2004), 771.

[24] Exod. 2:4–10.

[25] Exod. 15:20.

[26] Num. 12: 1–16. Evangeline Anderson, "Engendering Leadership: A Christian Feminist Perspective from India," in *Responsible Leadership: Global and Contextual Ethical Perspectives*, ed. Christoph Stückelberger and J. N. K. Mugambi (Geneva, Switzerland: WCC Publications, 2007), 14. (All italics in quotes are part of the original text unless otherwise noted.)

[27] Judg. 4:4.

[28] Judg. 4:21.

[29] William G. Braude and Israel J. Kapstein, trans., *Tanna Debe Eliyahu: The Lore of the School of Elijah* (Philadelphia, PA: Jewish Publication Society, 1981), 116.

In fact, *Tanna de Bei Eliyahu* 9 even states, in reference to Deborah, that God does not care whether a person is male or female, but God chooses a person to lead based on ability, not gender: "In regard to her deeds, I call heaven and earth to witness that whether it be a heathen or a Jew, whether it be a man or a woman a manservant or a maidservant, the holy spirit will suffuse each of them in keeping with the deeds he or she performs."[30]

Indeed, regardless of gender, the leader Deborah was not afraid of Sisera. This comes in stark contrast with King Saul, first king of a United Kingdom of Israel, who, possessed of doubt and increasingly erratic behavior, is ultimately divinely rejected in favor of David, whom Saul feared and, therefore, desired to kill. "David eluded him twice. Saul was afraid of David, for the Lord was with him and had turned away from Saul."[31]

From this example, one can swiftly conclude that leadership ability is not gender based but built on good character and leadership abilities, of which Moses is the paradigmatic example. After all, in modern times, we have seen evidence of powerful female leaders, such as Indira Gandhi, prime minister of India from the 1960s through the early 1980s; Golda Meir, prime minister of Israel during the 1970s; Margaret Thatcher, prime minister of the United Kingdom in the 1980s; Benazir Bhutto, prime minister of Pakistan from the 1980s through the 1990s; and Angela Merkel, chancellor of Germany since 2005, to name a few, all of whom demonstrate that leadership qualities were not gender based but character based. "Evidence suggests few differences in the actual behaviors of men and women leaders," argues Virginia Schein. She maintains that "effective leaders, male or female, seek[ing] to implement their visions, vary their behaviors contingent upon the situational requirements, and in general grapple successfully with the ever-changing and complex internal and external demands upon their organizations. Ineffective leaders, male or female, do not."[32] Moses revealed the importance of character as a key leadership quality.

## What Is Leadership?

While there are numerous leadership theories, the prominence of each has risen and fallen over time. What they share is a common attempt to try to encapsulate the leader's strengths, if not his or her weaknesses. The Great Man Theory that Freud espoused was prominent in the nineteenth century.

---

[30] Braude and Kapstein, trans., *Tanna Debe Eliyahu*, 112–13.

[31] 1 Sam. 18:11–12.

[32] Virginia Schein, "Would Women Lead Differently?", in *The Leader's Companion: Insights on Leadership Through the Ages*, ed. J. Thomas Wren (New York, NY: Free Press, 1995), 166.

It stressed that the leader possessed impressive inborn qualities even if those qualities could not be easily defined. But was the "great leader" born, or was the leader taught, or just a unique product of his or her time period? These questions were never adequately answered, but generated a view of "heroism" that one could characterize as "heroic leadership," since "heroes" had been leaders throughout history.

The effort to probe the traits of the Great Man, from 1910 to World War II, saw the rise of the Trait Theory of Leadership, which attempted to identify the personality traits, whether inborn or developed, that enhanced the roles of effective leaders. This led to the Behavioral Theory of Leadership from the start of World War II to the late 1960s, focusing on leadership behaviors rather than individuals' inner characteristics that were difficult to assess, taking the view that leaders were made, not born. Various contingency theories followed from the late 1960s onward that focused on situations, or the environment, that served to inspire particular desirable leadership behavior.[33] Situational Leadership Theory emerged that attempted to suggest that certain types of leadership might be better suited for making particular types of decisions,[34] perhaps an authoritarian style or a democratic style, for example. The 1970s saw the rise of other prominent management theories, namely transactional leadership, which put emphasis on follower compliance in comprehending the behavior of leaders.[35] Transformational leadership theories also became popular, attempting to show that leaders transformed their followers through their inspirational qualities, whether reflecting charismatic personalities or other aspects that enabled followers to identify with the leader's vision and its purpose.[36]

* * *

Leadership is not easily pigeonholed into one neat category, which might explain why there appear to be almost as many theories of effective leadership as the number of languages spoken. Hal Lewis warns that "the expectation that a punch list of effective leadership behaviors will simply alight [...] in ready-to-use fashion, is naïve and ill-conceived [since] the plethora of books from the general community, each purporting to contain *the* definitive listing of desirable behaviors, is the best proof that no such overarching taxonomy

---

[33] Martin M. Chemers, "Contemporary Leadership Theory," in Wren, *The Leader's Companion*, 83–90.

[34] Paul Hersey and Kenneth H. Blanchard, "Situational Leadership," in Wren, *The Leader's Companion*, 207–11.

[35] Chemers, "Contemporary Leadership Theory," in Wren, *The Leader's Companion*, 90–92.

[36] Richard A. Couto, "The Transformation of Transforming Leadership," in Wren, *The Leader's Companion*, 102–7.

exists anywhere."[37] Furthermore, Lewis asserts, while "serious students recognize that isolating the behaviors of effective leaders is often highly subjective," where Jewish leadership is concerned, the situation is more complicated because "no body of traditional Jewish literature, not the Bible, the Talmud, or any of the later classical writings, contains a singular, definitive work dedicated exclusively to leadership," even though Jewish thinkers certainly wrote about "aspects of leadership in a diversity of works across the ages."[38]

Still, writings on leadership do exist, and Lewis concedes that those seeking inspiration or guidance from the vast assortment of classical sources need to study them in order to interpret, contemplate and extrapolate "as serious Jews have always done."[39] According to Lewis' perspective, there are six behaviors that emerge from Jewish writings that characterize effective leaders, namely piety, tenacity, compassion, service to followers, humility, and consistency.[40] However, just as Lewis noted there is no succinct list of leadership behaviors, these six remain his own personal selections. Some—perhaps more if synonyms are considered—certainly apply, while one can still find others. This is the reason studying Moses provides such insight, as many characteristics of effective leadership are indeed found in his example of leadership.

According to John William Gardner, expert on leadership development, who served as the US Secretary of Health, Education, and Welfare under President Lyndon Johnson, "One hears and reads a surprising number of sentences that describe leaders in general as having such and such attributes and behaving in such and such a fashion—as though one could distill out of the spectacular diversity of leaders an idealized picture of The Leader," but, he asserts, "Leaders come in many forms, with many styles and diverse qualities [...] some find their strength in eloquence, some in judgment, some in courage."[41] As a result, some leadership theories appear more useful than others when considering Moses' biblical example of leadership.

In order to understand Moses' leadership style, it helps to consider several of the above approaches as each provides a glimpse of Moses' genius as a leader. First, however, it is useful to consider Moses as a prototype for religious leadership as, within Judaism, Moses' fame would spread by the community's religious teachers through the study of biblical texts, who then influenced general society by encouraging Torah study among the masses throughout the diaspora.

---

[37] Hal M. Lewis, *From Sanctuary to Boardroom: A Jewish Approach to Leadership* (Lanham, MD: Rowman & Littlefield, 2006), 111.

[38] Lewis, *From Sanctuary to Boardroom*, 111–12.

[39] Ibid., 112.

[40] Ibid., 112, 113–34.

[41] John W. Gardner, *On Leadership* (New York, NY: Free Press, 1990), 5.

## Moses as a Prototype for Leadership

After the exodus from Egypt, Moses and the Israelites he led subsequently wandered in the wilderness for 40 years, and just as they came within sight of entering Canaan, the Promised Land, Moses died.[42] While Moses never entered Canaan, he remained—particularly in Jewish history—the greatest leader, lawgiver and Prophet of the Israelites, the ancient Jewish people. Hence, Moses is arguably the most influential figure in the Jewish tradition. This is especially clear when contrasting Judaism's view of Moses with that of other religions prominent in Western civilization.

From the perspective of religious leadership, rabbis, who would later assume pivotal roles as Jewish teachers and community leaders, traced their own leadership authority or lineage to the first verses of the Mishnaic tractate *Pirkei Avot*, as mentioned earlier, through a chain of authority that led back to Moses. These influential early rabbis had to establish and reinforce their own authority as they contributed to what became the Mishnah and subsequently the vast Talmud that governed and influenced Jewish communities for nearly two millennia and continues to do so in many communities to this very day. After all, the sages and rabbis traditionally regarded the verses of the Torah as current, not merely historic, so they certainly would have proven influential as sources for leadership by rabbis and others in Jewish communities from ancient times through the present era.

The ancient rabbis saw themselves as the only legitimate interpreters of the Torah. With increasing recognition by the Jewish communities, they were elevated to significant communal leadership positions, at least with regard to their powerful religious legal influence through the communities' acceptance of their Torah interpretations. Since not all Jews accepted rabbinic authority, power was limited to those Jews who acknowledged their authority. Nonetheless, increasing numbers of Jews did, indeed, heed rabbinic wisdom.

Why wisdom? Rabbinic tradition focused on Torah study, at least in part, to gain wisdom, a source of leadership that Moses had demonstrated. While the later rabbis likely became smarter people due to a greater base of factual knowledge derived from careful study of the Written and Oral traditions, the rabbinic outlook was that wisdom brought them closer to God. For leaders in all walks of life, however, wisdom is not merely amassing stores of knowledge. Wisdom means using knowledge to become a more ethical and caring individual. As a result, if we view leadership qualities through a Jewish lens, we see that true leaders need to be wise.

---

[42] Deut. 34:5.

Hal Lewis relates, "Judaism's resistance to the concentration of power in a single individual, so apparent in the biblical period, is reflected in the rabbinic epoch as well."[13] Political leadership in ancient rabbinic times did not rest with the collection of rabbis who led in the religious realm, but rather with the Exilarch (*Resh Galuta*) in Babylonia and the Patriarch (*Nasi*) in Palestine. They dealt with the greater political powers on behalf of the Jewish community, representing the people's interests before Babylonian and Roman authorities, respectively.

Both the Exilarch and the Patriarch "had independent authority to make decisions and enact legislation which was binding on the *entire* Jewish people, regardless of geographic locale," Lewis notes, with the Patriarch holding "dominion over religious life in Palestine in his capacity as the head of the supreme court, the *Sanhedrin*" and also political and economic control by virtue of Roman approval.[14] In contrast, Lewis asserts, the Exilarch, who led Babylonian Jewry, did not lead based on rabbinic qualifications as did the Patriarch, but led according to heredity, with "each occupant claiming a direct descent from King David [and] serving with the full imprimatur of the Persian authority, without which he would not have been effective." This meant the Exilarch was treated much like "an imperial Persian officer who was expected to have extensive social contact with non-Jewish society."[45] The Exilarch influenced and controlled religious, political and economic matters by overseeing a "complex administrative infrastructure throughout the Jewish towns and villages of Babylonia."[46] Nonetheless, the attributes or characteristics of leaders arguably remained similar for effective religious and political leaders, perhaps with differing emphases.

Arguably, little has changed today, including the leadership skills necessary for corporate and organizational leaders. Various types of effective leaders emulate many of the characteristics of leadership that Moses exhibited. Therefore, it cannot be considered unusual to view Moses as among the most influential figures in the development of the subsequent rabbinic tradition.

Writing of the later Talmudic era in Babylonia, the American scholar Rabbi Jacob Neusner observes, "the pages of the Babylonian Talmud centered upon the figure of Moses and could be called the story of the Moses-piety of the rabbis." The Talmud told of Moses' report of a twofold revelation at Mount Sinai—a Written Torah and an Oral Torah, handed through an

---

[13] Hal M. Lewis, *Models and Meanings in the History of Jewish Leadership* (Lewiston, NY: Edwin Mellen, 2004), 69.

[14] Lewis, *Models and Meanings in the History of Jewish Leadership*, 69 70.

[45] Ibid., 72.

[46] Ibid., 73.

oral tradition "from master to disciple."[47] Neusner relates the rabbinic belief that "the whole Torah—oral and written—contained the design for the universe, the divine architect's plan for reality." It was therefore subject to study not merely for the purposes of information "but as an act of piety and reverence for the divine lawgiver."[48]

In Neusner's words, "Just as God had taught Torah to Moses, so the rabbi, modeling his life after Moses 'our rabbi,' taught his own disciples." Through diligent study of the Torah, the rabbis maintained their steadfast imitation of God. Schools for studying the Torah not only brought together masters and their disciples who preserved ancient traditions, but also, asserts Neusner, "the schools were holy because their men achieved sainthood through study of Torah and imitation of the conduct of the masters."[49] Thus, Neusner concludes, "they conformed to the heavenly paradigm, the Torah, believed to have been created by God 'in his image,' revealed at Sinai, and handed down to their own teachers."[50]

Neusner stresses that "obedience to the teachings of the rabbis" not only led "to ethical or moral goodness, but to holiness or sainthood." In other words, "discussion of legal traditions, rather than ascetic disciplines or long periods of fasting and prayer, was the way to holiness," observes Neusner, and "the rabbis believed that they themselves were projections of heavenly values onto earth." Neusner states that the rabbis never believed themselves to be of the same substance as the Divine, ensuring that "the distinction between the master of Torah and the giver of Torah was carefully preserved.[51]

From Neusner's description, and in light of subsequent Jewish religious tradition, one can see how Moses and the Torah would perpetuate and influence the thinking and behavior of later generations of Jewish leaders, particularly rabbis. After all, it was the rabbis who carefully studied the Hebrew Scriptures, among the larger corpus of Jewish writings, to a much greater extent than those from other religious traditions. This knowledge would spread throughout the Jewish communities of the diaspora. But this influence moved beyond religion into general culture, and subsequently Western civilization as a whole. After all, it "has been estimated that one-third of our Western civilization bears the marks of its Jewish ancestry," asserts Huston Smith, the child of American Methodist missionaries who worked in China,

---

[47] Jacob Neusner, *There We Sat Down: Talmudic Judaism in the Making* (Eugene, OR: Wipf & Stock Publishers, 1977), 73.

[48] Neusner, *There We Sat Down*, 73–74.

[49] Ibid., 74.

[50] Ibid.

[51] Ibid.

where he was born and raised.[52] However, Smith argues, "the real impact of the ancient Jews [...] lies in the extent to which Western civilization took over their angle of vision on the deepest questions life poses."[53] The role of leadership in society—or an organization in the microsense—is arguably among the pivotal questions to which Smith alludes.

The importance of the transmission of leadership from Moses down to the ancient and later rabbis, in a religious sense, was imperative to ensuring the tradition endured. In the opinion of Rabbi Samuel Hoenig, "it is the Oral Law as embodied in the Talmud that renders the Jewish people unique," because "the study of the Talmud has, throughout the ages, given meaning and vitality to Jewish existence."[54] His belief is based on the assertion of the rabbis in Midrash:

> When the Holy One came to give the Torah, He told Moses in succession the Bible, *Mishnah, Aggadah,* and Talmud. Moses said unto Him: "Master of the World, write it for your children." He replied: "My wish is to give it to them in writing, but it is foreseen by Me that the nations of the world are destined to rule over them and to take it (the Oral Law) from them, and My children will be as the nations of the world. Therefore, the Bible give unto them in writing, and the *Mishnah, Aggadah* and Talmud orally.[55]

Moses is hereby credited with transmitting more than just the Written Torah but the Oral Law as well, which gives him an even greater position of importance in Jewish tradition. But in speaking of leadership, Moses' leadership lessons are embedded in the Torah—and as Midrash asserts, the Talmud owes its creation to the Oral Law transmitted by Moses to the people from God—and therefore Moses' leadership model has been implicitly present for emulation until this very day, particularly as revealed in the Written Law of Torah, revered by Jews in particular for well over the past two millennia.

However, Moses' leadership is more than as a transmitter of law. There is no question that the Law guided the Israelites and subsequent generations of Jews, and this effect also impacted Western civilization since the Jews brought their religious texts wherever they traveled in the world. But Moses did not act solely as a "manager" sorting through paperwork. He actually led the people out of Egyptian slavery and then through four decades in the wilderness.

---

[52] Huston Smith, *Why Religion Matters: The Fate of the Human Spirit in an Age of Disbelief* (New York, NY: HarperCollins, 2001), xiii.

[53] Smith, *The World's Religions,* 271.

[54] Samuel N. Hoenig, *The Essence of Talmudic Law and Thought* (Northvale, NJ: Jason Aronson, 1993), 111–12.

[55] *Exodus Rabbah* 47:1, qtd. in Hoenig, *The Essence of Talmudic Law and Thought,* 111.

Considering Moses' achievements in exercising authority, therefore, how does one differentiate leadership from management? The answer involves a subtle line of distinction, but is an important one to draw since Moses was certainly a leader in the contemporary sense of the term and not confined to the biblical or religious realms.

# Chapter 3

# LEADERS AND MANAGERS

British leadership scholar Christopher Bones points out that leaders of modern organizations, particularly leaders of human resource departments, tend to blend notions of effective management and leadership without even realizing it. He cites a recent UK study on training needs that identified a series of problems related to leadership skills where the list of identified gaps included problems with people management, performance management, change management, strategic thinking, coaching and mentoring, communication/ interpersonal skills and innovation—"skill gaps," which Bones stresses do not "address the fundamentals of leadership; all are skills we require in managers at just about every level of the organization."[1] Bones believes that "this reflects a muddle amongst HR people specifically and the wider management population generally."[2] Identifying leadership skills is, therefore, imperative to understanding how they differ from management skills. Certain managerial skills are useful for the leader, and vice versa, but the roles of leader and manager fundamentally differ.

## The Leader and Transformational Leadership

American leadership scholar James MacGregor Burns outlines the implicit ideal of power and morality as crucial components of effective leadership but also articulates two key forms of leadership that a leader may possess, including his pioneering concept of "transformational leadership," representing intellectual leaders who focus on ideas for moral power; reform leaders; revolutionary leaders; and heroic leaders, and "transactional leadership," representing opinion leaders, group leaders, party leaders, legislative leaders and executive leaders.[3]

---

[1] Christopher Bones, *The Cult of the Leader: A Manifesto for More Effective Business* (San Francisco, CA: Jossey-Bass, 2011), 36.

[2] Bones, *The Cult of the Leader*, 36.

[3] See James MacGregor Burns, *Leadership* (New York, NY: Harper, 1979) for a discussion of each type in great detail.

In the contemporary business and political worlds, we might tend to focus more on the transactional leader, but, arguably, transformational leaders are profoundly important as they are likely to affect and influence the masses. However, each of these leadership types can be found in the effective leader, and both can certainly be identified in Moses' model of leadership.

Whereas a transactional leader might be found leading smaller-scale changes due to the focus on "the basic, daily stuff of politics," with modest change the result, transformational leadership is the leadership style of profound change—"revolutions that replace one structure of power with another."[4] After all, Moses succeeded as a transformational leader as he transformed the Israelites from slaves in Egypt into a functioning society in the wilderness. Transformational leadership also arguably reflects visionary leadership because focus on the "big picture," the ability to inspire the masses toward achieving meaning within that big picture, is enhanced by the skills of the visionary. Effective leadership also enables successful change—or in contemporary terms, "organizational change and development"—to occur. But what underlies the leader's skill is the ability to empower people.

Building upon MacGregor Burns' transformational leadership theory, American social researcher Bernard Bass added the significance of leaders deriving trust, respect and admiration from followers, stressing the importance of "empowerment" to the overall process.[5] In turn, Burns incorporated Bass' notions and believes that "leaders take the initiative in mobilizing people for participation in the process of change, encouraging a sense of collective identity and collective efficacy, which in turn brings stronger feelings of self-worth and self-efficacy, described by Bernard Bass as an enhanced 'sense of "meaningfulness" in their work and lives' [since] by pursuing transformational change, people can transform themselves"—a process embodied in the word *empowerment*.[6] Empowerment will be considered in a later chapter in connection with the very important skill of delegation, or power sharing.

Considering whether the transformational leader is just a remake of the Great Man Theory, Burns concluded the answer is no because "for leadership students the rise and fall of luminaries—many of them, indeed, more rulers and tyrants than leaders—dramatized the basic leadership issue of *agency* versus *structure*, the relation between the leaders' character and qualities

[4] James MacGregor Burns, *Transforming Leadership: A New Pursuit of Happiness* (New York, NY: Grove, 2003), 24.

[5] See, for example, Bernard M. Bass, *Leadership and Performance Beyond Expectations* (New York, NY: Free Press, 1985), and Bernard M. Bass and Ronald E. Riggio, *Transformational Leadership*, 2nd ed. (Mahwah, NJ: Lawrence Erlbaum, 2006).

[6] Burns, *Transforming Leadership*, 25–26.

and the social and political context in which they operated, and the role of each in charge."[7]

Twentieth-century leaders—like Winston Churchill, Clement Attlee and Margaret Thatcher in England; Harry S. Truman, John F. Kennedy and Lyndon Johnson in the United States; Joseph Stalin, Nikita Khrushchev and Mikhail Gorbachev in the Union of Soviet Socialist Republics; even China's Mao Tse-tung, among others—were all "titans" dependent on, and ultimately functions of, their place, time period, individual personality characteristics and overall circumstances. For instance, Burns maintains that Churchill "was a much-frustrated politician in peacetime who flowered in the demanding circumstances of two world wars," and that "Charles de Gaulle could not have assumed leadership in 1940 and 1958 without the collapse of transactional politics-as-usual," whereas "the limited transactional skills of Mao Tse-tung were nearly irrelevant to the dire needs of the followers who instead put their trust in his transforming powers."[8]

* * *

As a transformational leader, Moses was an intellectual leader who delivered ideas embedded in Divine laws. He was certainly a revolutionary given how he succeeded in leading the Israelites out of Egypt. Moses was heroic in his pivotal role where his faith in God prevented him from fearing the wrath of the powerful Pharaoh. Likewise, Moses was also a transactional leader as he helped cultivate opinions, groups and parties and delegated to subordinate judges and others he put in charge. Nevertheless, we cannot lose sight of the fact that Moses came first, while such descriptors as "transactional" or "transformational" leaders are modern terms for leadership roles that Moses represented through his actions.

Although what Gardner describes is largely true—that leaders come in many forms—one can still refine particular features that leaders have in common. However, first, it is necessary to distinguish between leadership and management because, in Gardner's words, "Leadership and management are not the same thing, but they overlap," with managers often exhibiting "some leadership skills, and most leaders on occasion find[ing] themselves managing."[9] This is certainly true in practice.

---

[7] Ibid., 25.
[8] Ibid.
[9] Burns, *Leadership*, 14.

## The Manager

In some respects, management is the task of a "small-group" leader. In other words, this is a person in charge of ensuring a task gets completed efficiently and on schedule. If management occupies the micro, leadership represents the macro. A leader is not necessarily driven by the same issues and concerns as the manager but has the "big picture" in mind. A "vision" of the end result and how to get there is the primary aim of the leader. In fact, a fundamental skill for a leader is to have a vision of the goal or end result that the group is being led to achieve. Such a person is often referred to as a "visionary leader," as described later, because of the big picture held by the leader who guides or inspires subordinates toward its achievement. Of course, there must be buy-in by those subordinates, and the Israelites did not always buy into Moses' vision.

For instance, before any plagues were sent down upon Egypt, after Moses with his brother Aaron first went to the Pharaoh to initially request that the Israelites be freed, the Pharaoh refused by saying, "Who is the Lord that I should heed Him and let Israel go? I do not know the Lord, nor will I let Israel go."[10] The Israelites were not initially willing to listen to Moses either. God's promise to Moses that, through Moses, the Israelites would be led out of slavery and bondage and into the Promised Land of Canaan—reflecting God's earlier covenant made with Abraham, Isaac and Jacob—fell on deaf ears when Moses related to the Israelites what he was told. As reported in Exodus, "But when Moses told this to the Israelites, they would not listen to Moses, their spirits crushed by cruel bondage."[11]

Even later on, after the Israelites agreed to follow Moses out of Egyptian bondage, with the Pharaoh's forces hot on their trail, a frightened community of Israelites having reached the sea over which they could not cross, complained to Moses, "What have you done to us, taking us out of Egypt? Is this not the very thing we told you in Egypt, saying, 'Let us be, and we will serve the Egyptians, for it is better for us to serve the Egyptians than to die in the wilderness'?"[12]

While the Israelites would subsequently not cease to complain or air their grievances, Moses would nonetheless prove his mettle as a leader of great skill. After all, in this case, he begins his approach to inspire the masses with strength and establish a vision to which they were to aspire. He responds, "Have no fear! Stand by, and witness the deliverance which the Lord will work for you today;

---

[10] Exod. 5:2.
[11] Exod. 6:9.
[12] Exod. 14:11–12.

for the Egyptians whom you see today you will never see again."[13] It was God who had to remind Moses not to rely on him but to be a leader of the Israelites. "Why do you cry out to Me? Tell the Israelites to go forward. And you lift up your rod and hold out your arm over the sea and split it, so that the Israelites may march into the sea on dry ground."[14] Moses did as God instructed. "Moses held out his arm over the sea and the Lord drove back the sea with a strong east wind all that night, and turned the sea into dry ground. The waters were split, and the Israelites went into the sea on dry ground, the waters forming a wall for them on their right and on their left."[15] The Egyptians stood no chance in pursuit of the Israelites, and Moses began to truly shine in his role as a leader. Until this stage, the people had yet to be moved by Moses' leadership as he lacked a solid sense of Divine visionary leadership.

Yet Moses became a visionary leader. As Hal Lewis stresses, Moses' "leadership served to transform the Israelites, to help former slaves transcend their psycho-spiritual shackles and reach for greater heights. In brief, he was able to do what effective leaders must do—to mobilize his followers, showing them a vision of the future which they themselves would not originally have discerned."[16] This leadership role transcends management. But Moses also represented other types of leadership.

Sigmund Freud alluded to a "heroic" form of leadership through his "Great Man" descriptor of Moses, such as when Freud speculated, "How is it possible that one single man can develop such extraordinary effectiveness, that he can create out of indifferent individuals and families one people, can stamp this people with its definite character and determine its fate for millennia to come?"[17] Indeed, this is outstanding leadership. But true leadership abilities must be concretely identified to see what Moses possessed, in order to recognize what kind of leader he represented. Such leadership abilities are not easily discernible, however, without first contrasting them with the role and skills of the manager.

\* \* \*

Although the word "manager" implies that such an individual "holds a directive post in an organization, presiding over the processes by which the

---

[13] Exod. 14:13.
[14] Exod. 14:15–16.
[15] Exod. 14:21–22.
[16] Hal M. Lewis, *Models and Meanings in the History of Jewish Leadership* (Lewiston, NY: Edwin Mellen, 2004), 13.
[17] Sigmund Freud, *Moses and Monotheism*, trans. Katherine Jones (New York, NY: Vintage Books, 1939), 136.

organization functions, allocating resources prudently, and making the best possible use of people," John Gardner notes, "many writers on leadership take considerable pains to distinguish between leaders and managers."[18] However, Gardner maintains, "in the process leaders generally end up looking like a cross between Napoleon and the Pied Piper, and managers like unimaginative clods," a depiction Gardner views as undesirable and inaccurate.[19]

According to Gardner, "Even the most visionary leader is faced on occasion with decisions that every manager faces: when to take a short-term loss to achieve a long-term gain, how to allocate scarce resources, whom to trust with a delicate assignment."[20] As a consequence, Gardner outlined different categories compared to the typical "manager versus leader," but rather had leaders *and* leader/managers occupying one category, and managers lacking leadership ability occupying another category.

Gardner recognized that both leaders and leader/managers "distinguish themselves from the general run of managers in at least six respects"—they are long-term thinkers; grasp the "larger realities" beyond their organization or community; influence people beyond their boundaries; emphasize "the intangibles of vision, values, and motivation"; possess the "political skill to cope with the conflicting requirements of multiple constituencies"; and "they think in terms of renewal" in light of an ever-changing reality, all in contrast with the typical manager who "tends to accept organizational structure and process as it exists."[21]

## Differentiating Leaders from Managers

Emerging as a leader, Moses certainly still had to "manage"—as Gardner concedes some leaders tend to do—such as when Moses took his father-in-law's advice and delegated the adjudication of common disputes to others, discussed later. David Baron, a congregational rabbi and business entrepreneur, includes a number of important leadership criteria in his book *Moses on Management*, like being a "visionary" and ultimately inspiring the Israelites as they fled Egypt and ended up in Sinai. He alludes to the importance of maintaining "vision" and describes how to stay focused, which is a challenge for all leaders today as it was for Moses. "Moses had plenty of distractions—water and food shortages, complaining compatriots, truculent neighbors, constant requests for advice—not to mention a very demanding boss," he notes, which

---

[18]  John W. Gardner, *On Leadership* (New York, NY: Free Press, 1990), 3.
[19]  Gardner, *On Leadership*, 3.
[20]  Ibid., 4.
[21]  Ibid.

led, at times, to discouragement.[22] What was the solution? "After communing with the Lord, Moses returns to the Israelites re-energized and with a clearer sense of purpose," demonstrating that solitary reflection is important, and "that in order to stay focused, leaders must periodically retreat from the crowd and consult their inner spiritual compass"—because, Baron asserts, "if we don't take time to refocus on our purpose, we may lose sight of it altogether."[23]

Baron observes that Moses was often criticized for spending "too much time in the Tent of Meeting" (*Mishkan*) or for being "too remote," but that some distance is necessary to retain the respect of the people, but not too much so that people become alienated.[24] This is a contemporary strategy Baron notes from Moses' example. Yet just as a CEO must report to a board of directors, Moses also knew when to report to his "boss" to deal with a problem—hence, regular visits to the Tent of Meeting were essential—but Moses had the security of knowing that his boss would listen to him and help him, indicating that God is also a good leader and the metaphorical contemporary embodiment of an effective singular board of directors.

While the best leaders also possess management skills, the roles still fundamentally differ from each other. Austrian-born, preeminent American management thinker Peter F. Drucker acknowledged, "There is no substitute for leadership. But management cannot create leaders. It can only create the conditions under which potential leadership qualities become effective—or it can stifle potential leadership."[25] Although this is an interesting perspective, one could also argue that effective leadership has the potential to encourage good management.

Though remaining a proponent of good management rather than focusing his intellectual interests on leadership, even Drucker concedes that "*leadership is lifting a person's vision to higher sights, the raising of a person's performance to a higher standard, the building of a personality beyond its normal limitations.*"[26] God does this for Moses. For Drucker, however, "nothing better prepares the ground for such leadership than a spirit of management that confirms in the day-to-day practices of the organization strict principles of conduct and responsibility, high standards of performance, and respect for individuals and their work."[27]

---

[22] David Baron and Lynette Padwa, *Moses on Management: 50 Leadership Lessons from the Greatest Manager of All Time* (New York, NY: Pocket Books, 1999), 140–41.

[23] Baron and Padwa, *Moses on Management*, 141.

[24] Ibid., 141–42.

[25] Peter F. Drucker, and Joseph A. Maciariello, *Management*, rev. ed. (New York, NY: Harper Collins, 2008), 288.

[26] Drucker and Maciariello, *Management*, 288.

[27] Ibid.

Nonetheless, American pioneer of the contemporary field of leadership Warren Bennis, former chairman of the Center for Public Leadership at Harvard University's John F. Kennedy School of Government, sharply differentiates the leader from the manager in more descriptive terms in his classic work, *On Becoming a Leader.*

Bennis' list is worth considering because the distinctions are crucial to appreciating Moses' leadership as legitimate precedent for contemporary qualities of leadership.[28] According to Bennis, the following distinctions can be made:

- The manager administers; the leader innovates.
- The manager is a copy; the leader is an original.
- The manager maintains; the leader develops.
- The manager focuses on systems and structure; the leader focuses on people.
- The manager relies on control; the leader inspires trust.
- The manager has a short-range view; the leader has a long-range perspective.
- The manager asks how and when; the leader asks what and why.
- The manager has his eye always on the bottom line; the leader has his eye on the horizon.
- The manager imitates; the leader originates.
- The manager accepts the status quo; the leader challenges it.
- The manager is the classic good soldier; the leader is his own person.
- The manager does things right; the leader does the right thing.

Bennis' description of leadership matches the depiction of Moses we know from the Bible. Indeed, Moses was innovative, original, developed a new path, focused on his people, inspired trust, had a long-range perspective that saw him through decades in the wilderness, was inquisitive of God about why he was selected to be a leader in the first place, always looked ahead, was unique among the masses, challenged the authority of the Pharaoh, was his own person rather than a follower and appears to have always tried to do the right thing. Although speculative, perhaps Bennis' own Jewish upbringing—whether cultural or religious—influenced his subsequent views on leadership?

In his autobiography, Bennis alludes to his personal Jewish origins but does not elaborate.[29] Bennis mentions the decades of quotas directed against Jewish students and academic faculty in the United States, and implies that

---

[28]  Warren Bennis, *On Becoming a Leader* (Cambridge, MA: Perseus Books, 1989), 45.
[29]  See Warren Bennis and Patricia Ward Biederman, *Still Surprised: A Memoir of a Life in Leadership* (San Francisco, CA: Jossey-Bass, 2010).

this quota system affected him as a faculty member in the late 1960s.[30] As a young American combat officer in Germany during World War II, Bennis relates, "Even as we got deeper into Germany, we had no idea of the nature or scale of Hitler's war against the Jews. [...] We didn't know about the death camps."[31] Bennis further concedes that he "didn't feel the full impact of what happened [to him] in 1944–45 until 2009" when he attended an exhibition of German art at the Los Angeles County Museum of Art. Describing himself standing before "a stark black-and-white photo of the German countryside," he notes, "all the old images came flooding back [...] and tears streamed down my face."[32] Hence, while Bennis was born into a Jewish family, we can only surmise how his Jewish upbringing, or perhaps a Jewish education, may have influenced his subsequent thinking on leadership.

Whether conscious of the biblical precedent of Moses or not, Bennis' differentiation between managers and leaders reveals qualities of leadership evident in Moses. Norman Cohen, professor of Midrash at New York's Hebrew Union College-Jewish Institute of Religion (HUC-JIR), maintains that the Bible and its innumerable rabbinical commentaries provides, in broad outline, "a significant portrait of leadership" applicable not only to the modern Jewish community but also the secular community.[33]

Cohen argues, "Imagine if every synagogue, communal organizational, or educational institution's board demanded that all who aspired to leadership in their communities had the following characteristics: strength; patience; faith in God; high ethical standards; the willingness to stand on principle and act on it in the face of aggressive opposition; a sense that life should not be solely dedicated to acquiring material wealth; [and] dedication to Torah (or Bible) study."[34] This list contrasts with Lewis' list of six leadership qualities, which, as mentioned in chapter 2, holds piety, tenacity, compassion, service to followers, humility and consistency as the distilled "Jewish" leadership characteristics, which only goes to show the significance of diversity of opinion. Yet, these lists are not entirely dissimilar but rather stress different elements.

Cohen's list is indeed a tall order. Despite the questionable legality in contemporary jurisdictions for demanding "faith" as a requirement for hiring a leader, the underlying implication from the qualities he identifies is that one would end up hiring a figure much like Moses. Bennis' list of qualities that

---

[30]   Bennis and Biederman, *Still Surprised*, 123.
[31]   Ibid., 18.
[32]   Ibid., 19.
[33]   Norman J. Cohen, *Moses and the Journey to Leadership: Timeless Lessons of Effective Management from the Bible and Today's Leaders* (Woodstock, VT: Jewish Lights, 2007), 94.
[34]   Cohen, *Moses and the Journey to Leadership*, 94.

differentiate a leader from a manager also conjures up a leader like Moses. To see why this is the case, leadership theories must be further explored.

* * *

In his biography of Freud, academic Mark Edmundson argues that "in Moses, Freud sees a new kind of authority," a heroic leader typically known as the Great Man, which is fundamentally important because of its significance to the history of modern leadership theories. Edmundson notes, "Up until this point, Freud's reflections on authority have ended up at the same place. Authority is inevitably male, narcissistic, overbearing, self-interested, arbitrary, and, quite often, tyrannical." Considering Moses, however, "Freud often (though not always) sees something different." Edmundson asserts that "Moses can project all the patriarchal qualities, true. But Moses is distinct from other sorts of leaders in that he is a hero of sublimation: he is a divided being who achieves his authority not by being self-willed and appetitive, but by intelligently rechanneling his impulses and teaching others to do the same." Freud maintained that while Moses rejects the pagan gods and provides laws that reflect prohibition, "when the Jews rebel, Freud argues in his early essay on the prophet, Moses succeeds in restraining himself from raging against them." In other words, Edmundson stresses, "Freud's Moses, unlike the archetypal leaders, lives with inner conflict and anxiety, and he does so in the interest of civilization." Hence, Edmundson concludes, "What Moses surely suggests to Freud—and should suggest to us—is that it may be possible to be an authority, to have an influence, without being a conventional patriarch."[35]

Edmundson's view rings true in light of the many successful female leaders who have followed Moses. For such a leader of any time period, the traits possessed by Moses are desirable and not tied to gender, other than perhaps a "paternal" view that some ascribe to Moses as his public leadership largely began when he was in his early eighties.[36]

[35] Mark Edmundson, *The Death of Sigmund Freud: The Legacy of His Last Days* (New York, NY: Bloomsbury, 2007), 236–37.

[36] Exod. 7:7, "Moses was eighty years old and Aaron eighty-three, when they made their demand on Pharaoh."

# Chapter 4

# HEROISM, CHARISMA AND THEIR LIMITATIONS

Sigmund Freud maintained that "the great man influences his contemporaries in two ways: through his personality and through the idea for which he stands."[1] Yet, according to James MacGregor Burns, in Freud's viewing Moses through the lens of the Great Man, whose personality and strongly held beliefs not only underscored the view that "Moses was one of the first of the towering 'charismatic' leaders," the essence of what Freud captured was "Moses' greatness and an ambiguity in the concept of charisma that has clouded understanding of the 'hero in history' to this day."[2] While aspects of the heroic and the charismatic leader apply to Moses, there are indeed limitations to these concepts that do not fully reflect the power of Moses' leadership.

## Heroic Leadership and the Great Man Theory

Hal Lewis feels that "the Great Man Theory exaggerates the importance of the individual leader" because it minimizes other factors or completely ignores them altogether. According to the Great Man model, Lewis asserts, "the success and failure of an entire enterprise rest largely upon the shoulders of the leader."[3] It is a hierarchical view of leadership. Lewis argues that this view of leadership means that followers—whether, in the modern sense, "employees" or other functionally equivalent roles as "citizens" or even "congregants"—implies a "leader-follower relationship" where the leader occupying the top position has something to offer, and, in turn, those who follow thereby depend upon that leader to address their needs, whether it be a "paycheck, physical protection, expertise" or something less concrete or even measurable, like "cures, validation, an inspired sense of purpose."[4]

---

[1] Sigmund Freud, *Moses and Monotheism*, trans. Katherine Jones (New York, NY: Vintage Books, 1939), 139.

[2] James MacGregor Burns, *Leadership* (New York, NY: Harper, 1979), 241–42.

[3] Hal M. Lewis, *From Sanctuary to Boardroom: A Jewish Approach to Leadership* (Lanham, MD: Rowman & Littlefield, 2006), 75.

[4] Lewis, *From Sanctuary to Boardroom*, 75.

Lewis notes that such a "top-down" view of leadership is believed to work best when the leader possesses particular personality traits deemed desirable, such as "strength, magnetism, single-mindedness, and forcefulness," almost making "heroic leaders" viewed in only superhuman terms. Lewis maintains, therefore, that "as Judaism has for centuries, today's most progressive leadership theories distance themselves from this archaic view," making the Great Man Theory obsolete, regarding which he points to leadership theorists like Warren Bennis and Robert Thomas as also believing that the era of the Great Man is over.[5]

Yet Lewis' certainty about the decline of the Great Man Theory may not be entirely warranted. The legitimacy of "heroic leadership," historically viewed in terms of the Great Man approach to leadership where inherent traits or qualities are viewed as the defining factors underlying the leader's strengths, appears to have received some support in a recent meta-analysis of the role of individual differences in effective leadership.[6] Finding support for the Great Man Theory of leadership, Brian J. Hoffman, David J. Woehr and Robyn Maldagen-Yongjohn suggest "leaders are born, not made."[7]

While no such finding can be simply accepted without more studies showing support, their conclusion adds credibility for views that emphasize the significance of traits. As Shelley Kirkpatrick and Edwin Locke explain, "The great man theories evolved into trait theories. ("Trait" is used broadly here to refer to peoples' general characteristics, including capacities, motives, or patterns of behavior.) Trait theories did not make assumptions about whether leadership traits were inherited or acquired. They simply asserted that leaders' characteristics are different from non-leaders" and reflect heredity as well as experience and learning.[8] However, Kirkpatrick and Locke concede that, on their own, traits "are not sufficient for successful business leadership" but are rather "only a precondition." In other words, they maintain, "Leaders who possess the requisite traits must take certain actions to be successful (e.g., formulating a vision, role modeling, setting goals)." Thus, Kirkpatrick and Locke's claim appears at least plausible if not convincing: "Possessing the appropriate traits only makes it more likely that such actions will be taken

---

[5]  Ibid., 76.

[6]  Brian J. Hoffman, David J. Woehr and Robyn Maldagen-Youngjohn, "Great Man or Great Myth? A Quantitative Review of the Relationship between Individual Differences and Leader Effectiveness," *Journal of Occupational and Organizational Psychology*, 84, no. 2 (2011): 347–81.

[7]  Hoffman, Woehr and Maldagen-Yongjohn, "Great Man or Great Myth?", 349.

[8]  Shelley Kirkpatrick and Edwin Locke, "Leadership: Do Traits Matter?", in *The Leader's Companion: Insights on Leadership Through the Ages*, ed. J. Thomas Wren (New York, NY: Free Press, 1995), 134.

and be successful."[9] Naturally, there can be no guarantees of success, but the argument remains compelling.

According to Kirkpatrick and Locke, evidence supports six traits—reflecting nature (through inheritance) and nurture (from experience and learning)—that differentiate leaders from nonleaders, namely drive, desire to lead, honesty/integrity, self-confidence, cognitive ability and business knowledge. Yet, regardless of whether leaders are born or made or are some combination of both, Kirkpatrick and Locke stress, "it is unequivocally clear that *leaders are not like other people*. Leaders do not have to be great men or women by being intellectual geniuses or omniscient prophets to succeed but they do need to have the 'right stuff' and this stuff is not equally present in all people." They argue, therefore, "that in the realm of leadership (and in every other realm), the individual *does* matter."[10]

Importantly, Hoffman, Woehr and Maldagen-Yongjohn emphasize that present reviews of the relationship between leadership and individual differences have not "considered the role of theoretically proximal individual differences," and that Edwin A. Locke—in his book, *The Essence of Leadership: The Four Keys to Leading Successfully*—has pointed out that "interpersonal skills, oral communication, written communication, administrative/management skills, problem-solving skills, decision making, and organizing and planning" are all crucial "antecedents to effective leadership," giving particular prominence to "interpersonal skills."[11]

Though it is questionable as to what degree such skills are truly necessary, many of these skills appear intuitive since the effective leadership of people understandably requires the ability to relate to others in a positive and efficacious manner. If a leader cannot do so, why would anyone with a choice agree to follow such a leader? As mentioned earlier, Rob Goffee and Gareth Jones asked this very question in the title of their work because leadership qualities matter.[12] Of course, most people do not get to choose for whom they work because, in need of a job, they must often simply put up with a terrible leader in order to earn money for their families. This is the reality of many workplaces today and has been the case over the course of history. This is also one of the reasons societies and organizations should want to hire or cultivate better leaders for the greater good.

---

[9]  Kirkpatrick and Locke, "Leadership," in Wren, *The Leader's Companion*, 134.
[10]  Ibid., 143.
[11]  Cited in Hoffman, Woehr and Maldagen-Yongjohn, "Great Man or Great Myth?", 352.
[12]  See Rob Goffee and Gareth Jones, *Why Should Anyone Be Led by You? What It Takes to Be an Authentic Leader* (Boston, MA: Harvard Business Review Press, 2015).

Hoffman, Woehr and Maldagen-Yongjohn assert, therefore, that "there does appear to be a systematic, dispositional-based component to being an effective leader, supporting the 'Great Man' approach to leadership; however, state-like individual differences were also important correlates of effective leadership, substantiating the expansion of leader-individual difference models to include more malleable individual differences." Each model, in isolation, only accounts for "modest amounts of variance in leader effectiveness." The final conclusion, therefore, is that there are other "correlates of effective leadership, such as leader behaviour, situational factors, and the interaction among individual differences."[13]

Given the above, when it comes to Moses, it is fair to conclude that Moses was heroic. He can be viewed in terms of the Great Man, but his leadership behavior, the situations in which he found himself, and how he interacted with others, each played important roles in developing his style of leadership. While these approaches might not all prove effective today, one can see how they would be effective for Moses' leading the Israelites out of bondage and then through the wilderness.

Even in contemporary times we often see leaders, from corporate CEOs to congregational rabbis and other religious leaders, being regarded by those who follow them as iconic leaders without whom success is impossible. Employees of Microsoft likely looked at a visionary like Bill Gates in similar terms, while those at Apple likely looked at Steve Jobs in a comparable fashion. Without these men's initial genius, their employees would not likely have attained their current occupations. Similarly, without a strong leader possessing leadership traits that inspire allegiance—like magnetism, forcefulness and single-minded focus on achieving the best for those being led—people would not likely follow (unless secure employment—or simply a regular paycheck—were the sole reasons).

* * *

We can only surmise why Moses was divinely selected to become a leader. Of Moses, God is reported as saying, "Hear these My words: When a prophet of the Lord arises among you, I make Myself known to him in a vision, I speak with him in a dream. Not so with My servant Moses; he is trusted throughout My household. With him I speak mouth to mouth, plainly and not in riddles, and he beholds the likeness of the Lord."[11] Clearly there was something about Moses that God believed represented true human leadership material.

---

[13] Hoffman, Woehr and Maldagen-Yongjohn, "Great Man or Great Myth?", 370.
[11] Num. 12:6–8.

But what is equally important to note is that God addressed these words to Moses' older siblings, Miriam and Aaron, who had cast aspersions on their brother's abilities or judgment. God merely ended by saying, "'How then did you not shrink from speaking against My servant Moses!' Still incensed with them, the Lord departed."[15] Miriam and Aaron's complaints suggest envy of their younger brother Moses. After all, Moses had benevolently included both of his older siblings in the exodus from Egypt and in his leadership over the Israelites, notes Rabbi Yitzchak Etshalom, making "Aaron one of his right-hand men" (Exod. 24:14), and Miriam leader of "the women" (Exod. 15:20).[16] But, as discussed previously, Miriam was a leader of more than women if Evangeline Anderson's persuasive Hebrew grammatical observation—that is, the use of the masculine plural for "them" in verse Exodus 15:21—indeed applies to both genders rather than just females.[17]

Moses cannot be viewed simply through heroic or Great Man terms, as he had other sources of leadership to draw upon and employed key managerial skills, like delegation, as will be discussed in more detail later. Moses had delegated responsibilities and tasks to his siblings Miriam and Aaron, as well as Joshua and Caleb, along with the many judges appointed to adjudicate over disputes, proving that power sharing was a very strong source of strength that fueled Moses' leadership. Hal Lewis maintains that "in the majority of cases, Moses understood that leadership, to be effective, must be a shared enterprise."[18] While this was true in Moses' practice of delegation of power to ensure that work got done, individual charisma—or personal charm—cannot be ignored.

Rabbi Jill Jacobs maintains that "charismatic leaders have transformed Jewish life and the Jewish community," citing their prominence among such early rabbis as Yochanan bar Nafcha and, in more recent centuries, among leading Hasidic rebbes, suggesting to her that "charisma can be an invaluable leadership tool" because leaders who possess charisma "can persuade a community to take risks, to explore new ideas to try out new modes of practice." Yet she warns that the qualities that underscore power for charismatic leaders "can easily be used for negative effect."[19]

---

[15] Num. 12:8–9.

[16] Yitzchak Etshalom, *Between the Lines of the Bible, Exodus: A Study from the New School of Orthodox Torah Commentary* (New York, NY: Orthodox Union Press, 2012), 50.

[17] Evangeline Anderson, "Engendering Leadership: A Christian Feminist Perspective from India," in *Responsible Leadership: Global and Contextual Ethical Perspectives*, ed. Christoph Stückelberger and J. N. K. Mugambi (Geneva, Switzerland: WCC Publications, 2007), 14.

[18] Hal M. Lewis, *Models and Meanings in the History of Jewish Leadership* (Lewiston, NY: Edwin Mellen, 2004), 17.

[19] Rabbi Jill Jacobs, "On Charisma and Jewish Leadership," *Contact: The Journal of the Steinhardt Foundation for Jewish Life* 11, no. 1 (Autumn 2008): 6.

## Charismatic Leadership

Charisma as a source of leadership authority was strongly asserted by the influential German sociologist Max Weber, who, notes Christopher Adair-Toteff, located charismatic power in the ethical and political behavior and beliefs of the biblical prophets Amos, Jeremiah and Isaiah.[20] As Adair-Toteff notes, "Weber believed that Amos and Jeremiah were," in Weber's words, the "'most powerful of the writing prophets'" and that Weber had made "considerable use of these three [prophets] in his own writings on ancient Judaism."[21]

According to Weber's book, *Ancient Judaism*, "During the later time of kings there was always a party in Israel—and, indeed, it included the most powerful scriptural prophets such as Amos and Jeremiah—who kept the memory of this condition alive."[22] Weber claimed, "The pre-exilic prophets from Amos to Jeremiah and Ezekiel, viewed through the eyes of the contemporary outsider, appeared to be, above all, political demagogues and, on occasion, pamphleteers."[23] Weber clarified this view. "This characterization of the prophets (as demagogues and pamphleteers) can indeed be misleading, but properly understood it permits indispensable insight. It means that the prophets were primarily *speakers*. Prophets as writers appear only after the Babylonian Exile. The early prophets addressed their audiences in public."[24] By operating in public, these prophets could easily reveal their charisma. However, while these prophets were significant male figures, charisma transcends gender and reflects other qualities.

Considering requirements for effective leadership, therefore, another aspect that can be dismissed besides gender, which was discussed earlier, is heredity. Harvey Minkoff observes that "though Moses has two sons, he designates Joshua of [the tribe of] Ephraim, who is unrelated to him, as his successor." Similarly, while Samuel, also of the tribe of Ephraim, has two sons, Samuel anoints Saul of the tribe of Benjamin "to establish the new monarchy."[25]

This tells us that—unlike the later tradition of hereditary kingship in Judah where the monarchy tended to remain in the House of David[26] (in contrast,

[20]   Christopher Adair-Toteff, "Max Weber's Charismatic Prophets," *History of the Human Sciences* 27, no. 1 (2014): 1.

[21]   Christopher Adair-Toteff, "Max Weber's Charismatic Prophets," 10.

[22]   Max Weber, *Ancient Judaism*, trans. and ed. Hans H. Gerth and Don Martindale (New York, NY: Free Press, 1952), 136.

[23]   Weber, *Ancient Judaism*, 267.

[24]   Ibid., 267–68.

[25]   Harvey Minkoff, "Moses and Samuel: Israel's Era of Charismatic Leadership," *Jewish Bible Quarterly* 30, no. 4 (2002): 257.

[26]   Even during Saul's earlier reign, his son Jonathan was considered heir to the throne rather than David, who ultimately succeeded Saul. See I Sam. 20:30–31.

the Northern Kingdom had frequent dynasty changes)—hereditary leadership between the period of Moses and Samuel was not seemingly necessary for effective leadership, but rather other attributes were important in leaders. Hence, Minkoff asserts, "Where there is no Divine mandate for hereditary elevation, Israel will have charismatic leadership."[27] Yet, for many, charisma alone is not considered a legitimate foundation upon which a leader should lead. This is apparent from the essentially negative assessment of the period of the Judges, who led primarily through charisma before the establishment of the monarchy. As the Bible reports, "In those days there was no king in Israel; everyone did as he pleased."[28]

For others, there may be justifiable reasons for hereditary leadership, such as religious bases like the transmission of the priesthood in Judaism through the paternal line of the tribe of Levi that began with Aaron. But genetics is secondary to the ability to lead, which may not have any genetic component for the leadership position beyond some common genes, without even considering nepotism as a means for making leadership appointments. Nepotism does not necessarily correlate with leadership ability. After all, as the Torah suggests, among the early priests, hereditary leadership did not necessarily work out so well as in the case of Aaron's sons Nadab and Abihu, the eldest two of Aaron's four sons, all of whom were appointed *kohanim*, or priests, but these two, according to the Book of Leviticus, were killed by God's own fire for disobeying his instructions.[29]

Rodney Hutton has observed that, from a sociological point of view, "both Weber and Durkheim romanticized charisma, seeing in it the generating power for society," but such romanticism "led them to long for what they believed to be in danger of extinction—whether the superhero of antirational passion or the coherent group bonded by a nearly mystical sense of primitive suprapersonal transcendence."[30] However, Hutton believed that Max Weber and Émile Durkheim differed from each other because, "for Weber, the romance of German Protestantism with its focus on the heroic individual; and for Durkheim, the romance of French Catholicism and the French Revolution, both [...] focused on the heroic community in fraternity."[31] Indeed, as mentioned, even Hutton maintains that the Judges of the Bible

---

[27]  Minkoff, "Moses and Samuel," 259.

[28]  Judg. 21:25.

[29]  Lev. 10:1–2. See Arthur J. Wolak, "Alcohol and the Fate of Nadab and Abihu: A Biblical Cautionary Tale against Inebriation," *Jewish Bible Quarterly* 41, no. 4 (2013): 219–26.

[30]  Rodney R. Hutton, *Charisma and Authority in Israelite Society* (Minneapolis, MN: Fortress Press, 1994), 206.

[31]  Hutton, *Charisma and Authority in Israelite Society*, 207.

"are often regarded as ideal paradigms of charismatic leadership,"[32] more so than Moses who preceded them.

In Hutton's view, "one no longer feels constrained by the need to position Weber's charismatic individual against Durkheim's charismatic community" because, focusing on the biblical Moses, he served, according to Hutton, "as the 'intimate outsider' who reflected both the community's 'effervescence' and its sense of being confronted by that which was determinative of its shape."[33] In other words, the Judges, according to Hutton's analysis, expressed "both of the community's own nurtured leadership and of the fiery hand of divine appointment," and, likewise, "the charismatic appointment of the kings was similarly anchored both in community endorsement and in divine designation." However, Moses was neither one of the later Judges nor was he a king. Moses preceded them as a prophet and community leader. "The prophetic experience was moored in traditional patterns of divine intermediation that were learned through socialization and were recognized by groups who would grant such charismatic attribution to the extent it met their expectations. Even limited social deviance was itself part of the expected patterning of such prophetic behavior."[34] In other words, there was some divine allowance for leadership error because leaders are only human, after all.

Charismatic leadership, therefore, is not inherently bad—though it can be bad if misused—provided that the leader possesses appropriate qualities that hereditary leadership alone cannot guarantee. Jill Jacobs notes that "those leaders blessed with charisma have the responsibility to maintain appropriate boundaries."[35] Indeed, Drucker, a critic of leadership qualities, maintains that "leadership is not by itself good or desirable" but rather "leadership is a means [...] to what end is, thus, the crucial question."[36]

Drucker focuses his suspicions and doubts on some eminently notorious examples. As Drucker relates, "History knows no more charismatic leaders than the twentieth century's [infamous] triad of Stalin, Hitler, and Mao—misleaders who inflicted as much evil and suffering on humanity as have ever been recorded."[37] Concerning these political leaders, Drucker is quite correct. But painting all leaders, even charismatic leaders, with such a singular brush of condemnation involves generalizing and, therefore, is possibly incorrect.

---

[32] Ibid., 43.
[33] Ibid., 207–8.
[34] Ibid., 208.
[35] Jacobs, "On Charisma and Jewish Leadership," 6.
[36] Peter F. Drucker and Joseph A. Maciariello, *Management*, rev. ed. (New York, NY: Harper Collins, 2008), 289.
[37] Drucker and Maciariello, *Management*, 289.

Regarding Moses' personal charisma, Burns asks, "Is the charismatic leader the spiritual and political father of his people, the source of authority, the lawgiver, the statesman, the mobilizer of popular support for the religious and political ideas that he defines and embraces? Or is he the idol and ikon [sic], the miracle worker, the prophet, the magic man, the 'personality' who arouses his people not because of the substance of his rule or his ideas but because of the halo effect of his magic?"[38] Such a question is legitimate. According to Burns' analysis, the answer is that

> Moses was all of these and more; he was prophet but also, as Martin Buber observed, 'leader of the people, as legislator.' Moses is brought up a prince; he has revelations; he casts a tree into the bitter waters of Marah to make them sweet; he smites the rock and water gushes out. Yet as God's agent he proclaims laws and values so explicit in form and so universal in meeting human needs that they have powerfully influenced Western political thought and behavior. Rare is the leader who can serve as both idol and ideologue, both hero and lawgiver.[39]

Was Moses a charismatic leader? The Bible suggests a qualified yes because it states in the Book of Exodus, even in the midst of the plagues descending across Egypt, that "Moses himself was much esteemed in the land of Egypt, among Pharaoh's courtiers and among the people."[40] His background in the Egyptian court meant "Moses was familiar with court protocol and etiquette," suggests Etshalom. Moses "had a sense of dignity, since he was not subject to the decrees of slavery nor was he culturally enslaved to the Pharaoh, which is often the blessing of those who are 'inside'" and, yet, "as an outsider, he also understood the basic unity of the Israelites."[41] When Moses returned to Egypt, however, he was not just a charismatic leader, which he had to have been to some extent—notwithstanding Hutton's qualifications— in order to engender some respect from the Egyptians, but also his leadership stood on firmer ground and therefore showed great power.

According to Hutton, biblical scholars have gone back and forth "on the question of whether Moses represents primarily a form of 'charismatic' leadership or 'institutional' authority." The latter is emphasized by some because of Moses' role at Sinai and the centrality of the "scribalization process" seen in the Bible, and the Mishnah and Gemara of later rabbinic writings as often

---

[38] Burns, *Leadership*, 242.
[39] Ibid.
[40] Exod. 11:3.
[41] Etshalom, *Between the Lines of the Bible, Exodus*, 48.

having "the last say *in the name of Moses*," which resolves "disparate and conflicting voices" or normalizing them "under the auspices of the Torah tradition" because of "the primary authoritative function of the figure of Moses."[12] Indeed, Moses became an authoritative figure in both Israelite society as well as among the later rabbis, but he arguably possessed certain charismatic traits that helped him rise to his authoritative position.

Hutton rightly asks, "Is Moses' authority that of 'charismatic empowerment' or rather that of 'institutional legitimation'? Does he symbolize the stable inertia of stasis or does he instead represent the potential dynamism of change? Does he speak for divine freedom against Israel's attempts to institutionalize religion or does he speak for those central institutions themselves?"[13] Hutton acknowledges there is no conclusive answer because, among other things, Moses functioned as a charismatic leader, prophet, judge, lawgiver and nation founder as well as mythological figure and literary hero.[14] Moses was each of these things, but charisma may not have been as essential to his leadership position as some suggest.

According to Drucker, charisma is not simply unimportant but effective leadership does not depend on charisma at all. Drucker observes,

> Dwight Eisenhower, George Marshall, and Harry Truman were singularly effective leaders, yet none possessed any more charisma than a dead mackerel. Nor did Konrad Adenauer, the chancellor who rebuilt West Germany after World War II. No less charismatic personality could be imagined than Abe Lincoln of Illinois, the raw-boned, uncouth backwoods man of 1860. And there was amazingly little charisma to the bitter, defeated, almost broken Winston Churchill of the interwar years; what mattered was that he turned out, in the end, to have been right.[15]

It is difficult to contradict Drucker's observations on these political leaders, though Churchill's charisma was evident in his wartime leadership based on Burns' earlier description. Yet, it is undeniable that charisma, if used appropriately, can enhance a leader's inspiring qualities. David Nadler and Michael Tushman argue that this can occur through such means as *envisioning, energizing* and *enabling*, in other words, by creating a picture of a desired future, providing motivation and helping people act to achieve challenging goals.[16]

---

[12] Hutton, *Charisma and Authority in Israelite Society*, 17–18.

[13] Ibid., 21.

[14] Ibid., 22.

[15] Drucker and Maciariello, *Management*, 289.

[16] David A. Nadler and Michael L. Tushman, "Beyond the Charismatic Leader: Leadership and Organizational Change," in Wren, *The Leader's Companion*, 109–10.

Bestselling author Bruce Feiler argues that Moses effectively shaped American identity in his book *America's Prophet: Moses and the American Story*. "In the tradition of nearly every great American icon—the seal, the flag, the Liberty Bell—Uncle Sam now took a turn as Moses." Feiler notes, "the Hebrew prophet [Moses] had become so ingrained in the country's consciousness that he served as a kind of American Hamlet, a role that every actor, in order to be considered great, had to play at least once."[17] Such a phenomenon, in a land so far removed from the original place and time of the events surrounding Moses, reflects the strong influence of Moses' leadership, his good reputation, his accomplishments and perhaps even charismatic aspects.

Similarly, Harold Kushner chose Moses as his vehicle to show how faith, strength and resilience were essential in Kushner's *Overcoming Life's Disappointments*. "Moses establishes the model of the Reluctant Prophet who, summoned by God to do daunting things, responds by recognizing the magnitude of the challenge and his own human limitations," observes Kushner. "Later Israelites called by God to the prophetic role will follow his example."[18] Charismatic leadership had power over the Hebrews and influenced their later religious and political leaders.

But not everyone will prove as strong or as motivated. "Hardly anyone," perhaps with the exception of Isaiah, suggests Kushner, "relishes the challenge of being God's prophet, telling people things they do not like being told."[19] Kushner notes that God had to tell Joshua, Moses' successor, "five times in eight sentences to be strong and not be intimidated (Joshua 1:2–9)."[50] The same reticence is evident in the warrior prophet Gideon, and the prophets Jeremiah[51] and Jonah, whom Kushner relates "famously tries to flee from God's presence instead of bringing God's word to the people of Nineveh, boarding a ship going in the opposite direction."[52] Kushner notes, "It is a daunting, thankless job to bring God's word to people who don't want to hear it," and knowing the Pharaoh as well as he did, Moses' initial trepidation at being asked to return to Egypt to negotiate with him is understandable.[53]

Based on their publication alone, each of these books, among so many others, attests to the powerful impact Moses has had on Judaism, Christianity,

---

[17] Bruce Feiler, *America's Prophet: Moses and the American Story* (New York, NY: William Morrow, 2009), 199.

[18] Harold S. Kushner, *Overcoming Life's Disappointments: Learning from Moses How to Cope with Frustration* (New York, NY: Anchor Books, 2007), 14.

[19] Kushner, *Overcoming Life's Disappointments*, 14.

[50] Ibid.

[51] See, respectively, Judg. 6:15 (Gideon) and Jer. 1:6 (Jeremiah).

[52] Kushner, *Overcoming Life's Disappointments*, 14.

[53] Ibid.

Islam and, ultimately, as Burns and others assert, the pervasive political thought and behavior of Western civilization. While Moses must have possessed some charismatic features, he also must have offered more from his leadership style to have been as successful as the biblical literature portrays.

* * *

Charisma alone is insufficient for effective leadership. There are a number of limitations on the value of the charismatic leader, making some charisma possibly useful or necessary but ultimately insufficient on its own, requiring organizational leaders to possess other qualities.[54] According to Drucker, "*charisma may [even] be the undoing of leaders. It may make them inflexible, convinced of their own infallibility, unable to change [...]* [as] happened to Stalin, Hitler, and Mao, and it is a commonplace in the study of ancient history that only Alexander the Great's early death saved him from becoming an ineffectual failure."[55] Strong words but, given such examples, arguably true, particularly where charismatic leaders operate in a system without checks and balances on their power. For instance, Dwight D. Eisenhower deferred to Congress; Winston Churchill deferred to the reigning monarch; and Moses deferred to God. Likewise, in Jewish terms, contemporary pulpit rabbis defer to the synagogue board. Adolf Hitler, Joseph Stalin and Mao Tse-tung arguably deferred to no one and, therefore, functioned as charismatic tyrants.

Hence, as Burns maintains, "at best, charisma is a confusing and undemocratic form of leadership," and "at worst, it is a type of tyranny."[56] He views charisma as an "exotic or lopsided form of transforming leadership," which he believes is best applied by "liberating and empowering" followers rather than "enslaving" them through the application of charisma.[57] Indeed, Moses did not enslave the Israelites; rather, he liberated them from slavery by relying on more than mere charismatic leadership. Of vital significance, Moses demonstrated empathy that tyrants—representing highly negative examples of leadership—would not typically possess.

---

[54] For a discussion of limitations, see Nadler and Tushman, "Beyond the Charismatic Leader," in Wren, *The Leader's Companion*, 110–12.

[55] Drucker and Maciariello, *Management*, 289.

[56] James MacGregor Burns, *Transforming Leadership: A New Pursuit of Happiness* (New York, NY: Grove, 2003), 27.

[57] Burns, *Transforming Leadership*, 27.

# Chapter 5

# EMPATHIC LEADERSHIP

Empathy is powerful. It is certainly innate but, arguably, also a teachable disposition for effective leadership that distinguishes Moses from other leaders, whether ancient or modern. One would be mistaken, however, in assuming that to feel empathetic means to reveal weakness, to be focused solely on feelings or to be completely ineffectual as a leader. In fact, just the opposite is true. Indeed, Moses' empathy deserves to be emulated by contemporary leaders. However, empathy is not the same as sympathy, which is just relating to, or agreeing with, the feelings of others. The *Financial Times* Lexicon holds that the essence of "empathic leadership is the ability to understand, relate to and be sensitive to customers, colleagues and communities." To emphasize its meaning even more, empathic leadership contrasts with sociopathic leadership, defined as "arrogant, self-centred, insensitive and manipulative."[1] Hence, empathy indicates that the leader is genuinely aware of the feelings or concerns of others, understands how other people are affected, and then is able to apply this knowledge in order to take action to address any problematic situation. Empathy, in other words, is an honest, humane and ultimately crucial leadership behavior.

## The Importance of Empathy

Empathic leadership is not necessarily an easy approach for leaders to effortlessly demonstrate, since it tends to contradict the myth of the heroic leader, and because it is not about egocentrism but a leader's humility. It is not about achieving personal agendas, but about helping communities—not to mention customers and colleagues—lead more desirable and satisfying lives.[2] Humility is indeed a key attribute of Moses' empathic personality and leadership style. Through the figure of Moses as a leader, it is evident that empathy means understanding the needs of others. According to Erica Brown, educator

---

[1] *Financial Times Lexicon*, s.v. "empathic leadership." Online: http://lexicon.ft.com/Term?term=empathic-leadership (accessed January 25, 2013).

[2] Ibid.

and director of the Jewish Leadership Institute at the Jewish Federation of Greater Washington, "Empathic leaders have curiosity about others. They listen with their whole face. They embody the pain of others. They are not afraid to be vulnerable. They do not back away from pain or conversations that prove emotionally entangling. They are big enough to make themselves small."[3] From the descriptions the Bible relates, Moses clearly demonstrates each of these capacities.

Moses understood the Israelites' need to escape slavery, to avoid starvation in the desert for which manna descended, and ultimately to comprehend why the sinful idol of the Golden Calf would be created in his absence. One reason a leader has great influence is because he or she has the ability to include or exclude people. "The leader can be callous or empathic and will set the standard of behavior for followers," observes Brown, "You cannot demand that others exhibit kindness to strangers; you can only model it and make others aware of situations that require additional attention and compassion."[4] Moses therefore serves as such a model that contemporary leaders should emulate.

Leadership theorist Stephen Covey, whose view of leadership is firmly based on what he considers to be deeply ingrained principles, includes empathy in his popular book *Principle-Centered Leadership* as a crucial aspect of leadership. Covey explains,

> Giving full attention, being completely present, striving to transcend one's autobiography, and seeking to see things from another's point of view takes courage, patience, and inner sources of security. It means being open to new learning and to change. It means moving into the minds and hearts of others to see the world as they see it. It does not mean that you feel as they feel. That is sympathy. Rather, it means that you understand how they feel based on how they see the world. That is empathy.[5]

Whether intended or not, Covey's definition of empathy relates well to Moses' leadership. Moses understood and empathized with his fellow Hebrews who were slaves in Egypt, even though he grew up in a privileged environment in the prior Pharaoh's court. Moses understood their worldview despite living an early life that differed markedly from theirs. He empathized, not merely sympathized. This key difference relates to his effective leadership. Moses did not just feel as his people felt but also understood how they

---

[3] Erica Brown, *Leadership in the Wilderness: Authority and Anarchy in the Book of Numbers* (Jerusalem, Israel: Maggid Books, 2013), 77.

[4] Brown, *Leadership in the Wilderness*, 76.

[5] Stephen R. Covey, *Principle-Centered Leadership* (New York, NY: Fireside, 1992), 116.

felt because of his comprehension of their perspective and general outlook. He essentially took a quick pulse of a nation-in-the-making and addressed its various needs. Hence, a brief review of Moses' early life is helpful for appreciating the origins of Moses' empathy as it provides a basis for learning about his personality and later motivation.

\* \* \*

According to the Book of Exodus, Moses was born into a Levite family in Egypt, where the Israelites, also known as the Hebrews, lived as slaves under the Pharaoh. The Pharaoh had ordered all the male children of the Hebrews killed, so Moses was hidden for three months until his mother, in desperation, decided to place him in a small wicker basket and hide him in a marsh near the Nile River, watched over by his sister Miriam, where he was eventually found by the Pharaoh's daughter, who, after he was weaned by a wet nurse who was actually his birth mother, was effectively adopted by the princess.[6]

The name "Moses" is typically translated from Hebrew as "drawn from the water."[7] Torah scholar and commentator Nahum Sarna surmises that "the narrative is subtly pointing to Moses' destiny as the one who safely led Israel to freedom [...] [when] in actual fact, the name that the princess conferred upon the child is of Egyptian origin."[8] Yet, aside from this detail, the biblical narrative is otherwise "silent on the years Moses spent in the palace, which is where he undoubtedly passed the formative period of his life," including his education that he would have begun at age four, lasting 12 years, like other "privileged boys in royal court and bureaucratic circles in Egypt."[9]

When Moses was a grown man, he killed an Egyptian whom he witnessed beating a Hebrew slave. He later fled from Egypt and settled in the land of Midian to hide from the Pharaoh and avoid capital punishment.[10] As Sarna notes, Moses' killing of the violent Egyptian came after Moses had spent years watching his kinsfolk work and become "sensitive to their sufferings"

---

[6] Exod. 2:1–10.

[7] Midrash provides some extensive, if not controversial, interpretations on the name "Moses." See Yitzchak Etshalom, *Between the Lines of the Bible, Exodus: A Study from the New School of Orthodox Torah Commentary* (New York, NY: Orthodox Union Press, 2012), 34–41.

[8] Etshalom notes that one theory regarding the meaning of the name Moses is based on the idea that, among the many hieroglyphics that Egyptologists have been able to translate, one of them represents "the consonantal string 'MSS,'" meaning "child," so the daughter of the Pharaoh possibly named the postweaned child "Moses," thereby declaring him "my son." Etshalom, *Between the Lines of the Bible, Exodus*, 37.

[9] Nahum M. Sarna, *Exploring Exodus: The Origins of Biblical Israel* (New York, NY: Schocken, 1996), 32–53.

[10] Exod. 2:11–12; 2:15.

to the point that he could not tolerate seeing an Egyptian beating a Hebrew. By striking down the Egyptian oppressor, "Moses has decisively thrown in his lot with his suffering people and [...] psychologically severed his ties to his aristocratic and privileged Egyptian past [with] his instinctive indignation at the maltreatment of his brethren," effectively overcoming his "self-interest."[11] Moses transcended any cognitive dissonance that may have weighed on his conscience to return to his earlier roots as a Hebrew.

This situation might be viewed by some Bible readers as evidence of sin, as Moses appeared to have covered up the matter and fled when he realized that the Pharaoh wanted to kill him for what had occurred.[12] Indeed, Moses did "kill," but he did not commit murder in the classical sense— that is, killing with the intent to kill. Instead, he appears to have committed homicide while defending another person from harm. Also, according to the biblical text, the injunction from God forbidding murder had not yet even been declared, as would take place years later at Mount Sinai. However, as Sarna notes, "That the order of the narratives in the Torah need not necessarily be chronological was well recognized in rabbinic times,"[13] so this might not serve as reliable justification. Nonetheless, God does not condemn Moses for the act. In fact, just the opposite occurred. "The Lord said to Moses in Midian, 'Go back to Egypt, for all the men who sought to kill you are dead.' So Moses took his wife and sons, mounted them on an ass, and went back to the land of Egypt; and Moses took the rod of God with him."[14] This particular rod would ultimately be Moses' undoing, but at this point Moses was just beginning his rise to leadership, having presumably demonstrated traits as a leader that were pleasing to God. Empathy was surely among them.

Moses' intervention upon seeing his kinsfolk attacked arguably points to a distinctively Jewish characteristic of leadership, which is indeed empathy, or, for leaders, concern for the oppressed and for human welfare in general. In articles published in the *Harvard Business Review*, Robert Goffee and Gareth Jones, as mentioned earlier, argued strongly that all leaders must empathize in order to show that they genuinely care for their employees—or the people they lead in other organizations or environmental settings.[15] Empathic

[11]   Sarna, *Exploring Exodus*, 34.
[12]   Exod. 2:12, 15.
[13]   Nahum M. Sarna, *The JPS Torah Commentary: Exodus* (Philadelphia, PA: Jewish Publication Society, 1991), 97–98.
[14]   Exod. 4:19–20.
[15]   See Robert Goffee and Gareth Jones, "Why Should Anyone Be Led by You?" *Harvard Business Review* 78, no. 5 (2000): 62–70; and Rob Goffee and Gareth Jones, *Why Should Anyone Be Led by You? What It Takes to Be an Authentic Leader* (Boston, MA: Harvard Business Review Press, 2015).

leadership is not simply a Jewish sentiment. As should now be readily apparent, this is not a new insight either. It has biblical origins in the example of Moses.

According to Ari Zivotofsky, in the early parts of Exodus and Moses' life four primary Torah stories show that "Moses is consistently portrayed as not only caring and concerned for others, but also as willing and ready to act upon those feelings." This makes Moses, in Zivotofsky's words, "the true Empath."[16] A quick reading of the above account from Exodus—the first story to which Zivitofsky alludes—in which Moses is described as having seen an injustice occurring, then looking again to make sure no witnesses were around, then proceeding to kill the Egyptian oppressor and hiding his remains, suggests that Moses was merely a "violent vigilante." Yet the ancient rabbis viewed this situation very differently, deeming "Moses' action as both appropriate and positive," notes Zivotofsky, because they focused on the repetition of the Hebrew word, va-yar—meaning, "he saw"—in Exodus 2:11.[17]

Zivotofsky observes that the rabbis—expressing their views in Midrash—comment in reference to the first instance of va-yar by answering the question "What is va-yar? He saw their burdens, wept, and lamented, saying: 'I am deeply distressed on your account, would that I could die for you. For there is no work harder than working with mortar.'"[18] But, Zivotofsky notes, the rabbis point out that "Moses did not just lament" because, as the Midrash states, "he would energetically help every one of them," which shows that, "just as with the second 'look,' Moses saw an injustice against a fellow Jew, felt pained, and took action," that is, by killing the Egyptian, "so too, the rabbis argue, was the case with the first 'look.'"[19]

"Commenting on the same word, va-yar, in Genesis 22:13," Zivotofsky notes that "Aggadat Esther 3:5 states: 'Rabbi Elazar said: '[As for] the wicked, the looking of their eyes is a stumbling block [for it exposes them to sources of temptation], but for the righteous it [the looking of their eyes] is an opportunity to be even greater.'"[20] A stronger defense of Moses comes from other sources of Midrash. As Zivotofsky relates,

If, as the Midrash contends, Moses' killing of the Egyptian was a legitimate act, why then did he, in a seemingly craven manner, look this way and that way to make sure that there was no man ('ish) around? If 'ish

[16] Ari Z. Zivotofsky, "The Leadership Qualities of Moses," *Judaism* 43, no. 3 (1994): 259.

[17] Zivotofsky, "The Leadership Qualities of Moses," 259.

[18] *Exodus Rabbah* 1:32.

[19] Zivotofsky, "The Leadership Qualities of Moses," 259.

[20] Ibid., 260.

is to be understood not only literally, as "person," but also as a *man*, a real man willing to take action, it becomes more understandable. The Talmud [*Bavli*, Sota 11b] says: "Rabbi Yehudah interprets [the meaning of "man," *'ish*, in this verse]: he saw that there was no *man* to show zeal [*kana'ut*] on behalf of the Almighty.' Leviticus Rabbah (32:4) adds: "He saw that there was no *man* to save the Jews."[21]

According to such interpretations, other people were certainly present, and Moses was not fearful of witnesses, but rather "the issue at hand was that there was no *man* to stand up and take action.[22] While Zivotofsky asserts that "Moses' chief leadership attribute [was] his readiness to act against injustice,"[23] underlying this positive attribute appears to be Moses' sense of empathy as a significant feature of his emerging leadership style, and as it would filter down to the present and be emulated by many in contemporary leadership positions.

Indeed, from a Jewish perspective, Orthodox rabbi and educator Nachum Amsel observes that Judaism holds that not only is there an obligation for Jews to help other Jews but also that "caring for other Jews is the mark of Jewish leadership."[24] He makes this point, in part, by alluding to the early stories in Exodus of Moses' intervention when people were in need, despite potential negative repercussions or reactions, such as following the serious incident when Moses killed an Egyptian attacking a Hebrew.[25] Likewise, the very next day, Moses tried to stop an argument between two Hebrews, only to receive a verbal thrashing for his efforts, ultimately resulting in his fleeing from Egypt in fear of Pharaoh's wrath.[26] Zivotofsky also relates this story as his second example.[27]

Moreover, empathy can be seen in the Jewish value concept of *Chesed* (loving-kindness), which became a major focus in the Jewish tradition. According to the Mishnah's *Pirkei Avot*, the ancient Jewish sage Simon the Righteous used to say, "The world stands on three things—the Torah [study for achieving wisdom], Divine worship [prayer after the destruction of the Temples made sacrifices impossible], and the practice of acts of loving-kindness [*Gemilut Chasadim*, of which *Chesed* is the singular]."[28] *Chesed* reflects "a loving deed

---

[21] Ibid.

[22] Ibid.

[23] Ibid., 261.

[24] Nachum Amsel, *The Jewish Encyclopedia of Moral and Ethical Issues* (Northvale, NJ: Jason Aronson, 1994), 197.

[25] Exod. 2:11–12.

[26] Exod. 2:13–15.

[27] Zivotofsky, "The Leadership Qualities of Moses," 261.

[28] *Pirkei Avot* 1:2.

that is completely unselfish; it is an act of love for which nothing is expected or awaited in return."[29] It echoes the spirit of Hosea's prophetic words, "For I desire goodness and not sacrifice."[30]

According to Jewish tradition, "Religious commitment to God was to be manifested in one's behavior directed toward other persons," observe Kravitz and Olitzky, "when an individual performed these acts of kindness, like giving to the poor, helping the widowed and the orphaned, and looking after the newcomer to a community, that person brought himself closer to God."[31]

\* \* \*

Since *Chesed* is an inherent quality of empathy, one could even argue that empathic leadership was the underlying stimulus for the social justice movement that emerged among liberal Jews in the United States. While Jewish involvement in social justice activities started early and continues today, it was particularly significant in the US between the 1950s and 1960s when many Jews became prominently involved in the civil rights movement, fighting against discrimination, helping alleviate poverty, defending civil liberties, and protesting America's involvement in the Vietnam War.

The focus on ethics of the biblical prophets is traditionally viewed as influencing the social consciousness of the Reform movement in Judaism. According to Eugene Borowitz and Naomi Patz,

> From its start, Reform Judaism has always said that acting ethically is the most important human obligation. Prayer, rituals and study are certainly all important parts of being a good Jew, but doing the right thing is the most important part of all. That, said the Reformers, is what God "wants" most from us. The reformers got this idea from the prophets. "Do Good, not evil" seemed to be the message of every prophet. The Reformers called their special emphasis on ethics "prophetic Judaism."[32]

While one can find evidence in such prophetic works as Amos for this notion,[33] in light of Moses' precedent-setting model of empathy, and since

[29] Harry A. Cohen, *A Basic Jewish Encyclopedia: Jewish Teachings and Practices Listed and Interpreted in the Order of Their Importance Today* (Hartford, CT: Hartmore House, 1965), 62.

[30] Hos. 6:6.

[31] Leonard Kravitz and Kerry M. Olitzky, eds. and trans., *Pirke Avot: A Modern Commentary on Jewish Ethics* (New York, NY: UAHC Press, 1993), 3.

[32] Eugene B. Borowitz and Naomi Patz, *Explaining Reform Judaism* (West Orange, NJ: Behrman House, 1985), 112.

[33] Borowitz and Patz, *Explaining Reform Judaism*, 113–16.

the final verses of Deuteronomy state "never again did there arise in Israel a prophet like Moses—whom the Lord singled out, face to face,"[34] one could just as easily point to Moses, traditionally regarded in Judaism as the greatest prophet and indeed a highly respected figure in both Christianity and Islam.

Based on prophetic biblical precedent, moving from "prophetic idealism" to "applied social justice" was not a huge stretch, particularly in such rapidly evolving societies as the United States. Historian Michael Meyer observes,

> A Reform Judaism in which moral action took precedence over religious observance could evoke commitment only if it presented its adherents with specific moral objectives that would be as Jewishly significant for them as ceremonials were for traditionalists. One of the weaknesses of European Liberal Judaism was that it failed to develop a program of applied social justice. In the United States, however, a favorable political climate and a parallel development in Christianity made possible a redirection of religious energies toward ameliorating inequities and cruelties in American society.[35]

Although the general Reform rabbinate may have transitioned from a prophetic Judaism that focused on individual conduct to conduct that focused on particular social issues—in part, because of "two outside influences," notes Meyer, "the American Progressive movement and the Christian Social Gospel"[36]—social justice concerns were not a monopoly held by Reform Jewish leaders, though Reform may have dominated Jewish participation in the movement. Other leaders in the Jewish community—representing Conservative, Modern Orthodox, Renewal and Reconstructionist Judaism—took on similar interests, such as Rabbis Abraham Joshua Heschel, Zalman Shachter-Shalomi, Mordecai Kaplan, Joseph Soloveitchik and writer (and future Nobel Peace Prize laureate) Elie Wiesel, to name but a few.

This empathic leadership interest in helping others comes clearly through the Jewish tradition and arguably stems all the way back to the biblical influence of Moses, subsequent prophets and later rabbinic commentary. Even Reconstructionist Judaism's founder Rabbi Mordecai Kaplan wrote that "Judaism as a religious civilization calls for the application of ethical principles and spiritual values to all human relations [...] [thus] Judaism, as a religious civilization, affirms the dignity of the human soul [...] [and]

---

[34] Deut. 34:10.
[35] Michael A. Meyer, *Response to Modernity: A History of the Reform Movement in Judaism* (New York, NY: Oxford University Press, 1988), 286–87.
[36] Meyer, *Response to Modernity*, 287.

asserts that freedom and security are both attainable and that neither can flourish without the other."[37] Regarding leading Modern Orthodox Rabbi Soloveitchik's views on "social action"—particularly in reference to dialogue with Christians—Rabbi Irving Greenberg relates that Soloveitchik deemed discussion on "social action and societal justice" as appropriate but was opposed to dialogue on matters related to religious doctrine and theology, because, regarding the latter, he felt "all religions spoke their own private language."[38]

Given the diversity of Jewish streams represented—with many influenced by early rabbinic notions of *Tikkun Olam*, or repairing the world through good deeds—they were undoubtedly at least partially influenced by prophetic precedent and Jewish values, besides the social influences of the day. Moses' impact could not have been far from Jewish leaders' minds.

Robert Aronson, president of the Steinhardt Foundation for Jewish Life, has argued that "great Jewish leadership" is distinguished by four key features:[39]

- People lead by displaying moral and ethical values through their behavior and by how they interact with others.
- Leaders are passionate about all of the Jewish people and Jewish knowledge, which motivates their behavior and decision making.
- When one leads troops into battle, one should look back and make sure they are following.
- Real power means never having to use it.

While the second point relates to Jewish learning and knowledge, and the third relates to visionary leadership and inspiring followers, the fourth relates to the appropriate use of power and a preference for inspiration to encourage others to follow rather than using a heavy hammer to achieve a particular aim. But the first point refers to empathy, because showing moral and ethical values while interacting with others implies an empathetic outlook since morality and ethics require thinking about others and relating to their experience.

However, considering the Midrash in connection with Moses in the story of his killing the Egyptian oppressor, it is clear Moses was a man of action

[37] Mordecai M. Kaplan, *Questions Jews Ask: Reconstructionist Answers*, rev. (New York, NY: Reconstructionist Press, 1966), 520.

[38] Irving Greenberg, *For the Sake of Heaven and Earth: The New Encounter between Judaism and Christianity* (Philadelphia, PA: Jewish Publication Society, 2004), 13–14.

[39] Robert P. Aronson, "On Jewish Leadership," *Contact: The Journal of the Steinhardt Foundation for Jewish Life* 11, no. 1 (2008): 7.

who could not stand by and witness injustice. He is shown as a bold empathic leader who was apparently capable of violence, which one can easily regard as necessary in a political or revolutionary leader. But even Zivotofsky stresses, Moses "was an *'ish*, a *man* of action, an Empath."[40]

Zivotofsky's third example shows similar sentiments. Arriving in exile in the land of Midian, in northwest Arabia, Moses again stood up (*va-yakam*) in the face of injustice, but, in doing so, revealed his underlying empathy. Standing near a well, Jethro's seven daughters, who had come to draw water for their father's flock, were driven away by some shepherds, but "Moses rose to their defense, and watered their flock." The daughters later credited "an Egyptian man" (*'ish mitzri*) for rescuing them from the shepherds, who then watered the flock for them.[41] "The Bible uses the word *va-yakom*—and Moses 'rose up,' as if to say that Moses (again) rose to the occasion," argues Zivotofsky, "despite the fact that he was fleeing from Egypt because of his previously being a *man*, he again 'rises,' *va-yakom*, and helps the helpless."[42] Justice and certainly empathy were Moses' primary drives.

The Midrash, suggests Zivotofsky, is preoccupied by why the word *'ish* (man) was used by the girls to describe Moses. Why not just an "Egyptian" rather than an "Egyptian man"? Zivotofsky points out that, because of the inclusion of this extra word "man," *Genesis Rabbah* 36:2 makes some comparisons between Moses and Noah, who was also referred to as an *'ish* (man) in Genesis 6:9. Zivotofsky maintains that "it is possible to suggest that the Bible is again stressing that Moses was an *'ish*, a *man*, someone willing to rise to the occasion when no one else was willing to assume the role."[43]

Zivotofsky maintains that in each of the sequential stories he describes, there is less reason for Moses to get involved as, in the story of the sisters and the shepherds, *none* of the characters were Jews, as was the case in the first story where a Jew was being beaten by an Egyptian, yet Moses could not help but intervene and attempt "to save the victim(s) from the aggressor(s)." Likewise, with each sequential story there is also a progression of a different sort in Moses' reaction to what he perceives as an injustice. In the first story, Moses responded by killing the Egyptian. In the third story, by watering the flocks, possibly even those of other shepherds, since the Torah

---

[40]  Zivotofsky, "The Leadership Qualities of Moses," 261.
[41]  Exod. 2:15–19.
[42]  Zivotofsky, "The Leadership Qualities of Moses," 262.
[43]  Ibid., 262–63.

does not specifically identify solely Jethro's flock, Zivotofsky again points to Midrash for insight.[14] He notes that *Exodus Rabbah* 2:3 states, commenting on Proverbs 30:5,

> God does not give greatness to a person until he tests him with a small thing and then he elevates him to greatness [...] David was tested with sheep [...] and so too Moses was tested with sheep, as it says: "He led the sheep to the desert" (Exod. 3:1) [...] and God took him as the shepherd of Israel, as it says: "You did lead your people like a flock, by the hand of Moses and Aaron" (Ps. 77:21).[15]

In this third story, therefore, "Moses acted in a manner that could bring about a harmonious peace between the parties involved." Zivotofsky points out that Moses' "mode of intervention had developed from rash violence [...] culminating, according to the Midrash, in peace-making," which showed that "regardless of the archetype of the nationalities or relationships of the persons involved or of the nature of the response, there is one common theme: Moses is a *man* in places where there are no *men*."[16] Regarding the act of peace-making, we will see later how this leadership skill is even better represented by Moses' brother, Aaron.

As for Moses, there is no surprise that he holds an extraordinary place in Jewish tradition, observes Wiesel, because

> his passion for social justice, his struggle for national liberation, his triumphs and disappointments, his poetic inspiration, his gifts as a strategist and his organizational genius, his complex relationship with God and His people, his requirements and promises, his condemnations and blessings, his bursts of anger, his silences, his efforts to reconcile the law with compassion, his authority with integrity—no individual, ever, anywhere, accomplished so much for so many people in so many different domains. His influence is boundless, it reverberates beyond time. The Law bears his name, the Talmud is but its commentary and Kabbala communicates only its silence.[17]

\* \* \*

---

[14] Ibid., 266.

[15] Qtd. in ibid., 266.

[16] Ibid., 263.

[17] Elie Wiesel, *Messengers of God: Biblical Portraits and Legends* (New York, NY: Touchstone, 1994), 182.

Empathy should not be equated with merely being "nice." After all, Moses had his moments of anger—a dispositional feature that may have helped him lead, but anger is rarely effective as a means of inspiring people in contemporary organizations—such as upon witnessing the injustice of a fellow Hebrew being attacked, or after descending from Sinai and witnessing a golden calf being idolized. In the latter case, Moses is described as having approached God in order to intervene on their behalf, successfully protecting them, which certainly demonstrated effective empathic leadership.[48] According to Nadia Goodman, "The best bosses employ empathy when and where it's needed, not as a panacea or a plea for approval."[49]

In the case of Moses, he applied empathy naturally. He often pleaded to God on behalf of the Israelites. Likewise in business leadership, empathy has its appropriate place. Goodman notes that Apple cofounder Steve Jobs "was known as controlling and harsh, but his former employees say he was incredibly in touch with others' strengths, weaknesses, and motivators."[50]

A sense of purpose, maintains leadership program director Lorin Woolfe, is what Jobs shared with Moses as "all the recent emphasis on mission and vision is something that the leaders of the Bible would have resonated with; indeed, they invented the terms, or at least lived with them daily."[51] For Drucker, in contrast, the sole essence of leadership *"is performance."*[52] However, Woolfe asserts,

> Moses did not always have an easy time of it, nor did […] [Steve] Jobs. Without an ongoing sense of mission and vision, Jobs's failures […] could have been as demoralizing as the near starvation of the Israelites during forty years in the desert. Jobs was thrown out of the CEO slot in the company he had so courageously created [Apple—to which he would subsequently return over a decade later in 1996, leading it back to profitability] because the company [by 1985] had outgrown his leadership style and business skills. Moses was also denied the honor of leading the Israelites into the Promised Land. Like Jobs, he was a great leader in times of calamity and innovation, but he was not the best man to lead a maturing group to the next stage of its development.[53]

---

[48] Exod. 32:11–14.

[49] Nadia Goodman, "How to Become a Better Leader," *Entrepreneur*, July 31, 2012. Online: http://www.entrepreneur.com/article/224097 (accessed January 25, 2013).

[50] Goodman, "How to Become a Better Leader."

[51] Lorin Woolfe, *The Bible on Leadership: From Moses to Matthew—Management Lessons for Contemporary Leaders* (New York, NY: AMACOM, 2002), 25.

[52] Peter F. Drucker and Joseph A. Maciariello, *Management*, rev. ed. (New York, NY: Harper Collins, 2008), 288.

[53] Woolfe, *The Bible on Leadership*, 25.

While a sense of "purpose" is certainly important and performance is essential, determining when a leader needs to pass the baton to another leader—the topic of leadership succession is discussed later—is debatable, and regarding both Moses and Jobs, Woolfe's opinion is well taken, but it remains just an opinion.

Although Moses was prevented by God from entering the Promised Land for disobeying God's command regarding providing water for the contentious Israelites in the wilderness,[54] Moses does not protest because he had achieved his leadership objective of bringing the Israelites to Canaan. It was never mandated that Moses must *enter* with them. However, that Jobs shared with Moses a sense of empathy appears crucial to their respective leadership careers. Moses was able to learn the strengths and weaknesses of those he led, whether of his own brother, Aaron, or the reliable and trusted Joshua, whom he would ultimately groom as his successor.

## Developing Empathy

As the Bible relates, Moses exhibited empathy and therefore drew upon this natural disposition—which does not come naturally to everyone—in his empathic leadership approach. It is an extremely important trait for leaders. In their White Paper entitled "Empathy in the Workplace: A Tool for Effective Leadership," William Gentry, Todd Weber and Golnaz Sadri, of the Center for Creative Leadership, argue that

> empathy is a construct that is fundamental to leadership. Many leadership theories suggest the ability to have and display empathy is an important part of leadership. Transformational leaders need empathy in order to show their followers that they care for their needs and achievement (Bass, 1985). Authentic leaders also need to have empathy in order to be aware of others (Walumbwa, Avolio, Gardner, Wernsing, & Peterson, 2008). Empathy is also a key part of emotional intelligence that several researchers believe is critical to being an effective leader (Bar-On & Parker, 2000; George, 2000; Goleman, 1995; Salovey & Mayer, 1990).[55]

Empathy—an awareness of the feelings of others and the possession of strong inner qualities to spontaneously work on others' behalf—is a powerful

---

[54] Num. 27:14.

[55] William A. Gentry, Todd J. Weber and Golnaz Sadri, "Empathy in the Workplace: A Tool for Effective Leadership," 2. Online: http://www.ccl.org/leadership/pdf/research/Empathy-InTheWorkplace.pdf (accessed January 25, 2013).

feature of effective leadership that helps in building and maintaining relationships with subordinates. Hence, leaders, and those aspiring to lead, should
recognize the possibility that empathy can actually be learned as an acquired
skill. Even if not an innate trait, studies show that it can be learned across
various leadership settings.

Joanna Shapiro has studied how to foster empathy in a medical setting,
arguing that teaching this ability to physicians as a skill-based process does
not reflect the reality of the clinical setting and, therefore, it is important to
teach "empathy in its totality, acknowledging both behavioral and attitudi-
nal tools for enhancing empathic awareness in learners."[56] However, empathy should not be viewed in isolation. Humility arguably contributes to its
development.

---

[56] Joanna Shapiro, "How Do Physicians Teach Empathy in the Primary Care Setting?" *Academic Medicine* 77, no. 4 (2002): 328.

# Chapter 6

# HUMILITY—THE ANTITHESIS
# OF ARROGANCE

Hal Lewis observes, "Of all the behaviors Judaism associates with effective leadership, none ranks higher than humility."[1] So strongly did the ancient rabbis view the trait of humility that, according to the Talmud, "a leader who guides Israel with humility shall lead them also in the World-to-Come."[2] Concerning its opposite—arrogance—the rabbis of the Talmud say God weeps "over the public leader who is arrogant in his leadership."[3] These references provide some indication of the importance the rabbis have given to humility as a desired quality in a leader. Its opposite, arrogance, is a leadership problem.

Yet William Berkson notes not only that humility has "become so unpopular in our time that it is often viewed as a vice" but also that "this rejection of humility is an offspring of Rousseau's view that our natural self is purely good, and only becomes corrupted by society."[4] However, this perspective that blames society for one's bad behavior negates the inner and innate human conflict that the ancient rabbis regarded as inherent in all people, namely the competing impulses to do good and to do bad. This notion is explored in a further chapter, but it is important to point out, as Berkson does, that "while the Rabbinic view of humility is vulnerable to criticism that it goes too far," the medieval Jewish rabbi, philosopher and moralist Bachya ibn Paquda "provides an important clarification" that helps support why "humility is a prerequisite to both reverence and compassion."[5]

In ibn Paquda's seminal work, *Duties of the Heart*, Paquda asserts that practicing humility "keeps a person from haughtiness, arrogance, pride, vainglory, domination, the urge to control everything, the desire for what is above

[1]  Hal M. Lewis, *From Sanctuary to Boardroom: A Jewish Approach to Leadership* (Lanham, MD: Rowman & Littlefield, 2006), 126.

[2]  Babylonian Talmud, *Sanhedrin*, 92.

[3]  Babylonian Talmud, *Hagigah*, 5.

[4]  William Berkson, *Pirkei Avot: Timeless Wisdom for Modern Life* (Philadelphia, PA: Jewish Publication Society, 2010), 143.

[5]  Berkson, *Pirkei Avot*, 143.

him, and similar outgrowths of pride."[6] Among the many situations where
Paquda asserts one has a duty to be humble includes while engaging in business with others and whenever one is praised for positive personal qualities. In
the latter case, Paquda maintains that one should remember "previous transgressions and sins" rather than rejoice.[7] However, Paquda also identifies a bad
type of humility. Berkson relates, "If we wrongly say we aren't good enough
to do something, and hence shrink from taking on responsibilities and doing
mitzvot we could [otherwise] do, this is a bad kind of humility," implying
that there is a "good kind of pride" located in identifying our own particular
strengths and regarding them as gifts to help serve other people, which is
positive, suggesting that true humility is "not underestimating our strengths
or overestimating our weaknesses, but rather honestly assessing ourselves,
and using our strengths in a way that benefits others, and not only ourselves."[8]

However, an outlook that elevates self-esteem over humility as a "core virtue" fails to appreciate that "some kinds of positive self-regard can be harm-
ful." As Berkson asserts, "In its current version, 'self-esteem' is seen as the
core virtue, and lack of it is the source of all evil," a notion he regards as "now
virtually a religion in America"[9] and not a view consistent with the ancient
rabbis or the Bible. Stressing self-esteem over humility therefore creates a
vacuum that has the potential of being filled by arrogance.

### The Problem of Arrogance

Arrogance is indeed one of the endemic problems in contemporary leadership. According to Jewish tradition, Lewis notes, "arrogance is a form of idolatry in which the conceited individual places his or her own concerns above
God's commands. Community leaders, therefore, are cautioned against
imperiousness and pomposity."[10] Hence, the purpose of humility is likely to
avoid its opposite—arrogance—very much frowned upon in Judaism because
of its traditional representation as idolatrous given the view that arrogant
individuals put their own interests above God's concerns.

The ancient rabbis were especially sensitive to arrogance because they saw
the Romans as supremely arrogant. American academic Lawrence Schiffman
observes that in Roman-controlled "Palestine, the gradual Christianization
of the Roman Empire and the resulting decline in Jewish fortunes eventually

---

[6]  Bachya ben Joseph ibn Paquda, *Duties of the Heart*, trans. Daniel Haberman, Vol. 2 (Nanuet, NY and Jerusalem, Israel: Feldheim, 1996), 549.

[7]  ibn Paquda, *Duties of the Heart*, 559.

[8]  Berkson, *Pirkei Avot*, 143.

[9]  Ibid.

[10]  Lewis, *From Sanctuary to Boardroom*, 126.

led to the elimination of Jewish self-government and to the premature end of amoraic [rabbinic] activity," unlike what Jewry was permitted in Babylonia around the same time period where "religious and scholarly creativity continued unabated throughout, as can be seen from the internal history of the Babylonian Talmud."[11] Roman arrogance was even more obvious because it could be compared with Babylonian rule at this crucial time period in the early centuries of the Common Era when Rabbinic Judaism—which was normative for well over a millennia until the emergence in the modern era of liberal streams among the Ashkenazi Jews that, in some ways, competed with what became regarded as Orthodoxy—was developing into a strong, intellectual force in Jewish life.

One may not require humility to sympathize—feel others' pain—or to show empathy—understand the perspective of others—but it helps, because being humble arguably makes the leader less self-absorbed and more attuned to the needs of others. Jewish tradition praises Moses for this particular character trait linked to the biblical verse that states, "Now Moses was a very humble man, more so than any other man on earth."[12] This description of Moses' humility contrasts with Aaron's and Miriam's apparent arrogance when they publicly criticized Moses because of whom he had married (a Cushite woman), and by suggesting God also spoke through them, not just Moses.[13] The former appears as pretext for the latter, maintains Jacob Milgrom, for Miriam and Aaron "were really after [...] a share in Moses' leadership"[14] and also the power he held in his leadership role over the Israelites, including his older siblings.

The Book of Numbers, chapter 12, is particularly important for understanding Moses because, as Milgrom points out, "the uniqueness of Moses is the sole theme of this chapter." It reflects "the challenge to his authority (v. 2); his humility (v. 3); God's affirmation of his uniqueness (vv. 6–8); the punishment of Miriam (vv. 9–10); and Moses' successful intercession on her behalf (vv. 11–15)."[15] From the biblical perspective, Nili S. Fox observes, "Moses' attribute of humility is underscored as praiseworthy."[16] Consequently, this attribute would be viewed as a crucial human quality for Jewish leaders, particularly in the view of the later rabbis.

---

[11]  Lawrence H. Schiffman, *From Text to Tradition: A History of Second Temple & Rabbinic Judaism* (Hoboken, NJ: Ktav, 1991), 219.

[12]  Num. 12:3.

[13]  Num. 12:1–2.

[14]  Commentary to Num. 12:2, see Jacob Milgrom, *The JPS Torah Commentary: Numbers* (Philadelphia, PA: Jewish Publication Society, 1989), 94.

[15]  Ibid., 93.

[16]  Nili S. Fox, commentary to Num. 12:3, *The Jewish Study Bible*, ed. Adele Berlin and Marc Zvi Brettler (New York, NY: Oxford University Press, 2004), 308.

Besides Moses' most humble reputation, Lewis suggests that "the Torah's characterization of the Jews as the humblest of all nations (Deuteronomy 7:7)" may have led "subsequent authorities to rank humility among a leader's most important behaviors."[17] However, this might depend on the translation or commentary used. The Jewish Publication Society (JPS) 1985 translation states, "It is not because you are the most numerous of peoples that the Lord set His heart on you and chose you—indeed, you are the smallest of peoples; but it was because the Lord favored you and kept the oath He made to your fathers that the Lord freed you with a mighty hand and rescued you from the house of bondage, from the power of Pharaoh king of Egypt."[18] Neither the word "humility" nor the word "humble" is mentioned in the JPS translation (1985), nor in the JPS (1917),[19] but perhaps such an interpretation was inferred from an unnamed commentator? Regardless, the Hebrew word used in the Torah is, *me'at*, meaning "smallest," not humble. In its adjectival use in Deuteronomy 7:7, *ha'me'at*—in *"Ha'me'at mee'kol ha'amim"*—means "the smallest, poorest of all peoples."[20]

Nonetheless, Lewis further cites "the prophetic commandment to 'walk humbly' [JPS 1985: "modestly"] with God (Micah 6:8)" as having a "particular resonance for those whom He authorized as leaders."[21] Indeed, this didactic verse said by Micah—"to walk modestly with your God"—is considered "one of the most influential and often quoted sayings in prophetic literature," observes Ehud Ben Zvi. He notes that "it was considered as a possible compendium of all the Mitzvot" because of the Talmudic dictum attributed to Rabbi Simlai, who preached that, of the traditional view that 613 *mitzvot* (Divine commandments) were communicated to Moses by God, "Micah came and reduced them to three [principles], as it is written, He has told you, O human, what is good, and what the Lord requires of you: only to do justice, and to love goodness, and to walk humbly with your God."[22] Ben Zvi observes that *"to walk modestly with your God"* is generally translated as "'to

---

[17] Lewis, *From Sanctuary to Boardroom*, 126.

[18] Deut. 7:7–8.

[19] The translation of Deut. 7:7 (per JPS: 1917) states, "HaShem did not set His love upon you, nor choose you, because ye were more in number than any people—for ye were the fewest of all peoples—," from *Devarim* (Deuteronomy), *Chapter 7:* www.breslov.com/bible/Deuteronomy7.htm#7, accessed February 7, 2013.

[20] William L. Holladay, ed., *A Concise Hebrew and Aramaic Lexicon of the Old Testament* (Grand Rapids, MI: Wm. B. Eerdmans, 1988), 206.

[21] Lewis, *From Sanctuary to Boardroom*, 126.

[22] Ehud Ben Zvi, commentary to Micah 6:8, in Berlin and Brettler, *The Jewish Study Bible*, 1215.

walk humbly with your God,' but its original meaning is likely to be 'to walk wisely with your God.' "[23]

Why is wisdom invoked? Because of the verse that follows, "Then will your name achieve wisdom."[24]

Ben Zvi observes that another prophet, Malachi—like Micah from the Twelve Minor Prophets, which is the last section of the *Nevi'im* (Prophets) occupying the middle part of the Tanakh—ends with a verse that states, "Be mindful of the Teaching [Torah] of My servant Moses, whom I charged at Horeb [i.e., Sinai] with laws and rules for all Israel."[25] Ben Zvi stresses that at this very conclusion, "Malachi asserts the dominance of Mosaic Torah over the prophetic tradition."[26] In other words, the Torah that contains the verse from Numbers 12:3—perhaps most central to Moses' character—which states that he was "a very humble man, more so than any other man on earth," assumes, again, a most central influence despite the significant impact of the prophets who came after Moses. His example, therefore, can be appreciated even more as a representation of great leadership material.

Lewis points out other prophets warned people in power to avoid allowing their egos to rise beyond acceptable limits, presumably to avoid becoming arrogant leaders. As he relates, "In Jeremiah's words, 'Let not the wise man glory in his wisdom, neither let the mighty man glory in his might, let not the rich man glory in his riches' (Jeremiah 9:22)."[27] Ultimately, asserts Lewis, Jewish literature of both the legal and the folklorist traditions assert "that humility not ego" is fundamental "to a leader's greatness."[28]

Hence, humility was highly regarded by rabbis as a key to the greatness of Moses. It was the antithesis of arrogance. Indeed, according to Lewis, "postbiblical leaders were also renowned for their humility, most notable among these, the Talmudic sages."[29] As Simon Glustrom relates, "It was this spiritual quality that enabled Moses to show such patience with his people, for he was painfully aware of his own short-comings."[30] Glustrom also emphasizes Moses' humility.

Yet humility is not strictly limited to the realm of religion. There is a secular basis that argues the importance of being humble. Julie E. Cooper asserts this very case in her book *Secular Powers: Humility in Modern Political Thought.*

---

[23] Ibid.

[24] Micah 6:9.

[25] Mal. 3:22. Ehud Ben Zvi, introductory remarks to "The Twelve," in Berlin and Brettler, *The Jewish Study Bible*, 1141–42.

[26] Ehud Ben Zvi, commentary to Mal. 3:22, in Berlin and Brettler, *The Jewish Study Bible*, 1274.

[27] Lewis, *From Sanctuary to Boardroom*, 136n41.

[28] Ibid., 126.

[29] Ibid., 127.

[30] Simon Glustrom, *The Language of Judaism*, 2nd rev. ed. (New York, NY: Ktav, 1973), 82.

Cooper notes that "in early modern philosophical discourse, modesty and humility were not only classed as passions—they were almost unanimously hailed as moral virtues." However, she concedes a strong religious element to the moral virtue of humility, of which modesty relates. "For Augustinians, humility was a signature of Christian ethics, the virtue that unites correct self-assessment with reverence toward God."[31] However, even though she confines her "discussion of traditional, theological ethics of humility to Christianity," humility is not rooted in Christianity but in Judaism. Cooper explains,

> Readers may conclude that I focus on Christianity because humility is a Christian innovation, unknown to Judaism, which advocates a more life-affirming ethic [...] In fact, while ideals of humility gain greater prominence in Christian traditions, they originate and flourish in Jewish texts [...] If humility plays an important role within Jewish ethics, it is nevertheless true that received portraits of secularity draw almost exclusively on Christian sources. Hence, I focus almost exclusively on Christian humility in this book.[32]

In other words, Cooper's investigation into secular humility and its relative virtue, modesty, relies on Christian sources because this is where she found sources of secularity. A religious basis is more relevant to Jewish sources as the very notion of humility is found in the Hebrew Bible. The notion spread from there to subsequent Jewish literature, notably the Talmud.

There is a story in the Talmud in which it is said that "whenever a man puts on *tefillin* [phylacteries, or prayer boxes affixed to the left arm and over the head during weekday morning prayers] he should make a blessing over them, says Rabbi. But if so, at any time [of the day whenever he puts on the garment he should say the blessing]?—Rav Judah was a most modest person and would not take off his cloak the whole day long."[33] It is therefore possible to see how modesty, or humility, is emphasized in the Jewish tradition, tracing back to the influence of Moses in the Bible.

* * *

As we shall see, humility linked to modesty is also linked to holiness, so one can assume that the ancient rabbis stressed humility, or humble behavior, not

---

[31] Julie E. Cooper, *Secular Powers: Humility in Modern Political Thought* (Chicago, IL: University of Chicago Press, 2013), 22.

[32] Cooper, *Secular Powers*, 166n1.

[33] Babylonian Talmud, *Menachot* 43a.

only because of its close tie to holiness, but to avoid its opposite, arrogance, something that the Tanakh is very much against, such as in the verse of the Psalms: "He who slanders his friends in secret I will destroy; I cannot endure the haughty and proud [that is, arrogant] man."[31]

After all, centuries later, the great medieval Jewish scholar Maimonides weighed in on this issue with a very significant statement. He declared,

> There are behaviors which a person is prohibited from doing even moderately. Instead he would distance himself from them in the most extreme fashion. An example of this is arrogance. For it is not sufficient for a person to be only humble, but he must be of lowly spirit, and his spirit should be very low, therefore it is written about Moshe [Moses] our teacher that he was "very humble" instead of merely stating he was "humble." Therefore, our sages commanded us to be of extremely lowly spirit, and they also said, "that anyone who has a haughty heart has committed heresy, as it is written: 'With the haughtiness of your heart you have forgotten the Lord your God.'" It was also stated, "A ban should be placed on the scholar who exhibits a haughty spirit—even if only a little bit."[35]

Humility, or being humble, is still deemed to be a powerful quality of modern leadership among contemporary leadership theorists. According to Stephen Covey,

> One of the characteristics of authentic leaders is their humility, evident in their ability to take off their glasses and examine the lens objectively, analyzing how well their values, perceptions, beliefs, and behaviors align with "true north" principles. Where there are discrepancies (prejudice, ignorance, or error), they make adjustments to realign with greater wisdom. Centering on unchanging principles brings permanency and power into their lives.[36]

Authenticity and wisdom are indeed fueled by humility. As it relates to human character, being humble is an admirable leadership quality. In contrast, while honesty is an important ideal, it does not necessarily go hand in hand with humility. It is interesting to note, as Lewis does, that the Jewish notion "that humility and effective leadership are not incongruous" has gained wider fame through such leadership theorists as Warren Bennis and Robert Thomas—in their book, *Geeks and Geezers*, which shows the effectiveness

[31] Ps. 101:5.
[35] Maimonides, *Laws of Behavior* 2:3.
[36] Stephen R. Covey, *Principle-Centered Leadership* (New York, NY: Fireside, 1992), 20.

of humble leaders in two different generations[37]—but, particularly, due to "Level 5 Leadership," which is based on ideas from management consultant Jim Collins in his book *Good to Great: Why Some Companies Make the Leap... and Others Don't*, which declares humility as among the key personality traits necessary for effective leadership.[38] As Lewis relates, "Unwittingly, no doubt, Collins proved what Judaism has taught for millennia: that personal humility, including shunning public adulation and a willingness to give credit to others, lies at the core of great leadership."[39]

The meaning of "humble" is fundamentally important. Milgrom notes that this use of the word humble—*anav* in Hebrew—is not found anywhere else in the Bible in its singular form as in its description of Moses in Numbers 12:3.[40] Milgrom maintains that the meaning of humble "is clarified by its synonymous parallel 'who seek the Lord' (Ps. 22:27), hence, 'devout, trusting,'" while it is also applicable to "the weak and exploited (Amos 2:7; Isa. 11:4)," but, most critically, he observes that humble "never means 'meek.'"[41] Some older biblical translations appear to use this English translation in error.[42]

Moses certainly showed no "meekness" when he killed the Egyptian while defending the Hebrew slave; nor when he approached the Pharaoh to release the Israelite slaves; nor when he led the Israelites against the dreaded enemy, the Amalekites; nor when he smashed the first tablets before the Israelites in apparent disgust at their Golden Calf at the base of Mount Sinai. Although Moses led the Israelites, he had delegated hands-on military leadership to Joshua in the battle against Amalek's forces.[43] Hence, Moses was humble but

---

[37] Warren G. Bennis and Robert J. Thomas, *Geeks and Geezers—How Era, Values, and Defining Moments Shape Leaders* (Boston, MA: Harvard Business School Press, 2002), 83; Lewis, *From Sanctuary to Boardroom*, 129 and 137n62.

[38] Lewis, *From Sanctuary to Boardroom*, 129. See Jim Collins, *Good to Great: Why Some Companies Make the Leap ... and Others Don't* (New York, NY: HarperCollins, 2001).

[39] Lewis, *From Sanctuary to Boardroom*, 129.

[40] Milgrom says the sole use of "humble" in the singular form exists in Numbers 12:3 in reference to Moses, but notes the use of "humble" in the plural exists beyond the Five Books of Moses, such as Zephaniah 2:3: "All you humble of the land" (*Kol Anevei Ha'aretz*) as well as in Amos, Isaiah and the Psalm verses cited (Milgrom, *The JPS Torah Commentary: Numbers*, 94). However, it should be mentioned that the word *Anav* in its plural form is also found extensively in other Psalms—such as in the famous verse, "But the lowly [other translations of disputed Hebrew translation include "meek"] shall inherit the land" (*Va'anavim yireshu-aretz*) (Ps. 37:11)—as well as some verses from Proverbs.

[41] Milgrom, *The JPS Torah Commentary: Numbers*, 94.

[42] For example, "Now the man Moses was very meek" (Num. 12:3), in J. H. Hertz, *The Pentateuch and Haftorahs*, 2nd ed. (London, UK: Soncino Press, 1960), 618. The use of "meek" in this context is not used by other *Chumashim*, including either Reform (*Torah: A Modern Commentary*), Conservative (*Etz Hayim*) or Orthodox (*Stone Edition Tanach*), each of which uses "humble" as the translation for *anav* in Num. 12:3.

[43] See Exod. 17:8–15.

he certainly was not meek. He was like a head of state instructing a field general. As a leader Moses' humility was profound.

According to Maimonides, a person ought not "be merely humble (*anav*), but [...] be humble-minded (*shfal ruah*) and lowly of spirit to the utmost."[44] Maimonides' point, asserts Daniel H. Frank, was to emphasize the importance of humility as a virtue as opposed to the Aristotelian view of humility as a vice. In Frank's words, "for Maimonides, humility is a—perhaps even *the*—virtue; for Aristotle, it is not."[45] In Aristotle's *Nicomachean Ethics*, humility was not included among virtues, observes Frank, because "for Aristotle, the proud man is not a pompous man" but ought to be distinguished "from the vain man who claims more than his due."[46] For Aristotle, therefore, as the proud man is liberal, temperate and courageous, pride is deemed to be virtuous and, as a result, the proud man has every right to the esteem of his peers as a humble man.[47] In strong contrast with Aristotle, Maimonides profoundly disagreed on the nature of pride. For Maimonides—as Frank relates from Maimonides' *Hilkhot De'ot*, contained in his *Mishneh Torah*—pride is a disposition that should be shunned. "The right way in this regard is not to be merely humble, but to be humble-minded and lowly of spirit to the utmost. As Maimonides wrote, Moses was not merely humble but "very humble" (Numbers 12:3) and, therefore, the Talmudic rabbis commanded that one should "be exceedingly humble in spirit" (*Avot* IV, 4), and anyone whose heart was haughty effectively denied the existence of God, underscoring this point by citing Deuteronomy 8:14: "beware lest your heart grow haughty and you forget the Lord your God—who freed you from the land of Egypt, the house of bondage."[48] Hence, Maimonides and Aristotle had very different views on the significance of humility. According to Frank, "Aristotle's vice becomes Maimonides' outstanding virtue. No longer bound by the norms of a secular society and a secular morality, Maimonides presents humility as a, maybe even *the*, virtue becoming a pious man, a man of God."[49]

Nachum Amsel maintains that it is not correct to equate humble people with those who think very little of themselves. He mentions that while Moses is said to have been the most humble person, even Moses knew that God had singled him out from many other people to become a leader, so deep down he likely knew

[44] Daniel H. Frank, "Humility as a Virtue: A Maimonidean Critique of Aristotle's Ethics," in *Moses Maimonides and His Time*, ed. Eric L. Ormsby (Washington, DC: Catholic University of America Press, 1989), 89.
[45] Frank, "Humility as a Virtue," 90.
[46] Ibid., 90–91.
[47] Ibid., 91–93.
[48] Ibid., 95.
[49] Ibid., 98.

he was a great man, but he was realistic and "humble" about this fact (after he finally agreed to take on the leadership role). Amsel says, "Jewish humility cannot be defined as a feeling of self-worthlessness."[50] So, he asks, what is Jewish humility? Amsel answers, "The quality that made Moses truly humble is that he did not ascribe any of his greatness to himself. He understood that all of his greatness came from the Almighty. This is true humility—acknowledging one's greatness, talents, and achievements in a realistic manner, but attributing all of life's achievements to God and not to oneself."[51] Thus, as Glustrom did earlier, Amsel also provides a useful definition of humility.

## Modesty and Holiness

As alluded to earlier, in Jewish tradition, humility relates to modesty—a word considered synonymous with humility—and, according to the Torah, modesty relates to holiness.[52] When Moses, still a shepherd, first meets God at the burning bush on Mount Sinai, God tells him that the place where he stands is holy ground, leading Moses to react by hiding his face.[53] Thus, Amsel asserts, "hiddenness and privacy seem to be the reaction to holiness."[54] For the traditional Jew, therefore, this idea of the connection between humility—or modesty—and holiness remains central.

This traditional Mosaic emphasis on humility and modesty became evident in a famous encounter between two major real estate moguls in New York's Manhattan when local property developer Donald Trump, not known for being humble in his business, media or future political pursuits, and Paul Reichmann, the head of a family-owned Canadian property development firm, Olympia & York, the largest development company in the world by the mid-1980s, who was regarded as modest, quiet and humble. "Many who crossed his path in business would come right out and say it: Paul Reichmann is a genius," observes Reichmann biographer Anthony Bianco, but "the man himself would advance no such claim, shrugging off the compliment whenever it was made in his presence. The word 'genius' is at once bombastic and imprecise, and thus offended Reichmann's sense of decorum and his verbal exactitude in equal measure."[55]

[50]   Nachum Amsel, *The Jewish Encyclopedia of Moral and Ethical Issues* (Northvale, NJ: Jason Aronson, 1994), 184.

[51]   Amsel, *The Jewish Encyclopedia of Moral and Ethical Issues*, 184–85.

[52]   According to Amsel, "Another aspect of Jewish modesty, *tzniut*, is related to another Hebrew word often translated into English as modesty, *anavah*, which is synonymous with humility. Jewish modesty, therefore, involves Jewish humility," ibid., 184.

[53]   Exod. 3:5–6.

[54]   Amsel, *The Jewish Encyclopedia of Moral and Ethical Issues*, 182.

[55]   Anthony Bianco, *The Reichmanns: Family, Faith, Fortune, and the Empire of Olympia & York* (New York, NY: Random House, 1997), 307.

After all, while his secular name was Paul, notes Bianco, "to his father, Paul would always be Moishe."[56] Whether Moishe, Moshe or Moses—variants of Moses from Yiddish, Hebrew and English, respectively—much like the biblical Moses, Paul "Moishe" Reichmann preferred humility to self-promotion, played down raving praises and certainly avoided appearing arrogant. Since his youth, Bianco asserts, "Paul was studious, and shy [...] a melding of parental personality. He inherited [his father] Samuel's retiring and gentle manner but his mother's drive and dauntless self-confidence. Paul was, in short, a most aggressive introvert."[57]

Although Trump and Reichmann were both celebrated international property developers, their personal backgrounds could not be more different. Trump is an American-born business magnate from a non-Jewish family,[58] while Reichmann was not only a European-born Canadian business magnate raised in a traditional Ashkenazi Orthodox Jewish home but also an Orthodox rabbi trained at numerous yeshivot, who, prior to coming to Canada, had been responsible for helping educate Morocco's Jewish community.[59]

While Trump graduated from the Wharton School of Business at the Ivy League University of Pennsylvania,[60] Reichmann studied, from 1947 onward, first at a yeshiva in Antwerp, Belgium, then, relocating to London due to an expired transit visa he obtained from Tangier, to which the Reichmann family had fled at the start of the war, began his studies at the first of four Lithuanian-style yeshivot, where he would learn over the subsequent five years. As Bianco explains, these Talmudic academies were distinguished institutions in their own right.

Like the colleges of the Ivy League, the various Lithuanian yeshivoth stress[ed] their marginal differences while remaining essentially identical. First and foremost, they were bastions of Torah lishma—of Talmudic

---

[56] Bianco, *The Reichmanns*, 25.

[57] Ibid., 193.

[58] It is interesting to note that Donald Trump's eldest daughter, Ivanka Trump, converted to Orthodox Judaism in 2009 prior to her marriage to Jared Kushner. While remaining a devoted daughter who works in her father's business and is a graduate of his alma mater, the University of Pennsylvania, Ivanka's public behavior is noticeably different from her father's and perhaps a subconscious result of her Jewish studies. While retaining the image of a strong business professional, she is more modest, humble and careful with her words compared to her father. See Debra Kamin, "How Jewish Values Help Ivanka Trump Stay Classy," *Haaretz* (August 11, 2015). Online: http://www.haaretz.com/jewish/news/1.670584 (accessed November 22, 2015).

[59] Bianco, *The Reichmanns*, 221.

[60] Donald J. Trump and Tony Schwartz, *Trump: The Art of the Deal* (New York, NY: Random House, 1987), 93.

study for its own sake, as opposed to vocational purpose. In other words, the Lithuanian yeshiva was neither a rabbinical academy nor a teacher's college, though many of its graduates did in fact go on to join the rabbinate or teach professionally. This did not mean that the yeshiva existed merely or even mainly to indulge the intellectual curiosity of its students, or bachurim. These were institutions of high religious purpose, Torah study being both an obligation and an aspect of worship, and they were as devoted to building moral character as to increasing knowledge.[61]

Bianco relates, "In yeshiva life there were three orders of merit: brilliance, diligence, and piety. Everywhere he went, Reichmann earned top rank in the latter two categories and was just a cut below the pinnacle in the former," so, following two years at London's Torat Emeth, Reichmann headed north for the next three years at Yeshiva Ben Joseph, considered the most renowned yeshiva in Gateshead, near Newcastle, where "there had evolved a group of strictly Orthodox schools that emerged after the war as the Jewish educational capital of Europe."[62] At Gateshead, relates Bianco,

> Reichmann was exposed to a half-dozen prominent Talmudic scholars on the faculty, including Rabbi Leib Gurwitz, a product of the great Lithuanian yeshiva at Mir [...] [and] it would be a source of deep satisfaction to Paul Reichmann that the younger and more scholarly of his two sons, Henry, not only would go to Gateshead but also be taught by the son of Rabbi Gurwitz.[63]

In 1950, Paul left England to spend the High Holidays in Israel rather than in Tangier. where his father had established a bank but had his eyes on future immigration to North America given the unpredictable situation in northwest Africa.[64] But Paul "decided to stay and attended two of the best of Israel's transplanted Lithuanian yeshivoth," notes Bianco, "Mir and Ponovezh, the latter of which today is widely considered 'the Oxbridge of yeshivas.'"[65] However, after nearly a year of study at the Mir yeshiva in Israel, he was called back to Morocco in order to become the educational director of Ozar Hatorah in Casablanca in 1953.[66] He worked in Morocco for three years until immigrating to Canada.

In 1953, as the educational director of Ozar Hatorah in Morocco, Paul changed the organization's religious curriculum and upgraded its teaching

---

[61] Bianco, *The Reichmanns*, 202.
[62] Ibid., 204.
[63] Ibid., 205.
[64] Ibid., 217.
[65] Ibid., 212.
[66] Ibid., 224 25.

staff, helping establish Jewish schools all over Morocco, including the first girl's seminary in Tangier. In 1956, he resigned from Ozar Hatorah, sailed to New York and came to Canada, where the family had settled in Toronto. In 1964, Paul and two of his brothers, Albert and Ralph, established Olympia & York Industrial Development Company, which, at its peak, was the largest real estate empire in the world. By the 1980s, the Reichmanns became one of the ten wealthiest families globally, ranked just beneath the British Royal family. Nonetheless, while Paul Reichmann was "among the most resourceful and resilient entrepreneurs of the 20th century," he was determined to lead "a rigorously devout, modest private life."[67]

Hence, as a religiously educated Jewish immigrant to Canada, Rabbi Paul Reichmann, asserts Bianco, became "the most accomplished property man of his generation," and for this longtime yeshiva student, "real estate was an accidental calling."[68] For Trump, in contrast, real estate had been his father's business and Donald's academic major at the Wharton School.

Although the mid-1950s saw Conservative Judaism on the ascendancy in Canada, with most new synagogues built during the rising tide of demand in suburban North America being non-*haredi*, Bianco asserts that "the forecasters had got it exactly wrong: instead of expiring on cue, strict Orthodoxy quietly but inexorably gained strength to emerge in the 1970s and 1980s as the new eight-hundred-pound gorilla of North American Judaism."[69]

The reason for this development was that, at a minimum, 300,000 European Jews had immigrated to the United States and Canada in the mid-twentieth century, asserts Bianco, and while "only a minority of these newcomers, perhaps 10 percent, were strictly observant, their religious identities had been tempered into steel by the ordeals of the Holocaust era."[70] These Jewish immigrants were not about "to compromise the strict Orthodoxy that had sustained them [as that] would have been the basest form of self-betrayal," argues Bianco, "so, in contradistinction to all the preceding waves of Orthodox immigrants, this latest group wanted nothing more than to be left alone."[71]

In the Canadian setting, however, while Montreal "was exceptional among North American cities in that traditional Orthodoxy never ceded much ground to the Conservative movement," Bianco notes, "in Toronto, Orthodoxy not only had faded according to form but its reemergence had

---

[67] See "Paul Reichman." Online: http://www.shemayisrael.com/ozerhatorah/reichman.htm (accessed February 8, 2013).
[68] Bianco, *The Reichmanns*, 256.
[69] Ibid., 245.
[70] Ibid.
[71] Ibid., 246.

been retarded by the federal policies that prevented large-scale Jewish immigration until the 1950s"—when the Reichmanns arrived only to discover a "multidenominational landscape lightly dusted with recently founded, makeshift Orthodox prayerhouses and day schools. Over time, the family's money and initiative would prove a crucial catalyst in the coalescence of these isolated and impoverished pockets of immigrant settlement into one of North America's most vibrant haredi communities."[72]

Traditional Jewish life, observance, values and outlook were therefore far from extinct in this "new world" where Reichmann now resided. Reichmann's business manner, reflecting his religious training and piety, would demonstrate a strong sense of modesty and humility, while he and his family's property development company earned a reputation for great integrity. However, as Bianco observes,

> extreme piety of any denomination is not in and of itself a guarantee of integrity in business [...] And yet Paul Reichmann's protests notwithstanding, the Reichmanns' founding approach to real estate development exemplified the code of the lifnin Mishuras Hadin—or the Extra-Righteous Jew—as articulated by Maimonides in the Mishneh Torah.[73]

Indeed, the preeminent medieval Jewish philosopher and rabbi Maimonides—the Rambam—held high standards for Jews engaged in business, and Reichmann lived up to this ideal, even though, Bianco observes,

> most of the Reichmann's early enthusiasts did not know Maimonides from Hippocrates, it was expected that they would frame their appreciation in secular, even non-Jewish terms. [...] In Toronto, bastion of Britishness, it was not Lifnin Mishuras Hadin that provided the context for understanding the Reichmanns but the Protestant equivalent: the Code of the English Gentleman.[74]

Yet, all people needed to know to understand Paul Moishe Reichmann, was the characteristics of the biblical Moses, who embodied many of the values fostered in the yeshivot at which Reichmann had studied.

In the 1980s, the Canadian billionaire Reichmann family was making major inroads in the New York property market, with Trump's development interests among their primary competition. Canadian business writer Peter Foster notes that, in describing Trump Tower's glamour on Fifth Avenue,

---

[72] Ibid.
[73] Ibid., 269.
[74] Ibid.

"perhaps Trump's most significant contribution to the building's design was to intercept the shop drawing and double the height of his own name at the entrance," making "Trump a trademark for glitz," which worked to legitimately enhance Trump's business image beyond mere ego inflation.[75] Accounting for their different styles, Foster explains,

the Reichmanns perfectly understood Trump's approach. Just as he had very deliberately built a high-profile image as part of his business franchise, they had cultivated a low-profile one as part of the creation of a very deliberate "mystique." As Trump had once said: "The name sells. It's all a game really." In the Reichmanns' case, the name of the game was "integrity." But the Reichmanns' "integrity" never represented any kind of contradiction or business sacrifice. Despite the frequent horrors reported in the business pages, integrity was not exceptional for businessmen. For the Reichmanns, it was part of their franchise. It made business smoother and brought business back.[76]

While the fortunes of both Trump and Reichmann would rise and fall in dramatic cycles in the 1990s, Foster notes,

what made the Reichmanns exceptional was the genius of Paul Reichmann.[...] The roots of his skill were apparently as much a mystery to his family as to anyone else. Even his own mother, Renée, would be astonished at her son's success. Paul Reichmann would transform his Talmudically trained brain into a powerful analytical tool and a commercial weapon. He would turn his studious mind from rumination on arcane points of scholarship to thoughts of how to build a business empire.[77]

This dramatically different demeanor separating Trump from Reichmann, while puzzling for some, is clear when viewed through a traditional Jewish lens. The point that Foster did not emphasize in his fascinating work on the Reichmann family—to which Bianco alluded in his equally interesting account of the Reichmanns—is the profound role their Judaism played in their behavior. Not only was Reichmann inherently modest but also the company's global construction projects stopped each week for Shabbat, the Divinely mandated day of rest.

---

[75] Peter Foster, *Towers of Debt: The Rise and Fall of the Reichmanns* (Toronto, ON: Key Porter Books, 1993), 228.

[76] Foster, *Towers of Debt*, 228–29.

[77] Ibid., 17–18.

For a rabbi who was certainly no stranger to Talmud study, Judaism and business were entirely intermingled. As Bianco explains,

> for the observant Jew, commercial ambition is an intrinsically touchy subject. [...] Within haredi society, the study of Torah is regarded not merely as the highest form of achievement but as every adult male's solemn religious duty. As a product of some of the world's finest yeshivas, Paul Reichmann was steeped in the culture of the Book and would remain unswervingly loyal to it. During Olympia & York's life, he would distribute hundreds of millions of dollars among yeshivoth and other schools around the world, ranking him the greatest patron that Orthodox education has seen or is likely to see. And yet Reichmann rarely would be found at the kollel that he founded in 1970 a few blocks from his house in North York. By all accounts but his own, Reichmann devoted himself so obsessively to business after he had discovered his calling as a developer that he had little time left for study.[78]

Nonetheless, for someone like Reichmann, humility meant modesty, and modesty meant holiness. Such a focus could not be more different than the often arrogant or pompous public image Trump had intentionally cultivated for himself.

Larry Kahaner notes that the Reichmann family "had built a reputation based on integrity, honesty, and on-time delivery of projects, while adhering to their core values of charity and generosity."[79] Concerning the Talmud, however, Kahaner relates an interesting story (with no mention of whether Trump also followed this trend):

> When competitors discovered that Paul Reichmann and his brothers studied the Talmud daily, they also began reading it to see if they could glean some of the family's business secrets from this esoteric document. To their dismay, there were no hidden secrets. The Reichmann's business acumen stemmed from the Talmud's practical advice, moral guidance, and ethical values—teachings that the family precisely followed.[80]

The rivalry between Trump and Reichmann not only revealed a major contrast between arrogant and humble leadership but also shed light on the significance of humility that many within the business world may not have

[78]  Bianco, *The Reichmanns*, 303.
[79]  Larry Kahaner, *Values, Prosperity, and the Talmud: Business Lessons from the Ancient Rabbis* (Hoboken, NJ: John Wiley & Sons, 2003), xi.
[80]  Kahaner, *Values, Prosperity, and the Talmud*, xi.

taken seriously in their own careers. Hence, for modern organizations, humility ought to be an important trait for leaders to emulate. Nielsen, Marrone and Slay have theorized that humility plays a major role in "socialized charismatic leadership" primarily because it "prevents excessive self-focus" while allowing for self-understanding.[81] Likewise, Owens and Hekman maintain that humility among leaders is a successful trait because leaders provide a model of behavior for their followers, which helps them to understand that feelings of uncertainty are legitimate and that positive outcomes for organizations can be achieved.[82] Through his business and leadership behavior, Reichmann of Olympia & York arguably was able to achieve this demonstration without intending to do so.

* * *

Indeed, humility is hardly exclusive to Jewish leadership despite its historic and biblical precedence. This feature is considered by introspective leaders of various backgrounds. During the 2016 US political primaries, while at a CNN-hosted town hall meeting in New Hampshire for Democratic Party leadership candidates Hillary Clinton and Bernie Sanders, Clinton, regarded as a formidable political fighter, was asked a question by Rabbi Jonathan Spira-Savett of New Hampshire's Temple Beth Abraham. He inquired, "How do you cultivate the ego, the ego that we all know you must have, a person must have to be the leader of the free world, and also the humility to recognize that we know that you can't be expected to be wise about all the things that the president has to be responsible for?"[83]

The aspiring presidential nominee gave a reflective response. "I think about this a lot," Clinton answered. "I feel very fortunate that I am a person of faith, that I was raised in my church and that I have had to deal and struggle with a lot of these issues about ambition and humility, about service

---

[81] Rob Nielsen, Jennifer A. Marrone, and Holly S. Slay, "A New Look at Humility: Exploring the Humility Concept and Its Role in Socialized Charismatic Leadership," *Journal of Leadership & Organizational Studies* 17, no. 1 (2010): 33–43.

[82] Bradley P. Owens and David R. Hekman, "Modeling How to Grow: An Inductive Examination of Humble Leader Behaviors, Contingencies, and Outcomes," *Academy of Management Journal* 55, no. 4 (2012): 787–818.

[83] Rabbi Spira-Savett's question posed to Hillary Clinton is available from a number of sources including YouTube. See "Hillary Clinton Answers a Rabbi's Question on Ambition and Humility." YouTube video, 4:34. Posted by "Hillary Clinton," February 4, 2016, https://www.youtube.com/watch?v=CWS2IzYx6J8&feature=youtu.be (accessed March 11, 2016). The question also appears verbatim in Ron Kampeas, "How a US Rabbi Opened Hillary Clinton's Heart—in His Own Words," *Jerusalem Post*, February 5, 2016. Online: http://www.jpost.com/Diaspora/How-a-US-rabbi-opened-Hillary-Clintons-heart-in-his-own-words-443969 (accessed March 11, 2016).

and self-gratification—all of the human questions that all of us deal with, but when you put yourself out into the public arena, I think it's incumbent upon you to be as self-conscious as possible. This is hard for me [...] I always wanted to be of service."[84] This was a remarkable moment of unbridled honesty for a politician seeking the most powerful political office in the United States—and arguably the world.

Clinton continued, "I have had to come to grips with how much more difficult it often is for me to talk about myself than to talk about what I want to do for other people. [...] So I am constantly trying to balance how do I assume the mantle of a position as essentially august as president of the United States, and not lose track of who I am, what I believe in, and what I want to do to serve." Clinton shared that she not only receives a "scripture lesson" every morning by e-mail from a minister she knows well but also that "friends who are rabbis" also send her notes and readings from upcoming sermons that she appreciates receiving. "It gets me grounded," she said.[85]

One can only assume that Hillary Clinton had become acquainted with the notion of humility from her study of the Bible, and quite possibly through the Mosaic example. Wherever she acquired this outlook that happens to be consistent with Moses, she articulated the view that, in politics, humility is concerned with preserving a balance between one's skills and one's limitations, conceding that "I don't know that there is any ever absolute answer." However, Clinton added, "It's that balance that I keep to try to find in my life, that I want to see back in our country."[86]

According to Jewish tradition, however, humility is linked to modesty, which is connected to holiness, which ideally leads to integrity. Moses' concern for others and personal qualities showed him to be a man of great spiritual integrity and, as such, serves as a profound role model for leaders—perhaps even including Hillary Clinton.

## Mercy—Demonstrating Compassion

Moses also exhibits the quality of "mercy"—perhaps more clearly expressed as compassion—a character trait Israeli economist Meir Tamari stresses as a significant "leadership quality."[87] While Moses was spending time atop Mount Sinai where he communed with God for what turned out to be

---

[84] Hillary Clinton's response can be viewed on YouTube. See "Hillary Clinton Answers a Rabbi's Question on Ambition and Humility."

[85] Ibid.

[86] Ibid.

[87] Meir Tamari, *Jewish Values in Our Open Society: A Weekly Torah Commentary* (Northvale, NJ: Jason Aronson, 2000), 138.

40 days and 40 nights,[88] receiving the revelation—the "mission statement" for the Israelites, discussed in more detail later—they, in turn, lacking faith and patience that Moses would return, convinced Aaron to melt down their gold to build a golden calf that they could worship. They exclaimed to Aaron once the statue was finished, "This is your god, O Israel, who brought you out of the land of Egypt!"[89] Aaron seems to have succumbed to the pressure of the people, and the people reverted to old Egyptian ways of cultic worship.[90]

While Moses was receiving many important guidelines from God, such as "you must keep My sabbaths, for this is a sign between Me and you through-out the ages,"[91] the Israelites were worshipping a false idol, the Golden Calf. God was angry and told Moses, "I see that this is a stiffnecked people. Now, let Me be, that My anger may blaze forth against them and that I may destroy them, and make of you a great nation."[92] But Moses revealed the quality of mercy—or compassion—that helped change God's mind.

Moses pleaded with God, while showing his own mercy for a people he knew had done wrong, declaring,

> "Let not Your anger, O Lord, blaze forth against Your people, whom You delivered from the land of Egypt with great power and with a mighty hand. Let not the Egyptians say, 'It was with evil intent that He delivered them, only to kill them off in the mountains and annihilate them from the face of the earth.' Turn from Your blazing anger, and renounce the plan to pun-ish Your people. Remember Your servants, Abraham, Isaac, and Israel, how You swore to them by Your Self and said to them: I will make your offspring as numerous as the stars of heaven, and I will give to your off-spring this whole land of which I spoke, to possess forever." And the Lord renounced the punishment He had planned to bring upon His people.[93]

According to Jewish custom, the above verses from Exodus 32:11–14 (and also those from Exodus 34:1–10 that relate the restoration of the covenant between God and Israel), Jeffrey Tigay notes, "are read in the synagogue on the public fast days that commemorate national disasters or near-disasters."[94] In other words, these biblical verses are very significant

---

[88] Exod. 24:18.
[89] Exod. 32:4.
[90] Exod. 32:1–3.
[91] Exod. 31:13.
[92] Exod. 32:9–10.
[93] Exod. 32:11–14.
[94] Jeffrey H. Tigay, commentary to Exod. 32:11–14, in Berlin and Brettler, *The Jewish Study Bible*, 184.

because they show both human—through Moses—and Divine mercy for the Jewish people.

Tamari notes, Moses "entreated God not to destroy Israel, rejected the offer of being the beginning of a new Chosen People, and asked for his own life to be destroyed rather than this sinful people."[95] Indeed, Moses must have been annoyed given that this people he had come to Egypt to save from bondage, was showing—under the watch of his brother Aaron no less—a lack of fortitude, a lack of belief in the monotheistic God who directed their escape, and a lack of confidence in Moses.

Moses must have felt great disappointment considering, in utter disgust, he would smash the first stone tablets containing God's words. Sarna asserts, "It is evident that Moses played the role of the exclusive mediator between Israel and God. He was the only recognized and acceptable channel through which the Divine energy could flow to Israel, through which God's immanence could be perceived and His communication transmitted."[96] In doing so, Moses showed mercy on these people, which, in turn, convinced God to show mercy on them. By making these verses part of the synagogue experience, successive generations are constantly reminded of the value of mercy, so it would be expected to have an impact on many who study how Moses behaved on behalf of the people and how God responded.

In the people's defense, however, Sarna points out that they merely wanted some "material, visible entity that would fill the spiritual void created by Moses' absence," which is why Sarna states that "Aaron could declare in all sincerity, after making the image, that the next day would be 'a festival of the Lord,'" indicating that there had been "no rejection of the national God."[97]

So important is mercy and compassion in the Jewish tradition, it has become a core of the *Selichot* prayers—uttered for Divine forgiveness of sin—that are typically said the Saturday night prior to Rosh Hashanah, the start of the most solemn period of the Jewish calendar. The "Thirteen Attributes of Mercy" represent the very words that God taught Moses for the Israelites to use if they required pleading for Divine compassion—based on the Golden Calf incident when God threatened to punish the people.[98] God taught Moses the Thirteen Attributes of Mercy[99] following the restoration of the covenant

[95] Tamari, *Jewish Values in Our Open Society*, 138.
[96] Nahum M. Sarna, *Exploring Exodus: The Origins of Biblical Israel* (New York, NY: Schocken, 1996), 217.
[97] Sarna, *Exploring Exodus*, 217.
[98] Exod. 32:10.
[99] Ronald L. Eisenberg, *The JPS Guide to Jewish Traditions* (Philadelphia, PA: Jewish Publication Society, 2008), 180.

when new tablets were carved by Moses to replace those he had smashed earlier—smashed, after being confronted by the Golden Calf—based on the two Torah verses to which Tigay alludes:

> The Lord! The Lord! a God compassionate and gracious, slow to anger, abounding in kindness and faithfulness, extending kindness to the thousandth generation, forgiving iniquity, transgression, and sin; to the thousandth generation, forgiving iniquity, transgression, and sin; yet He does not remit all punishment, but visits the iniquity of parents upon children and children's children, upon the third and fourth generations.[100]

This latter part of the final verse, suggesting that God does not completely absolve those who sin but makes later generations pay for transgressions of their ancestors, was not in sync with the general spirit of God's merciful and forgiving nature, suggests Ronald Eisenberg, so rabbinic authorities "ingeniously cut off the verse [...], thus changing the meaning to indicate that God does forgive all sins!", a Midrashic transformation that has evolved as the format for this verse whenever read in synagogue services.[101]

Eisenberg notes that the later Jewish mystics, "the kabbalists[,] introduced the custom of also reciting the Thirteen Attributes of Mercy before taking the Torah from the ark during the three pilgrimage festivals of Passover, Shavuot, and Sukkot."[102] In other words, Jews who attended synagogue were traditionally presented with this characteristic of God's mercy, found in Moses' defense of the Israelites, and preserved in the Thirteen Attributes linked to God, which whenever heard—as on the holidays above, certain fast days when these verses from Exodus are read, and *Selichot*—would have served as a source of emulation, and constant reinforcement, by Jews across the generations, evolving into a highly desirable character trait for Jewish people to imitate, particularly leaders from all walks of life who hear these attributes articulated in synagogues.

\* \* \*

The sense of mercy evident in Moses' actions also showed his perseverance, which is the first word that comes to Harold Kushner's mind when he ponders "the greatness of Moses."[103] According to Kushner, "perseverance in the face of frequent criticism" was necessary for Moses' "dedication born of keeping

---

[100] Exod. 34:6–7.

[101] Eisenberg, *The JPS Guide to Jewish Traditions*, 181.

[102] Ibid., 182.

[103] Harold S. Kushner, *Overcoming Life's Disappointments: Learning from Moses How to Cope with Frustration* (New York, NY: Anchor Books, 2007), 27.

his mind constantly focused on the presence and the promise of the God who summoned him and assured him that He would be with him."[104] After all, Kushner observes,

> Moses' career as a leader began with an act of helpfulness that was met with resentment rather than gratitude, and continued in that vein for the entire forty years of his leadership. He led the people from slavery to freedom; they complained that freedom was too demanding, too unpredictable. He fed them in the wilderness; they complained that the food was monotonous. At one point, they nostalgically recalled what they were fed as slaves: 'We remember the fish we used to eat free in Egypt, the cucumbers, the melons, the leeks, the onions and garlic' (Numbers 11:5). [...] Where did Moses get the strength of soul to overcome these frustrations and continue to serve as a leader?[105]

Moses' strength undoubtedly came, at least in part, from his leadership qualities, including his perseverance. However, in order to be a leader of what Elie Wiesel describes as a "flighty, ungrateful people,"[106] Moses required considerable inner strength and patience, but he also had cause for frustration. "Moses had good reason to despair, to castigate—and he did so often," Wiesel acknowledges, "some commentators say: too often and too severely."[107] Sometimes his frustration led to anger, for which one of his actions was punished by his not being allowed to enter the Promised Land. Anger can be justifiable and defendable, but it can also be misplaced and exaggerated. After all, whenever Moses was confronted by evidence of injustice, or his people sinned against God, he occasionally had outbursts of anger that could be justified.

Examples of Moses' anger that are arguably defendable include his outrage over the Pharaoh's rebellion against God. Moses said to the Pharaoh, "Then all these courtiers of yours shall come down to me and bow low to me, saying, 'Depart, you and all the people who follow you!' After that I will depart," after which Moses angrily left Pharaoh's presence.[108] The Golden Calf was a famous incident that aroused Moses' anger because it was related to the people's idolatry: "As soon as Moses came near the camp and saw the calf and the dancing, he became enraged; and he hurled the tablets from his hands and shattered them at the foot of the mountain."[109] Frustrated at the burden

---

[104]  Kushner, *Overcoming Life's Disappointments*, 27.
[105]  Ibid., 30.
[106]  Elie Wiesel, *Messengers of God: Biblical Portraits and Legends* (New York, NY: Touchstone, 1994), 199.
[107]  Wiesel, *Messengers of God*, 199.
[108]  Exod. 11:8.
[109]  Exod. 32:19.

of leadership, questioning his ability to be successful, Moses even got angry at God: "Moses heard the people weeping, every clan apart, each person at the entrance of his tent. The Lord was very angry, and Moses was distressed. And Moses said to the Lord, 'Why have You dealt ill with Your servant, and why have I not enjoyed Your favor, that You have laid the burden of all this people upon me?'"[110] Hence, sometimes Moses' anger was appropriate, but not always. His quickness to anger is arguably Moses' greatest leadership failing.

The most serious failure occurred over the Israelites' complaints about the lack of water to drink. Moses' anger led to frustration and an error in judgment when he misused the Divine rod to get water from a rock, but, in doing so, publicly disobeyed God, who had already given the instruction to "order the rock to yield its water."[111] But Moses stuck the rock twice instead of issuing the order.[112] God responded, "Because you did not trust Me enough to affirm My sanctity in the sight of the Israelite people, therefore you shall not lead this congregation into the land that I have given them."[113] This was a serious consequence of Moses' anger, which led, in turn, to frustration and arrogance—the opposite of humility—that led to his judgment error, constituting a serious offense against God. Moses, like a CEO, was essentially being held accountable for his error by God, who behaved like a board of directors in contemporary terms.

Nonetheless, Wiesel concedes, "Moses defended [the Israelites] not only against their enemies but, at times, even against God."[114] This contrast between valid and inappropriate or excessive anger indicates that leadership is not easy, but Moses' qualities of humility, modesty, integrity, mercy and perseverance undoubtedly helped him carry out his empathic leadership role despite this sin of arrogance, which was addressed by God in a most serious manner because it was a matter between Moses and God rather than between Moses and the people he led. On balance, Moses' leadership revealed good character, which a later Yiddish term—"mensch"—would encapsulate in a single word. Indeed, Moses decisively fit the modern criteria of a mensch.

## The "Mensch Factor"—a Leader's Good Character Matters

The three early stories that revealed Moses' character "represent the course of Moses' development toward becoming a leader," maintains Ari Zivotofsky,

---

[110] Num. 11:10–11.
[111] Num. 20:8.
[112] Num. 20:11.
[113] Num. 20:12.
[114] Wiesel, *Messengers of God*, 199.

whereby "in each he displays the traits of empathy and of standing up to an injustice as a *man*," even before he emerges as a heroic, empathic leader to whom God has yet to speak.[115]

The mercy, or compassion, Moses later shows in regard to the Golden Calf only emphasizes Moses' quality of empathy. Perhaps the essence of a leader who possesses the collective traits of humility, modesty, integrity, mercy, perseverance, empathy and wisdom is one who has "good character." It is interesting to note that the use of the Hebrew word, *'ish*, or man, evokes the later Yiddish term mensch, derived from the German *Mensch*, which literally means "person." In the Yiddish language, which is infused with Jewish sensibilities, the word reflects a more nuanced meaning describing a "human being" who is "an upright, honorable, decent person," or "someone of consequence; someone to admire and emulate; someone of noble character."[116]

It is difficult to express the special sense of respect and dignity that is conveyed by calling someone a "real mensch." Leo Rosten states, being a mensch does not relate to "success, wealth, or status," but the secret to being a real mensch "is nothing less than character: rectitude, dignity, a sense of what is right, responsible, [and] decorous."[117] Character is a "central, important element of leadership," assert Canadian management theorists Mary Crossan, Jeffrey Gandz and Gerard Seijts, because "character fundamentally shapes how we engage the world around us, what we notice, what we reinforce, who we engage in conversation, what we value, what we choose to act on, [and] how we decide."[118]

Moses proved to be a mensch, which made his subsequent rise to public leadership that much more appropriate. Above all, the Jewish religious texts studied by countless generations over the past two millennia have served to provide considerable exposure to the Mosaic example. Since Moses' qualities would have been learned, internalized and respected by those who espoused them, even those who did not benefit from a traditional Jewish education would have likely been influenced—through the power of cultural immersion—by the ideas of good character and good leadership emanating from the Mosaic ideal.

According to Crossan, Gandz and Seijts, "When it comes to leadership, competencies determine what a person can do. Commitment determines

---

[115]   Ari Z. Zivotofsky, "The Leadership Qualities of Moses," *Judaism* 43, no. 3 (1994): 263.

[116]   Leo Rosten, *The New Joys of Yiddish* (New York, NY: Three Rivers Press, 2001), 232.

[117]   Rosten, *The New Joys of Yiddish*, 233.

[118]   Mary Crossan, Jeffrey Gandz and Gerard Seijts, "Developing Leadership Character," *Ivey Business Journal* (January/February 2012). Online: http://iveybusinessjournal.com/publication/developing-leadership-character/ (accessed November 24, 2015).

what they want to do, and character determines what they will do." It is little surprise, therefore, that the top two of their ten leadership virtues include
humility—because it is regarded as essential for "learning and becoming a
better leader"—and integrity—due to its necessity for building "trust and
encouraging others to collaborate."[119] It just so happens that these traits are
not only associated with Moses but they are also traits of a mensch who is a
good and decent person and, therefore, regarded as someone who possesses
good character.

* * *

Zivotofsky poses an interesting question, namely, why was there such an
apparent need for "midrashic embellishments" to supplement and build on
the biblical accounts? Zivotofsky maintains that the rabbis who wrote the
Midrash

> recognized that the absolute empathy displayed by Moses included a vio-
> lent action and, fearing that this would serve as a precedent for others, saw
> a need to limit and to channel the empathy in specific directions. They
> therefore embellished the stories of the Egyptian and of the daughters of
> Jethro with so many sins and supernatural actions so as to make them dif-
> ficult to use as precedent. In the midrashic scheme, it is unlikely that an
> ordinary person would find himself in a situation identical to Moses', one
> so replete with sin as to demand violence. These embellishments are thus
> intended to prevent people from being overly zealous and recklessly mur-
> dering others, or getting involved in quarrels where they do not belong,
> and using Moses as the role model.[120]

If this is true—and it is a compelling argument—then the rabbis were
indeed gifted with tremendous insight because, by helping establish Moses as
a leader to be emulated, one would want to dissuade people from emulating
the less attractive elements of the leader's actions but rather those that emphasized a good and noble character. Hearing and studying the verses from the
Torah that show these positive leadership traits would serve to underscore
their significance and potential emulation by later generations. After all, the
Torah reports, when Moses "came down from Sinai with the second tablets and with God's forgiveness, his face shone with the Divine Presence,"
which served as "his reward, *karnu p'nai Moshe*," suggests Tamari, "his reward

[119] Crossan, Gandz and Seijts, "Developing Leadership Character."
[120] Zivotofsky, "The Leadership Qualities of Moses," 265.

for the great love he had for his people, the ultimate role model for Jewish leadership."[121]

In Zivotofsky's view, the rabbis were trying to draw a picture of a leader solely driven by the right motivation to instigate action. Moses represented a leadership role model because of his character and his strong beliefs. "There is no need for unique talents, great miracles, or a special position in life," Zivotofsky asserts. "The rabbis were trying to impress upon the reader, the Jewish masses, that ordinary caring is truly great." In other words, Zivotofsky stresses from the ancient Jewish tradition, "this is what leaders are made of; this, and not supernatural acts, is what led to the selection of Moses and what made Moses great as a *man*."[122] Or, even more categorically, what made Moses a mensch—a person of special and desirable human qualities—as expressed in Yiddish, the Jewish vernacular for much of the past millennia among those who resided in, or descended from, the Central and Eastern European Jewish diaspora, whose population grew in size to such a degree that it became the largest proportion of Jews among the global Jewish population until the horrors of World War II. Before then, it was the Ashkenazi Jews who provided the main source of Jews who went to North America and the Land of Israel in the nineteenth and early twentieth centuries. They represented a major presence, though the Sephardi population increased greatly over the past century.[123] Nonetheless, whether among Ashkenazi or Sephardi Jews, the Jewish textual sources—with Moses as a central figure—remained a major source of influence that they carried with them wherever they settled.

Of course, gender is not at issue when the word "man"—or *'ish* in Hebrew—is used. In the words of Rabbi Jonathan Sacks, former chief rabbi of the Orthodox United Hebrew Congregations of the United Kingdom and the Commonwealth, "an *ish* in the context of leadership is not a male but rather someone who is a *mensch*, a person whose greatness is lightly worn, who cares about the people others often ignore [...] who is courteous to everyone equally and who receives respect because he gives respect."[124] Moses just happened to be a male, but he was certainly a man of action who could not tolerate injustice and emerged as a talented empathic revolutionary leader.

---

[121] Tamari, *Jewish Values in Our Open Society*, 138.

[122] Zivotofsky, "The Leadership Qualities of Moses," 265.

[123] Cecil Roth, ed., *The Concise Jewish Encyclopedia* (New York, NY: The New American Library, 1980), 48.

[124] Rabbi Jonathan Sacks, *Lessons in Leadership: A Weekly Reading of the Jewish Bible* (New Milford, CT and Jerusalem, Israel: Maggid Books, 2015), 223.

# Chapter 7

# MOSES' ESSENTIAL
# LEADERSHIP SKILLS

Transformational leadership tends to reflect visionary leadership because of its focus on the larger picture, combined with the leader's ability to inspire people to work toward the achievement of a particular organizational vision. Empowerment helps foster leadership ability in those who receive delegated authority, and is a management tool that can contribute to effective leadership. Moses both empowered people and provided a vision and shared a mission statement, actions that remain essential for leadership success. Moreover, effective leadership requires trust that leaders must earn, asserts Peter Drucker, "otherwise there won't be any followers," and, for Drucker, "the only definition of a leader is someone who has followers."[1]

Warren Bennis, in his list of differences mentioned previously, maintains that "the leader inspires trust," while "the manager relies on control," underscoring the importance of trust as a leadership quality.[2] Furthermore, "trust is the conviction that the leader means what he says," because, according to Drucker, "it is a belief in integrity [since] a leader's actions and a leader's professed beliefs must be congruent, or at least compatible." Drucker asserts, "Effective leadership [...] is not based on being clever; it is based primarily on being consistent."[3] Consistency in leadership is imperative in order for followers to understand the message and goals of the organization as articulated by the leader.

Ultimately, however, even a twentieth-century management authority like Drucker can appreciate that "an effective leader knows that the ultimate task of leadership is to *create human energies and human vision*."[4] Robert Rosen, a theoretical biologist who applies scientific views to business, similarly asserts

---

[1] Peter F. Drucker and Joseph A. Maciariello, *Management*, rev. ed. (New York, NY: HarperCollins, 2008), 290.

[2] Warren Bennis, *On Becoming a Leader* (Cambridge, MA: Perseus Books, 1989), 45.

[3] Drucker and Maciariello, *Management*, 290.

[4] Ibid.

that "trust is the glue that holds relationships together [and] without trust, no vision ever becomes a reality," yet, just as "trust takes a long time to earn," it can be "lost in a moment's thoughtlessness."[5]

## Visionary Leadership

Erica Brown argues that "being visionary involves not only reflecting on the future, but also on taking a sharp, sometimes painful look at what currently exists."[6] In Midian, Moses was confronted, first, by a messenger, or angel, of God from a burning bush—whether simply serving to get Moses' attention or to get him prepared for his encounter with the Divine—the voice of God emerged from the fire declaring, "'I am [...] the God of your father, the God of Abraham, the God of Isaac, and the God of Jacob.'"[7]

This scene at the burning bush, suggests Nahum Sarna, serves "to establish an unbroken historic continuity between the present experience of Moses and the revelation received by his forefathers the Patriarchs, beginning with Abraham," to whom God had promised to redeem his Chosen People, and, in this spot, will soon choose Moses to be the agent to achieve his promise.[8] While there might be an element of heredity here, it does not apply to everyone, but rather to Moses and the particular role God had for him, perhaps inspired by his forefathers. However, his ancestors were by then quite remote; therefore, it is difficult to suggest genetics was of particular relevance. Nonetheless, at this point, Moses was compelled to become a "visionary leader," knowing that a major task was ahead, while reflecting on the current situation and the events that brought him together with the Israelites to Midian in the first place.

In their response to the episode in Exodus 3:1–4 when God calls out to Moses from the burning bush, the rabbis explained in Midrash their views on what occurred:

6. AND MOSES SAID: I WILL TURN ASIDE NOW AND SEE (III, 3). R. Joanan said, Moses took five steps then, as it is said: *"I will turn aside now, and see."* R. Simeon b. Lakish said: He simply turned his face to see, as it is said: *And when the Lord saw that he turned aside to see.* When God saw this, He said: This

[5] Robert H. Rosen, *Leading People: The 8 Proven Principles for Success in Business* (New York, NY: Penguin, 1997), 74.

[6] Erica Brown, *Inspired Jewish Leadership: Practical Approaches to Building Strong Communities* (Woodstock, VT: Jewish Lights, 2012), 71.

[7] Exod. 3:6.

[8] Nahum M. Sarna, *Exploring Exodus: The Origins of Biblical Israel* (New York, NY: Schocken, 1996), 43.

man is worthy to tend Israel. R. Isaac said: What is the meaning of: HE
TURNED ASIDE (SAR) TO SEE? God said: "This man is downcast (*sar*) and trou-
bled at seeing Israel's affliction in Egypt, he is, accordingly, worthy of being
their shepherd." Immediately, *"God called unto him out of the midst of the bush."*[9]

This Midrash emphasizes Moses' "seeing." In other words, Moses saw the
troubles of his brethren in Egypt, which can be inferred as a strong sign of
empathy for their situation. He was not intentionally casting his gaze aside
to ignore them in order to avoid becoming involved and protect his own
interests. This made Moses worthy in God's eyes to become the "shepherd,"
or leader, of the Israelites. So, as the rabbis maintain, that was when God
decided to call on Moses from the burning bush.

This episode at the burning bush represents Ari Zivotofsky's fourth example of biblical preselection stories for Moses' call to leadership.[10] According
to Zivotofsky, it is particularly interesting that "the verse does not say 'to see
the bush' or 'to see the spectacle,' but simply that Moses turned 'to see,'"[11]
reflecting on Midrash *Exodus Rabbah* 1:32, which quotes Rabbi Eliezer, the
son of Rav Jose the Galilean, as saying with regard to Moses when he was still
in Egypt that, having seen a child, a woman, a young man, and an elderly
man each carrying heavy items not suited for them, Moses rearranged their
burdens. The Midrash states that the

> Holy One, blessed be He, "You put aside your own affairs and went to share
> in Israel's suffering. [...] Therefore I will leave [...] and speak only to you."
> That is the meaning of "the Lord saw that he turned aside to see" (Exod.
> 3:4): He saw that he had turned aside from this own affairs to see their bur-
> dens; therefore, "He called to him out of the midst of the bush." (Exod. 3:4)[12]

Hence, argues Zivotofsky, "the Midrash, using a play on words, is telling
us one of the reasons behind Moses' selection: He was willing to put aside his
own needs and help another person. God therefore selected him as a prophet
to be spoken to directly."[13]

Brown asserts, while "vision and attentiveness—hearing and seeing—form
the foundation for strong biblical leadership," with the same criteria apply-
ing to leaders in the present, "to make good on the vision the leader must

[9] *Exodus Rabbah* 2:6.
[10] Ari Z. Zivotofsky, "The Leadership Qualities of Moses," *Judaism* 43, no. 3 (1994): 263.
[11] Zivotofsky, "The Leadership Qualities of Moses," 263.
[12] Cited in ibid., 263–64.
[13] Ibid., 264.

be attuned to the complexity of the situation and the possibility of crisis," a reality that requires both inner strength and acute sensitivity to direction.[14] Moses appears to exhibit these traits in the Midrashim above, and the Bible shows Moses taking on the responsibility that God presented to him. Moses' "seeing" went beyond physical sight and reflected a grander "vision" that was and remains an important basis for strong leadership.

God commanded Moses to return to Egypt and lead the Hebrew slaves out of Egyptian bondage.[15] After showing initial reticence or, rather, over-whelming humility—for as Simon Glustrom notes, "the modest man is God's greatest ally, for he recognizes his limitations and readily admits to error and fallibility"[16]—Moses returned to Egypt with his brother, Aaron, and told the Pharaoh of God's command. In God's name, the declaration was made to "let my people go."[17] When the Pharaoh refused to release the Hebrews from slavery, God afflicted the Egyptians by sending ten plagues to Egypt in order to convince the Pharaoh to change his mind.[18] Ultimately, the Pharaoh relented, and Moses led his people out of Egypt.[19] The exodus journey therefore began.

Shortly thereafter at Mount Sinai, Moses, as leader of the Israelites, received from God the Decalogue[20]—Latin, based on the earlier Greek term for "ten words," though popularly known in English as the "Ten Commandments,"[21] even though in Hebrew it is *Aseret Ha'Devarim*, or "ten words"—which, notes Tigay, represents the "initial stipulation of the covenant" directed to the people. The Decalogue implicitly recognized "God as Israel's king, hence its legislator," with Moses occupying a very important human leadership role because God only spoke directly to Moses, who later shared God's words with the people. As an aside, Tigay observes, the Talmud resolves the inconsistency in communication by stating that the first two commandments—in which God spoke in the first person—came from God directly, while the rest were spoken by Moses in reference to God in the third person.[22]

[14] Brown, *Inspired Jewish Leadership*, 72.
[15] Exod. 3:10.
[16] Simon Glustrom, *The Language of Judaism*, 2nd rev. ed. (New York, NY: Ktav, 1973), 81–82.
[17] Exod. 5:1.
[18] Exod. 7:14–11:7; 12:29.
[19] Exod. 13:17.
[20] See Exod. 34:28: "And he [Moses] was there [atop Mount Sinai also known as Horeb, see Deut. 5:2] with the Lord forty days and forty nights; he ate no bread and drank no water; and he wrote down on the tablets the terms of the covenant, the Ten Commandments"; and Deut. 10:4: "The Lord inscribed on the tablets the same text as on the first, the Ten Commandments that He addressed to you [the Israelites] on the mountain out of the fire on the day of the Assembly; and the Lord gave them to me [Moses]."
[21] The Decalogue appears twice in the Torah. See Exod. 20:2–14 and Deut. 5:6–18.
[22] Jeffrey H. Tigay, commentary to Exod. 20:1–4 and 20:1, *The Jewish Study Bible*, ed. Adele Berlin and Marc Zvi Brettler (New York, NY: Oxford University Press, 2004), 148.

Nonetheless, the Ten Commandments represented a covenant. As Sarna asserts, a covenant

> embraces a treaty as an instrument of international diplomacy, a compact between a king and his subjects, a pact that defines mutual understanding and responsibilities between two individuals, and is even used in matrimony. Without doubt, the overwhelming usage of the "covenant" is to designate the function and effect of the great national experience at Sinai. By so doing, the Bible describes a living reality, an actual legal circumstance, nothing less than the assertion of the conclusion of an eternally binding pact between God and His people. Thereafter, the entire history of Israel, as portrayed in the Bible, is governed by this outstanding reality. Covenant consciousness suffuses all subsequent developments.[23]

In contrast to the general context of the ancient world, where, notes Sarna, "the legislators are kings, princes, and sages," in this situation, both the king and the state represent the source of law and its authority. Sarna stresses, however, "The only name connected with law is that of Moses, and he is not its source but a prophet who mediates the divine communication to Israel."[24] Sarna relates, therefore, that "the source of sanction in law" distinguishes the Decalogue from other ancient Near Eastern texts because "no biblical law is ever attributed to Moses personally or to any prophet. The narratives know nothing of a lawgiver-sage or a lawgiver-king."[25] As clearly related in the Torah, Moses is not divine but received the law from the Divine at Mount Sinai. Moreover, these Ten Commandments, Sarna stresses, "are general precepts of universal applicability unconditioned by temporal considerations and unaffected by shifting political conditions. They are truly of binding validity for the present and the future," which is because "the 'suzerain' [sovereign] who dictates the terms of the covenant is none other than God Himself."[26]

Hence, despite some differences in interpretation and implication, Christianity's New Testament authors still unambiguously associate the Ten Commandments with Moses as the receiver who related the Divine laws to the people (for example, John 7:19, Mark 7:10, and Ephesians 6:2). In Islam, while the Koran features its equivalents to the content of the biblical Ten Commandments, it nevertheless appears to acknowledge the validity and significance of the Ten Commandments transmitted from God to Moses to the

[23] Sarna, *Exploring Exodus*, 134.
[24] Ibid., 140–41.
[25] Ibid., 141.
[26] Ibid.

Israelites, since the Koran says, "Of the people of Moses there is a nation who guide by the truth, and by it act with justice."[27]

* * *

This Divine communication—the Ten Commandments—can appropriately be viewed as a "mission statement" in contemporary terms. Moses' visionary leadership and this mission statement were certainly closely connected. On this point, Judaism, Christianity and Islam all appear in agreement. It was Moses, as leader of the Israelites, who was assigned the role of bringing this mission statement to his people for their understanding, acceptance and observance.

## Implementing a Mission Statement

Mission statements are essential for organizational focus, and to achieve such focus people must be encouraged to embrace the tenets of their organization's mission statement. As Stephen Covey relates in *Principle-Centered Leadership*, "One of the best ways I know of bringing about [a] shared vision is in creating a mission statement," because, Covey maintains, "a mission statement has the potential of being a living constitution—something that embodies deeply held values and that is based on timeless principles." Covey asserts, "In a world of such tremendous global change, what is needed is a compass in the hand of each associate. A mission statement that results from broad-based involvement and that is based on principles is such a compass."[28] One can only speculate whether Covey realized just how significant his words were in context of Moses and the Israelites at Sinai.

* * *

Early on, when Moses was first confronted by God at the burning bush "at the mountain called Horeb, which many scholars view as Mount Sinai," notes Norman Cohen, this was deemed as "inextricably bound up with the events that will take place later at Sinai, as the text intimates: 'This shall be a sign for you [...] that you shall worship God at this place' (Exodus 3:12)."[29]

---

[27] Koran 7:159. *The Koran: Interpreted*, trans. Arthur J. Arberry (Oxford, UK: Oxford University Press, 1983), 162.

[28] Stephen R. Covey, *Principle-Centered Leadership* (New York, NY: Fireside, 1992), 184–85.

[29] Norman J. Cohen, *Moses and the Journey to Leadership: Timeless Lessons of Effective Management from the Bible and Today's Leaders* (Woodstock, VT: Jewish Lights, 2007), 98.

Later, after Moses brought the Israelites out of Egypt to Mount Sinai, the Bible relates,

Israel encamped there in front of the mountain, and Moses went up to God. The Lord called to him from the mountain, saying, "Thus shall you say to the house of Jacob [that is, the Israelites] and declare to the children of Israel: 'You have seen what I did to the Egyptians. [...] Now then, if you will obey Me faithfully and keep My covenant, you shall be My treasured possession among all the peoples [...] you shall be to Me a kingdom of priests and a holy nation.' These are the words that you shall speak to the children of Israel."[30]

In Cohen's words, Moses' prior experience leads him to implicitly know "what must be done and he does not hesitate to act."[31] Moses is catapulted into the very strong role of "visionary leader" in order to inspire the people to follow the mission statement as revealed to Moses by God. This was a leadership role of the highest order.

Indeed, Moses then assumed the role of biblical CEO, of sorts, because he became a leader entrusted with transforming God's mission statement into a viable entity wherein the masses of Israelites will look to Moses as a human leader who occupies a special role, one possessing authority, power, compassion and, especially, vision.

At Sinai, the Israelite people, who had been quite divided in their rebellion against God and Moses, finally came together. The Book of Exodus reports that, upon their arrival, as noted by Cohen, "'Israel camped (va-yihan) in front of the mountain'" (19:2), indicating that finally they have drawn together as a people, perhaps in anticipation of God's revealing of the Divine Self to them." In other words, Cohen asserts, "they have finally become one people, responding with one heart, and as such they are worthy of the revelation."[32]

Rashi, the renowned eleventh-century French rabbi whose commentary on both the Talmud and the books of the Tanakh remain closely studied to this day, indicated that until this point in the Scriptures all verbs in reference to the Israelites had been in the plural form (such as "they journeyed" or "they entered"), but Exodus 19:2—"Israel encamped there"—represents the first time that the Hebrew verb for "encamped" is in the singular form, signifying that only when they rose above their differences and arguments

[30] Exod. 19:2–6.
[31] Cohen, *Moses and the Journey to Leadership*, 99.
[32] Ibid., 101.

and became one people were they deemed fit to receive the Torah.[33] Hence, the rabbis observe that this verb (va-yihan) was in the singular, implying that Israel was united as if they were one entity.[34] This was perhaps why the Decalogue was given at this particular point, because it was as if the Israelites, as the People of Israel, were united and therefore more receptive to the message.

Cohen observes that at Sinai, "everything has changed for the Israelites—they are now expected to live by God's commandments, so each and every Israelite has to understand and internalize these commandments. Thus, when the task is to adapt the organization to a radically new reality, every leader must recognize that each member must be engaged in the mission."[35] Indeed, Moses was the preeminent visionary leader now in charge of an enormous number of Hebrews who would be intimately connected with fulfilling the mission.

Yet, according to Rabbi Nathan Laufer, "a long-term vision, by its very definition, takes a protracted period to actualize," so leaders need to work to achieve "small victories along the way" that help people "reach the longer-term goal."[36] Such small victories, asserts Laufer, are the series of "mini crises" that the Israelites had to confront even prior to arriving at Mount Sinai, such as the need for water just three days following the sea split that enabled them to cross to the other side. Moses—under the guidance of God—made the waters of Marah sweet to drink with the help of a tree (Exod. 15:22–25). A second water crisis is averted when Moses led the people to an oasis where there was lots of water and shade (Exod. 15:27). And then the third water scarcity crisis occurred, but God had shown Moses how to bring water from a desert rock (Exod. 17:3–7).[37]

However, according to Laufer, at this stage "the people were not only lacking in water, they were also lacking spiritual faith that God was really with them, which in turn undermined their faith in themselves and in the viability of their journey to the Promised Land," so, he asserts, "this third provision of water had to slake the people's physical thirst and satiate their spiritual qualms."[38] As a result, the people saw some small achievements toward the

---

[33]  See D'rash commentary to Exod. 19:2, edited by Harold Kushner, in Etz Hayim: Torah and Commentary, ed. David. L. Lieber (New York, NY: The Rabbinical Assembly of the United Synagogue of Conservative Judaism, 2004), 437.

[34]  Ibid.

[35]  Cohen, Moses and the Journey to Leadership, 102.

[36]  Nathan Laufer, The Genesis of Leadership: What the Bible Teaches Us about Vision, Values and Leading Change (Woodstock, VT: Jewish Lights, 2006), 126.

[37]  Laufer, The Genesis of Leadership, 127–28.

[38]  Ibid., 128.

overall vision of their aim to reach the Promised Land. Now at Sinai, both the vision and the mission became much clearer.

After Moses had delegated power by appointing judges—discussed later in greater detail—he then had to codify values and policies to establish and actualize the vision. As Laufer notes, "For the Israelites to merit settling the Promised Land and displace the native populations residing there, they needed to fulfill God's purpose in selecting them in the first place: to consti- tute a nation that could fulfill God's dream for humanity at creation and the Israelites' role in the community of nations." Laufer argues, therefore, that not only did they need to "develop the character to be, in effect, God's partner, God's agent in history" but they also "needed to embody a set of values and behavioral norms that would be a vast improvement over the indigenous and morally corrupt nations of Canaan that they were to displace (see Deut. 9:5)."[39]

After all, maintains Laufer, "the purpose of the Exodus was to create a new civilization with radically different ethical values and social norms than those that existed in ancient Egypt and Canaan" and an "innovative, humane society, what has been since called 'ethical monotheism'" that both God and Moses had envisioned firmly "taking root in the Promised Land."[40] Hence, after Moses appointed a "hierarchical judicial authority" in Exodus 18, notes Laufer, and God described "the vision of covenantal responsibility in [Exodus] chapter 19, the Bible begins to spell out in [Exodus] chapter 20 the fundamental strategic values necessary for achieving that vision."[41] These strategic values, Laufer asserts, were embodied in the Decalogue, as revealed in Exodus 20:2–14 (and repeated in Deuteronomy 5:6–18), which were "Ten Commandments [...] not merely ten specific laws governing human behav- ior," but instead, "they conveyed the large, axiomatic, strategic values that were to guide the Israelites on their historic mission."[42]

According to David Baron, Moses "reading the commands aloud, writing them down, establishing a special place for them, reciting them again—this is how Moses reinforced his message and infused the Israelites with the ideals of Judaism."[43] Laufer agrees, but goes further by stressing that

> leaders need to set out in writing the nonnegotiable values and principles that are the bedrock of their organizations. Whether those principles are con- tained in a mission statement, a "covenant," or a simple list of "what we stand

---

[39] Ibid., 137.
[40] Ibid., 138.
[41] Ibid.
[42] Ibid.
[43] David Baron and Lynette Padwa, *Moses on Management: 50 Leadership Lessons from the Greatest Man- ager of All Time* (New York, NY: Pocket Books, 1999), 33.

for," such a body of values is the key for anchoring the organizational culture on firm ground. The values must be clear, reiterated, and explained at every opportunity. Most important, they must be consistently implemented by the organization's leadership.[11]

These were ten fundamental values to which the Israelites needed to conform in order to become a cohesive, decent and ethical people worthy of entering the Promised Land. While not embodying all of the laws found in the Torah (traditional Judaism holds that 613 commandments are found in the Torah[15]), the Decalogue's ten commandments established a code of behavior, acknowledging (in commandments, 1–3) the significance of respect for God (Exod. 20:2, 3–4, and 7), (4) the Sabbath (Exod. 20:8–10) and (5) one's parents (Exod. 20:12). The last five commandments regulated human interactions by teaching respect for other human beings through the prohibition of (6) murder (Exod. 20:13), (7) adultery (Exod. 20:13), (8) theft (Exod. 20:13), (9) bearing false witness (Exod. 20:13) and (10) coveting (Exod. 20:14). In Laufer's words, "The Ten Commandments address the fundamental spiritual and ethical values that the nation as a whole needed to internalize and inculcate in their children to become the kinds of people and the type of nation that God and Moses envisioned in the Promised Land. The commandments are the medium by which to teach the people how to be responsible to God and responsible to each other."[16]

* * *

The call that Moses received from God at the burning bush was, initially, like what Erica Brown refers to as a mission "addressed to a religiously gifted or charismatic personality."[17] Just as the burning bush was not just about God's revelation to Moses to lead the Israelites out of Egypt and bring them to the Promised Land, the vision was to bring them there "only after they underwent a national transformation on God's mountain and became God's special emissaries to the world (Exod. 3:12, 19:5–6)," because, as Laufer argues, "Moses' task was to lead the people out of Egypt geographically, culturally, and morally," with the "geographical exodus" taking about one year, the "cultural and moral exodus" taking about 40 years. Even then not all of the

[11] Laufer, *The Genesis of Leadership*, 141–42.
[15] Babylonian Talmud, *Makkot* 23b records Rabbi Simlai's statement that 613 commandments were communicated to Moses and written in the Torah, specifically 365 negative commandments and 248 positive commandments that cover a whole range of different responsibilities.
[16] Laufer, *The Genesis of Leadership*, 141.
[17] Brown, *Inspired Jewish Leadership*, 72.

corruption of ancient Egypt was expunged (see, for example, Numbers 25:1–6, 31:9, 32:5–8), yet, "whatever success was achieved can be attributed to God and Moses's teaching of the Ten Commandments and the laws of the covenant."[18]

The Decalogue of Exodus chapter 20 was just the start because a set of detailed legal positions followed in Exodus 21 through 23, building on the underlying values that the Ten Commandments articulated for this "newly constituted Israelite nation." Laufer maintains that, together, "these laws constituted the Book of the Covenant that Moses read to the people and to which they voiced their enthusiastic consent in Exodus 24:7."[19] The Torah is explicit in relating what Moses did and said: "Then he took the record of the covenant and read it aloud to the people. And they said, 'All that the Lord has spoken we will faithfully do!' "[50] Hence, Laufer contends—in the spirit of the Torah—that "if the Ten Commandments were the overall strategy, then the Book of the Covenant was the more detailed game plan for how a 'kingdom of priests' was to evolve."[51]

## Leading with Management Skills

The general distinction between management and leadership was discussed previously in considerable detail. The fundamental implication is that, in general, leaders *lead* and managers *manage*. Role crossover exists, as John Gardner noted, but the leader's particular qualities—which Moses possessed in abundance—must be acknowledged for the power they wield.

It should be further noted that, while a "manager is more tightly linked to an organization than is the leader," Gardner asserts, "the leader may have no organization at all." Just as Florence Nightingale showed extraordinary leadership in the field of health care after she left the Crimea, without any organization for her to command, and Mohandas Gandhi proved an effective leader before ever having an organization to head, Gardner observes, "some of our most memorable leaders have headed movements so amorphous that management would be an inappropriate word."[52] This is definitely true concerning Moses, who was the indisputable leader of a people, the Israelites, who would grow in number and become a formidable force that, over a long time period, exercised considerable influence on Western civilization as a whole.

---

[18] Laufer, *The Genesis of Leadership*, 141.
[19] Ibid., 142.
[50] Exod. 24:7.
[51] Laufer, *The Genesis of Leadership*, 142.
[52] John W. Gardner, *On Leadership* (New York, NY: Free Press, 1990), 4.

"The truly great cultural changes in human history are rarely attributable to individuals, but individuals play key roles," Gardner maintains, and "in the emergence of monotheism, for example, Moses was surely the most central figure of whom we have extensive knowledge."[53] This is what makes the Great Man Theory of leadership not easily disposable, as Moses was a Great Man in his time as related in the biblical literature. Likewise, he was a genuine transformational leader.

* * *

What motivated Moses to go to the Pharaoh—who held considerable power—against overwhelming odds to tell him that holding the Israelites as slaves was not right? What gave Moses the courage to lead in this way, to speak truth to power? Presumably God chose Moses because he had faith in Moses to accomplish such a mission. Moses must have had faith in God's support. But, in undertaking the mission, Moses showed strong qualities of leadership. Moses spoke the truth and addressed the Pharaoh. In other words, he spoke truth to power. Speaking truth is a character attribute that shows courage and, arguably, inspires others to follow.

Moses was neither an autocrat nor a tyrant, as Sigmund Freud conceded. He did not appear to have as his objective self-glorification or ego gratification. He came to know he had a crucial role to play, a goal to achieve and a mission statement to follow. God provided the mission statement at Sinai in the form of the Decalogue, or Ten Commandments, and the Written and Oral Torah became the guiding principles for generations to come. Meir Tamari notes that "the spiritual and ethical teachings of the Ten Commandments are prefaced with the acknowledgment that they flow from the God who took us out of Egypt. We were strangers in a foreign land."[54] Tamari further relates,

Experienced in and familiar with the feeling of hopelessness, exploitation, and alienation, which are the lot of the strangers, the Torah said we should not oppress the stranger, both in word and in action, but also in the provision of one legal system for native born and stranger alike. The mandatory resting of servants and animals on *Shabbat* is in the Decalogue in *Devarim* [Deuteronomy], linked to the Exodus. Such linkage is not a function of ethnic memory but of the teachings inherent in the Exodus, so the Torah tells us that the basis for the injunction against the interest-bearing loan is

---

[53] Gardner, *On Leadership*, 136.
[54] Meir Tamari, *Jewish Values in Our Open Society: A Weekly Torah Commentary* (Northvale, NJ: Jason Aronson, 2000), 96.

because God took us out of Egypt. [...] The whole concept of just weights and measures, which come to prevent fraud and exploitation in daily business dealings, is linked in the Torah to the God that took us out of Egypt.[55]

While God is traditionally viewed in the Bible as the one who is ultimately in charge—like a singular board of directors to which the CEO, personified by Moses, reports—who actually led the Israelites out of Egypt? Moses was the human leader in charge of this task. Regarding the demonstration of leadership, however, Moses led the Israelites through the wilderness for 40 years, overcoming many problems along the way. This process revealed macro competencies that the best leaders possess.

As the Bible relates, once he accepted his Divine mission, and later encountered God atop Mount Sinai, Moses received a strong vision and objectives to achieve—in Moses' case, one major objective was to get the Israelites to Canaan—and this vision was ultimately achieved under Joshua, groomed for succession to assume his leadership role. As mentioned earlier in reference to the notion that heredity does not guarantee effective leadership, it is remarkable that Moses appears to have implicitly understood this and, therefore, neither felt the need to groom either of his sons to take over after him nor to establish a personal biological dynasty.

Yet Moses understood the importance of leadership succession. Not only did Moses prove an effective heroic, visionary and empathic leader but he was also a mentor through his fostering of key leadership skills in those who followed him, especially Joshua. Such a skill was evident as a subdivision of his leadership strategy that involved the management principle of delegation, or power sharing, as part of Moses' leadership strategy.

## Empowerment and Delegation

Humility was raised earlier as a crucial character trait possessed by Moses,[56] which, it was argued, is also the mark of a good leader. Another observation in praise of humility as a leadership quality is that an arrogant person who lacks humility will be less likely to delegate; hence, the ability to effectively delegate is arguably a mark of a good leader. According to Jewish tradition, observes Glustrom, an arrogant person—in Hebrew, *Ba'al Ga'avah*—is deemed to be "the greatest adversary of God" because such a person "places himself in God's stead, seeking "to play the role of God."[57] Such a

---

[55] Tamari, *Jewish Values in Our Open Society*, 96–97.

[56] Num. 12:3.

[57] Glustrom, *The Language of Judaism*, 83.

person is boastful and proud. However, Glustrom notes that the language of Hebrew

> contains several expressions, each signifying different shades of arrogance. In the [Jewish] morning [prayer] service we petition God to be saved from *azei panim*—insolent men, hardened and shameless people who ignore the feelings of others. We also ask that we ourselves be delivered from *azut panim*, that same "boldness of face," that insolence which corrupts so many human beings. Then there is the incisive expression, *hutzpah* [often spelled chutzpah in English] [...] denoting outright impudence—the epitome of arrogance. *Hutzpah* is also used in a positive way [for example, in Yiddish and English] to express nerve or boldness, but it still expresses a form of arrogance which leaves little room for restraint or regard for another person's feelings.[58]

It is written in the Psalms, "I cannot endure the haughty [arrogant] and proud man."[59] Proverbs states, "Every haughty person is an abomination to the Lord; Assuredly, he will not go unpunished."[60] Thus, as Glustrom points out, according to the Talmud, "no human failing is condemned as vigorously as the sin of the arrogant man," since self-centeredness is abhorred as a vile sin.[61] Indeed, the Talmud finds arrogance incompatible with being close to God, as the following story asserts:

> Rabbi Alexandri said: Every man in whom there is haughtiness of spirit [arrogance], will be disturbed by the slightest wind. As it is said: But the wicked are like the troubled sea. If the sea, which contains so many quarters of gallons of water, is ruffled by the slightest wind, how much more so a human being who contains but one quarter of a gallon.

> Rabbi Hiyya b. Ashi said in the name of Rav: A disciple of the Sages should possess an eighth [of pride]. Rav Huna the son of R. Joshua said: [This small amount of pride] crowns him like the awn of the grain. Raba said: [A disciple of the Sages] who possesses [haughtiness of spirit] deserves excommunication, and if he does not possess it he deserves excommunication. Rabbi Nahman bar Isaac said: He should not possess it or part of it; as it is written: "Every one that is proud in heart is an abomination to the Lord!" [Prov. 16:5].[62]

[58] Ibid., 83.
[59] Ps. 101:5.
[60] Prov. 16:5.
[61] Glustrom, *The Language of Judaism*, 84.
[62] Babylonian Talmud, *Sotah* 5a.

Hence, arrogance is clearly viewed negatively in the Jewish tradition, particularly as reflected in the Tanakh and the Talmud. However, its opposite—humility or being humble—is viewed positively. One can see in Moses why this would be so. Without practicing delegation—possibly a reluctant exercise by the arrogant leader—a true leader cannot lead because such a leader cannot carry out all that is needed to effect change or achieve objectives. Delegation is ultimately about empowering people to be responsible while holding them accountable for their actions. Effective leaders delegate and empower with expectations of accountability. Arrogance impedes this process.

"Empowering others and sharing leadership authority should be a basic part of the playbook of every leader," argues Cohen, because "in empowering others to share the burden of leadership, the leader must recognize that people can play very different kinds of roles."[63] Indeed, Cohen asserts, "not every potential leader is equipped to fulfill every role; choices must be made based on the individual's skills and talents," and from Jethro's advice to delegate, "Moses learns that there are indeed different levels of leadership, and each person can play a role for which [he or] she is uniquely suited." For, as Cohen points out, "all leaders must recognize the importance of what" Peter Senge in *The Fifth Discipline: The Art & Practice of the Learning Organization*, calls "distributed leadership."[64]

This notion is reflected in other terms, from delegation to power sharing, the latter being the preferred term of Hal Lewis, who justifiably critiqued Cohen in a review of *Moses and the Journey to Leadership* for using "leadership and management synonymously in the book's full title," implying that Cohen, a specialist in Midrash rather than business, may not have been as well-versed in the research from "the field of leadership studies."[65] Nonetheless, Cohen makes a good point with regard to empowering leaders through their use of "distributed leadership," or rather delegation and other forms of power sharing.

When God first approached Moses to lead the Israelites, Moses objected because he felt his lack of oratory skill would prevent him from achieving the task. Moses first asks, "Who am I that I should go to Pharaoh and free the Israelites from Egypt?"[66] Later, Moses concedes, "'Please, O Lord, I have never been a man of words, either in times past or now that You have spoken to Your servant; I am slow of speech and slow of tongue.'"[67] Even after God

---

[63] Cohen, *Moses and the Journey to Leadership*, 92–93.

[64] Ibid., 93.

[65] Hal M. Lewis, review of *Moses and the Journey to Leadership: Timeless Lessons of Effective Management from the Bible and Today's Leaders*, by Norman J. Cohen, *Shofar: An Interdisciplinary Journal of Jewish Studies* 27, no. 1 (2008): 112.

[66] Exod. 3:11.

[67] Exod. 4:10.

assures Moses that this is no obstacle, that God will instruct Moses in what
to say, Moses continues to object: "'Please, O Lord, make someone else Your
agent.'"[68] God, now slightly angered, tells Moses that his brother, Aaron,
"speaks readily," possessing the oratory skill Moses lacks and will perform
this role and serve as Moses' spokesman before the people.[69]

God's recommendation—to use Aaron's inherent skills in aid of Moses'
mission—represents the important management concept of delegation (or job
sharing, as Lewis prefers), successfully delegating speaking duties to Aaron
who, years later, would emerge as a leader in his own right, becoming the
high priest of the line of *Kohanim*, or priestly class of the tribe of Levi, who
would serve God at the Tent of Meeting, the *Mishkan* (Tabernacle). Aaron's
descendants down the paternal line would continue to serve as priests at the
First Temple built by Solomon and, following the First Temple's destruction,
at the Second Temple.

After Moses led the Israelites out of Egypt, he "sat as magistrate among
the people, while the people stood about Moses from morning until evening."[70] This judicial role obviously took up considerable time and may not
have been the best use of Moses' time as a leader. Moses' reliable and sup-
portive father-in-law, Jethro, a non-Israelite Midian priest, took note of the
situation and encouraged Moses to appoint others to share in the burden
of administering justice among the nation of Israelites through delegation.
Seeing how much Moses was doing for the people, Jethro said, "'Why do
you act alone, while all the people stand about you from morning until evening?' Moses replied [...] 'When they have a dispute, it comes before me, and
I decide between one person and another, and I make known the laws and
teachings of God.'"[71]

Jethro recognized this micromanagement problem and did not hesitate to
point out to Moses, "you will surely wear yourself out, and these people as
well. For the task is too heavy for you; you cannot do it alone."[72] An autocratic
leader requiring total control would likely find it very difficult to delegate
responsibility, but, as a responsible leader, Moses recognized the wise counsel
of Jethro.

First, Jethro pointed out the problematic situation to Moses: "You represent the people before God: you bring the disputes before God, and enjoin
upon them the laws and the teachings, and make known to them the way they

---

[68] Exod. 4:11–13.
[69] Exod. 4:14–16.
[70] Exod. 18:13.
[71] Exod. 18:14–16.
[72] Exod. 18:18.

are to go and the practices they are to follow."[73] Second, Jethro recommended a solution:

> You shall also seek out from among all the people capable men who fear God, trustworthy men who spurn ill-gotten gain. Set these over them as chiefs of thousands, hundreds, fifties, and tens, and let them judge the people at all times. Have them bring every major dispute to you, but let them decide every minor dispute themselves. Make it easier for yourself by letting them share the burden with you. If you do this—and God so commands you—you will be able to bear up; and all these people too will go home unwearied.[74]

Moses accepted Jethro's advice, allowing more cases to be heard while Moses could continue doing what he was chosen to do—lead! And that is exactly what Moses did. "The judicial machinery itself [remained] decentralized to a certain extent by an internal hierarchy of authorities," Sarna points out, with Moses acting "as a supreme judicial authority" functioning "as the mediator of divine will, but not as lawmaker or as one who dispenses justice by virtue of superior wisdom."[75]

Moses appears to have recognized that, while he may have been the leader of the Israelites, there were wise people among the Israelites and they should be appointed to positions of authority and adjudicate over issues that Moses acknowledged he might be incapable of ruling. He tells the people, "Pick from each of your tribes men who are wise, discerning, and experienced, and I will appoint them as your heads."[76] Bernard Levinson suggests that this use of the word "wise" in Deuteronomy 1:13 refers particularly to "experienced" or knowledgeable, as it underscores Moses' emphasis on wisdom as a worthwhile "criterion for leadership."[77] This is a step up from Exodus 18:21 where Jethro focuses on the desired leadership characteristic of trustworthiness in judges, or their being "men of truth."[78] Trust is certainly an important leadership quality, as alluded to earlier, but is insufficient in itself to accomplish effective leadership.

Tigay asserts that "Deuteronomy regards justice and piety as expressions of wisdom [...], and wisdom literature regards the very qualities named in

---

[73] Exod. 18:19–20.

[74] Exod. 18:21–23.

[75] Nahum M. Sarna, *The JPS Torah Commentary: Exodus* (Philadelphia, PA: Jewish Publication Society, 1991), 100.

[76] Deut. 1:13.

[77] Bernard M. Levinson, commentary to Deut. 1:13, *The Jewish Study Bible*, ed. Adele Berlin and Marc Zvi Brettler (New York, NY: Oxford University Press, 2004), 364.

[78] Jeffrey H. Tigay, commentary to Exod. 18:21, in Berlin and Brettler, *The Jewish Study Bible*, 144.

Exodus as expressions of wisdom."[79] According to Tigay, "That morality is a form of wisdom is one of several concepts which Deuteronomy shares with wisdom literature,"[80] such as the biblical books of Psalms, Proverbs, Ecclesiastes, Job and Song of Songs.

The later Sages, however, assert in the Mishnah's *Pirkei Avot* that the wise person learns from everyone; the mighty or strong person controls natural urges (particularly that associated with the "evil inclination"); the rich person is one who is happy with what he has; and the honored person is one who honors others.[81] Interpreting these views, the great French medieval rabbinic scholar Rashi said that "one who learns from everyone" implies a person who is "not too conceited to learn from even those who may be less learned." Regarding personal strength, the rabbis maintained that every human being has two conflicting drives, the *yetzer ha-ra*, or the human propensity to do evil, and the *yetzer ha-tov*, or the human drive to do good. If one could control the former, this meant one had inner strength. "One who honors others" is an honored person because, as Rashi asserted, it is only fitting that human beings "who are merely flesh and blood" should honor others who are similarly just people comprised of flesh and blood.[82]

In other words, leaders are human beings and so should not be worshipped; leaders are strong if they can control their impulses; and wise leaders are capable of learning from any individual without regard to their position or social standing. Indeed, as discussed earlier, the Sages were describing humility as the very essence of quality leadership material. As William Berkson observes, "humility is a core virtue in the eyes of the Sages, as well as in the Bible," for in the view of the Sages, human beings struggle between good and bad impulses, and it is arrogance that "unleashes many of the bad impulses, whereas humility keeps them in check and enables our good side to flourish." However, being humble does not equate with being a pushover, or in Berkson's words, "humility is not the same as timidity." He cites Rabbi Yehudah ben Teima, who lived toward the end of the period of the Sages of the Mishnah and was a student of Judah HaNasi, as advocating "being extremely bold and assertive in pursuit of the right goals."[83] A wise leader is a humble yet strong

[79] Jeffrey H. Tigay, *The JPS Torah Commentary: Deuteronomy* (Philadelphia, PA: Jewish Publication Society, 1996), 11.

[80] Tigay, *The JPS Torah Commentary: Deuteronomy*, 345n52. Tigay cites Prov. 31:10, 26 (for the use of "capable"); Ps. 111:10 and Prov. 1:7 ("fear of the Lord"); Prov. 23:23–24 ("truth"); Prov. 29:16 ("spurning ill-gotten gain").

[81] See *Pirkei Avot* 4:1.

[82] Leonard Kravitz and Kerry M. Olitzky, eds. and trans., *Pirke Avot: A Modern Commentary on Jewish Ethics* (New York, NY: UAHC Press, 1993), 56–57.

[83] William Berkson, *Pirkei Avot: Timeless Wisdom for Modern Life* (Philadelphia, PA: Jewish Publication Society, 2010), 142–43.

leader, one of conviction who understands personal limitations yet works to mitigate them.

Moses' recognition of his personal limitations, and his willingness to delegate responsibilities, exemplified mature and appropriate leadership qualities.[84] It also implicitly recognized trustworthiness and wisdom—not in isolation but among various characteristics—as being of paramount importance in exercising the function of leadership. However, Moses did not limit leadership to judges or military leaders, as outlined in Exodus.[85] "A just and moral society requires more than just a judiciary," Tamari notes, "there is need for leaders in all walks of life, officials to enforce the law, and a sociopolitical establishment."[86] Other leadership roles appear in Deuteronomy that fill the numerous and diverse aspects that are essential for a society to function, with the result that Moses appointed leaders of thousands, hundreds, fifties and tens until each thousand Israelites were guided by 131 people. Rabbinic commentators saw rational and functional reasons for such a large number, as Tamari explains: "There were military officers for each thousand soldiers, there were judges for each hundred people, teachers of Torah for each fifty, and police for each ten."[87]

* * *

Indeed, delegating authority represents a form of power sharing that a leader can use to great advantage. According to Lewis, "Because even the greatest individuals must limit their powers and because no single leader can ever expect to succeed in a vacuum, the traditional wisdom insists that the most important task any leader can perform is to empower and nurture the leadership potential of others."[88] Moses had granted the military authority of a general to Joshua during the war with the Amalekites.[89] Moses certainly delegated. However, Burton Visotzky, a scholar of Midrash, observes,

> At the battle of Amalek [...] Moses was able to share some of his leadership. He had Joshua act the general. Joshua was further delegated to

[84] Tigay points out that Maimonides believed both character and intellect were crucial qualifications for judges (*Hilkhot Sanh.* 2.7). Tigay, commentary to Exod. 18:21, in Berlin and Brettler, *The Jewish Study Bible*, 144.

[85] Ibid. Tigay notes that *"chiefs of thousands, hundreds, fifties, and tens"* are "military ranks, consistent with the fact that the Israelites are [in Exodus] organized as an army," having just fought a battle against the Amalekites [Exod. 17:8–16] and that "military officers sometimes held judicial responsibilities in the ancient Near East."

[86] Tamari, *Jewish Values in Our Open Society*, 291.

[87] Ibid.

[88] Hal M. Lewis, *From Sanctuary to Boardroom: A Jewish Approach to Leadership* (Lanham, MD: Rowman & Littlefield, 2006), 146.

[89] Exod. 17:8–16.

choose platoon leaders. Moses went even farther in quite literally receiving support from Aaron and Hur. Yet in every one of these instances of power-sharing, Moses remained an unequal compatriot. He was unquestionably the leader, the man calling the shots, the one on whom responsibility devolved in the end.[90]

Visotzky makes a crucial observation. With delegation, power sharing or distributed leadership—whatever term is used—there must be someone ultimately in charge or else anarchy could be the end result. Moses delegated roles, but he also led. Though each person in their respective role remained accountable, Moses ultimately remained accountable for his strategy of delegation and for his giving of leadership roles.

Empowering people is a crucial leadership strategy, which Moses exercised. However, Covey maintains that empowerment is only possible provided there exists a framework comprising four components: win-win agreements, accountability, self-supervision and helpful systems and structures.[91] In other words, those to whom power is shared must be accountable and be able to take charge of their tasks, with adequate support to help them achieve their stated goals or successfully fulfill their roles. Everybody wins if this occurs. Yet, for Covey, "at the heart of empowerment must be basic character."[92]

Good character, as suggested by the model of the mensch outlined earlier, requires that the leader at the top—and those to whom power is delegated—possess strong, positive values as this book has discussed. They are crucial at the top, however, because the leader's values and character influence everyone below, like the shape of a pyramid. But as Moses learned with regard to the requirements for judges appointed as part of a delegation or power-sharing strategy, wisdom was also an important trait for responsible leaders to possess.

## Wisdom and Values

Although Moses had already cultivated leadership qualities in Joshua—those associated with "leadership succession," a significant topic discussed in more detail later—he did not initiate the selection of Joshua as his successor, as God is quoted as telling Moses, "Single out Joshua son of Nun, an inspired man […] Invest him with some of your authority, so that the whole Israelite community may obey."[93] This verse says that Moses was to invest only "some" of his

---

[90]  Burton L. Visotzky, *The Road to Redemption: Lessons from Exodus on Leadership and Community* (New York, NY: Crown, 1998), 189.

[91]  Covey, *Principle-Centered Leadership*, 214.

[92]  Ibid., 215.

[93]  Num. 27:18–20.

authority because it came directly from God. As a human being, Moses could only transmit some of what he received from God. Yet this did not detract from Moses' leadership role, which was akin to a contemporary CEO. Developing new leadership talent and ensuring leadership succession are part of an effective leader's skills. Significantly, however, Moses accomplished this important leadership function by transmitting some genuine wisdom to Joshua.

According to the Torah, "Now Joshua [...] was filled with the spirit of wisdom because Moses had laid his hands upon him [transferring attributes for investiture into office]; and the Israelites needed him, doing as the Lord had commanded Moses,"[94] underscoring the expectation of communal respect for the leadership successor. After all, Moses, like any contemporary CEO, is responsible to, and requires some direction from, his board of directors. For Moses, the "board" to which he reported just happened to be represented by the God of the Torah.

\* \* \*

Values are of key importance to effective leadership because they are transmitted by leaders to the people, who are influenced by them. Yet James MacGregor Burns observes that "value setters are established throughout society and are all the more influential because they are implicit, taken for granted, and thus not overtly concerned with reforming their fellow human beings."[95] This can make the process of delegation dangerous if those put in charge are not well trained or do not share the visionary leader's values, such as Moses' values of empathy, trustworthiness and wisdom. Given the biblical source, it may be safe to assume that Moses chose the right people to assume responsibilities and that the people at large also chose appropriately from among the tribes, but we can never assume the same is true in all places and at all times. Leaders of organizations must pay careful attention to whom responsibilities are delegated, or these leaders will fail as a result of unaccountable incompetence that can arise at any given level.

"There is considerable slippage in the communication of values," Burns asserts, because "it is unlikely that leaders who serve as 'value communicators' convey the precise values adumbrated from official purveyors on high—except perhaps in wars or other crises." Burns notes that "Aaron did not interpret the Ten Commandments as Moses handed them down," which suggests that such power sharers or those to whom power is delegated tend to

---

[94] Deut. 34:9.
[95] James MacGregor Burns, *Leadership* (New York, NY: Harper, 1979), 76.

"exact a price in serving as transmitters, modifying values as they express or impart them."[96]

The transmission of positive values from one leader to another is crucial. In Deuteronomy 34:9, as noted, Joshua received wisdom from Moses. Levinson argues that

> Deuteronomy revises earlier traditions to stress wisdom as the essential qualification of office, and thus what Joshua receives from Moses. In Num. 27:18, Joshua was already "an inspired man" (often associated with prophecy or possession), while Moses was to transfer [some of] his "authority" to him. Here "the spirit of wisdom" is what Joshua receives from Moses. *Because Moses had laid his hands upon him:* as at Num. 27:22–23, a means of transfer of attributes (Lev. 16.21; Num. 8:10–13), here used for investiture into office.[97]

While cultivating leadership may not involve investiture into office—other than perhaps in the traditional rabbinic practice of rabbinic ordination or, perhaps, in the office of leader of the Israelites in this case—this "transfer of attributes" is key because it reflects the transfer of values and wisdom to a future leader, thus underscoring the importance of leaders having solid values that they can transmit to those they lead and inspire in leaders to whom power is delegated as well as share with leadership successors. The possession of positive, solid values is indeed an aspect of wisdom that is essential for effective leaders to possess. Moreover, wisdom is certainly helpful for the resolution of conflicts.

## Conflict Resolution

According to British philosopher and religious scholar Rabbi Jonathan Sacks, "One of the hardest tasks of leaders—from prime ministers to parents—is conflict resolution. Yet it is also the most vital."[98] In the Bible, Moses was often faced with the task of resolving conflict. Indeed, Sacks affirms that Moses was one with his people, and that "God Himself says of him, 'He is [supremely] loyal in all My house (Num. 12:7).'"[99] Hence, Moses intervened on the people's behalf when the Pharaoh mistreated them in Egypt, and continued to do so with God when their situation had not improved.[100] Moses intervened during

[96]   Burns, *Leadership*, 76.
[97]   Bernard M. Levinson, commentary to Deut. 34:9, in Berlin and Brettler, *The Jewish Study Bible*, 449–50.
[98]   Rabbi Jonathan Sacks, *Lessons in Leadership: A Weekly Reading of the Jewish Bible* (New Milford, CT and Jerusalem, Israel: Maggid Books, 2015), 217.
[99]   Sacks, *Lessons in Leadership*, 219.
[100]   Exod. 5:22–23.

the Golden Calf incident when God threatened the people with destruction.[101] Moses did so again when the negative report of the spies led many to express their wish to return to Egypt, enraging God in the process.[102] The Torah is filled with Moses' attempts to resolve conflict and achieve peaceful resolutions.[103] While Moses had attempted to mediate, resolve conflict and essentially make peace between God and the Israelites, this strong leadership quality was one at which Moses' brother, Aaron, appeared particularly adept.

Aaron had stayed with the people during his younger brother's absence spent atop Mount Sinai. From a superficial reading of the biblical text, one might conclude that Aaron allowed the people to build their Golden Calf either because he lacked sufficient leadership training from his brother Moses (who was being schooled in the art by none other than God himself) or he lacked the kind of leadership skills Moses had already developed or inherently possessed. After all, an outraged Moses said to Aaron, "What did this people do to you that you have brought such great sin upon them?"[104] The Bible states that "Moses saw that the people were out of control—since Aaron had let them get out of control—so that they were a menace to any who might oppose them."[105]

Yet Moses, under God's instruction, would later effectively delegate a leadership role to Aaron—as high priest leading over the Priesthood derived from his family tribe of Levi—but in this early case at Sinai, Aaron failed to achieve the expectations one might anticipate of a leader. Indeed, upon Moses' return from his second sojourn up Mount Sinai, he helped guide the Israelites back to their senses. Moses would spend several decades doing so since the Israelites were sent wandering through the wilderness for 40 years due to their ceaseless complaining against God.[106]

Although the Israelites had promised God they would obey and serve Him, they complained so much and angered God to such a degree, the Bible reports, that God swore that the first generation would never enter the Promised Land, with the exceptions of Caleb and Joshua. "None of the men from twenty years up who came out of Egypt shall see the land that I promised on oath to Abraham, Isaac, and Jacob, for they did not remain loyal to Me—none except Caleb [...] and Joshua [...] for they remained loyal to

---

[101] Exod. 32:32.

[102] Num. 14:3, 19.

[103] Sacks, *Lessons in Leadership*, 219.

[104] Exod. 32:21.

[105] Exod. 32:25.

[106] According to Numbers 14:34, "You shall bear your punishment for forty years, corresponding to the number of days—forty days—that you scouted the land: a year for each day. Thus you shall know what it means to thwart Me."

the Lord."[107] Hence, in a modern context, a leader may not always have the most worthy of followers and termination of employment may be necessary in extreme cases. As the Bible relates, the second generation of the new nation of Israel inherited the Promised Land, later called Israel.[108]

* * *

Regarding the sin of idol worship of the Golden Calf, Moses may have exercised an extreme reaction that was perhaps unwarranted. Lewis describes Moses as both a "revolutionary and a reactionary" because "in Egypt, he was the iconoclast, the critic *par excellence*, who challenged the pharaonic establishment at every turn." But following the Exodus, "as the leader of his own enterprise, Moses became the voice of conservatism, the one to squelch revolution."[109] Lewis maintains that "as both the founder of the Jewish nation and its supreme administrator, Moses walked the line between visionary and chief operative." In defense of the people, in this particular episode, Aaron Wildavsky asserts that "early rabbis argued that the people could not be held responsible for their actions unless and until all the law had been taught to them in the Tent of Meeting [the Tabernacle]." Nevertheless, Wildavsky reasons, certainly "by that time the people knew idolatry was forbidden to them and that it carried the ultimate penalty. If they did not know that, what did they know?"[110] Hence, Aaron was not an obstacle for Moses but proved to be a helpful leader in his own right because leaders are not perfect and can lack certain qualities that one might deem essential but that, in truth, can be compensated for through effective delegation and training.

Probing the texts closely, however, we see that rabbinic tradition holds that Aaron's main virtue was his peacemaking skills and genuine love of peace. In other words, Aaron practiced conflict resolution, even if unsuccessfully at first. Aaron was arguably motivated by the desire to keep peace among the Israelites when he permitted the building of the golden calf.

Covey notes that "principle-centered people don't overreact to negative behaviors, criticism, or human weaknesses. [...] They are not naive; they are aware of weakness. But they realize that behavior and potential are two different things. They believe in the unseen potential of all people. They feel grateful for their blessings and feel naturally to compassionately forgive and

---

[107] Num. 32:11–12.
[108] Josh. 10:42.
[109] Hal M. Lewis, *Models and Meanings in the History of Jewish Leadership* (Lewiston, NY: Edwin Mellen, 2004), 12n11.
[110] Aaron Wildavsky, *The Nursing Father: Moses as a Political Leader* (Tuscaloosa: University of Alabama Press, 1984), 103.

forget the offenses of others. They don't carry grudges."[111] If one can label Moses a "principle-centered leader"—as is quite plausible in modern terms— we can assume that Moses may not have been at all naive when he gave his brother Aaron leadership roles. In turn, Aaron became a leader of his own type because, indeed, the desire for peace—the resolution of conflict— among people is an appropriate trait in a leader. A leader, Covey advocates, "in the middle of confusion or contention or negative energy, [should] strive to be a peacemaker, a harmonizer, to undo or reverse destructive energy."[112]

Aaron, after all, did possess humble traits, perhaps cultivated from closely working with his brother, Moses. As instructed by God, therefore, Aaron, along with his four sons, was chosen "from among the Israelites" to serve God as priests.[113] God tells Moses to create Aaron's garments, "sacral vest- ments [...] for dignity and adornment."[114] Why ask Moses to perform this task? Arguably, Moses either possessed the best qualities to help put together Aaron's garments, or, more plausibly, Moses could serve as a model for those leadership attributes that Aaron would require, given that Moses was regarded by the Bible as the humblest person in the world.[115]

Later, reflecting on his time in the wilderness, Moses states, "The Lord said to me, 'Up, resume the march at the head of the people, that they may go in and possess the land that I swore to their fathers to give them,'" but he continues, "'And now, O Israel, what does the Lord your God demand of you? Only this: to revere the Lord your God, to walk only in His paths, to love Him, and to serve the Lord your God with all your heart and soul.'"[116]

Even God recognizes the importance of delegation by modifying this directive. God tells Moses "to instruct all who are skillful, whom I have endowed with the gift of skill, to make Aaron's vestments."[117] Tigay observes, "Artistic skills, no less than intellectual ones, are recognized as forms of wis- dom."[118] We already know the importance of wisdom as ascribed to Moses for positions of leadership, so it is intriguing to note that, regarding Moses, wisdom can come in many forms, including through the demonstration of special skills.

The requirements of the garments are outlined in detail in Exodus 28:4– 39, 42. "Put these on your brother Aaron and on his sons as well; anoint

---

[111] Covey, *Principle-Centered Leadership*, 35.

[112] Ibid.

[113] Exod. 28:1. Aaron and his four sons Nadab, Abihu, Eliezer and Ithamar.

[114] Exod. 28:2.

[115] Num. 12:3.

[116] Deut. 10:11–12.

[117] Exod. 28:3.

[118] Jeffrey H. Tigay, commentary to Exod. 28:3, in Berlin and Brettler, *The Jewish Study Bible*, 171.

them, and ordain them and consecrate them to serve Me as priests."[119] God further instructs Moses that these garments "shall be worn by Aaron and his sons when they enter the Tent of Meeting or when they approach the altar to officiate in the sanctuary, so they do not incur punishment and die," and that this "shall be a law for all time for him and for his offspring to come."[120] In other words, these vestments were like a uniform of sorts. Aaron was the designated leader of the priestly class, and the uniform served various functions, including distinguishing this particular leadership group from others, of which Aaron was high priest, and protecting this group while they were in the sanctuary, representing a "law for all time" for Aaron and his descendants. Perhaps it also served to remind the wearer of the holiness associated with the priestly leadership role.

Aaron, rather than Moses, was chosen by God as high priest, a significant leadership position but different from Moses' leadership role, for Aaron also had positive leadership traits including humility. His traits just seemed to need more refining over time spent in the wilderness.

Talmudic scholar Rabbi Adin Steinsaltz maintains that, while Moses was indeed special, unique and without parallel, "Aaron has had more extended influence than his illustrious brother" because Aaron "was the head of a line, father of a long succession of priests, who were called the sons of Aaron and constitute a vital part of the Jewish people for all time. [...] [Whereas] the sons of Moses vanished from sight; the sons of Aaron became a permanent feature of national existence."[121] While this is undoubtedly true, which serves to underscore the unique differences among leadership roles, Aaron, his sons and their descendants would still have been influenced by the leadership example of Moses.

Steinsaltz keenly observes that, in the Jewish tradition, the priest "became the symbol of one who 'loves peace and pursues peace, who loves people and brings them to the Torah,' a teacher of the common folk, a guide and support." Furthermore, Steinsaltz effectively relates, "the priest was not merely a functionary who performed rituals; he was a teacher of the people and had a broad and vital part to play in the community. And this archetypal image was established by Aaron."[122]

\* \* \*

---

[119] Exod. 28:41.
[120] Exod. 28:43.
[121] Adin Steinsaltz, *Biblical Images* (Oxford, UK: Rowman & Littlefield, 2004), 81–82.
[122] Steinsaltz, *Biblical Images*, 83.

While pursing conflict resolution—which is another way of describing seeking peace—is an important trait in a leader, it is not an absolute requirement as it depends on the leader's role. "Moses and Aaron represent two kinds of leader," Steinsaltz observes. "The difference between them only reinforced the bond, cemented an alliance and a lasting friendship," but, concurrently, "Moses never could descend altogether from the higher sphere; he did not even try to be liked or understood by the people."[123] This is important to recognize because it underscores different styles of leadership depending on an individual's leadership position.

Though one can argue that there exist common traits that all effective leaders should possess—as has been argued with regard to Moses' traits—Moses was a different type of leader. He held a different role as a political, heroic and authoritative leader who inspired the people while also remaining largely aloof from them. Whereas Aaron supported his brother Moses as his primary orator, translator and assistant, he was nonetheless "a leader in his own right," maintains Steinsaltz, since Aaron

> was the popular chief, one of the tribe, a Levite, and a spokesman. Because he understood the people and sympathized with their shortcomings, he could guide them toward a goal that Moses had reached in a different way. Moses operated from the higher to the lower: he was the authority figure, giving orders and hardly ever explaining or educating. Aaron, on the other hand, functioned from the lower to the higher, trying to lead the people carefully, teaching and guiding them.[124]

Regarding the shameful Golden Calf incident, the above sheds some light on what occurred. Steinsaltz suggests that Aaron was placed in a particularly difficult, if not painful, situation that was not so different than what Moses encountered later after he descended from the mountain. However, according to Steinsaltz, the main difference between Moses and Aaron is that

> Moses had clear authority from above and could destroy the Golden Calf, overawe the main culprits, and even kill many of them. Aaron could do none of these things; he had no such authority from above. His authority came from below, from the people; and he was compelled to do their bidding. What he endeavored to do in this predicament was to raise popular sentiment into something more subtle and noble and more in keeping with his own concepts. When he agreed to cooperate in the casting of the Golden

---

[123]  Ibid., 84.
[124]  Ibid., 84–85.

Calf, he was undoubtedly proceeding along his own mode of leadership—given to compromise and acquiescence—with the accompanying perils of "distorting the truth for the sake of peace." So was the pattern of Aaron's personality fixed for the ages, [as Hillel said]: "One who loves peace and pursues peace, loves the people and brings them to the Torah."[125]

Aaron was placed in the role of the "popular leader" who was a compromiser, an "intermediary between the people and God," which became the function of his sons as members of the priesthood, but, as Steinsaltz emphasizes, "in Aaron himself it was an intrinsic aspect of his personality: that is to say, he was both a vehicle of the people's will and able to draw from Moses something of the special authority and power from above," making Aaron "a beloved man of the people."[126] Aaron tried to resolve conflict because he desired peace, though he was a different kind of leader from his younger brother Moses. Aaron would become a genuine and important leader but with fewer leadership attributes as compared to Moses.

God appointed Aaron as high priest; however, as Jonathan Sacks observes, "There is more than one kind of leadership, and priesthood involves following rules, not taking stands and swaying crowds." Nonetheless, leaders reflect different talents. "The fact that Aaron was not a leader from the same mould as Moses does not mean that he was a failure," asserts Sacks, but simply "means that he was made for a different kind of role."[127] Moses was a leader of action besides empathy; Aaron preferred to avoid conflict. As Sacks notes, "there are times when you need someone with the courage to stand against the crowd, others when you need a peacemaker. Moses and Aaron were different [leadership] types."[128]

\* \* \*

The brothers' importance as leaders is evident by the Bible's accounts that both Aaron and Moses were mourned by the Israelites equally for thirty days rather than the customary seven days.[129] Regarding Aaron, the Torah reports, "all the house of Israel bewailed Aaron thirty days."[130] Similarly,

---

[125] Ibid., 85–86.
[126] Ibid., 86.
[127] Sacks, *Lessons in Leadership*, 108–9.
[128] Ibid., 109.
[129] In the Tanakh, mourning typically lasted seven days (a period of time that remains today for the most intensive period of mourning, known as shiva, derived from the word "seven" in Hebrew). See Gen. 50:10; 1 Sam. 31:13; and Job 2:13.
[130] Num. 20:29.

the Torah states, "And the Israelites bewailed Moses [...] for thirty days."[131] Hence, a leader would benefit from the ability to strive for peace—resolving conflicts—among those being led. After all, in contemporary terms, strikes are the end result of inherent conflict. If a leader can either prevent or resolve strikes that arise from anger against the organization, so much the better for all involved. If not, then delegation to those who can resolve conflict is entirely appropriate. In certain circumstances, delegation is also a form of leadership continuity when the primarily leader is unable, for one reason or another, to carry on the role.

## Leadership Continuity

As seen in the examples of Moses and Joshua, effective leadership includes ensuring leadership continuity. Moses fits the leadership role as defined earlier by John Gardner. Moses was to lead the Israelites out of Egypt toward the Promised Land of Canaan. The fact that he ultimately fails to enter the land himself may have been a just outcome in accordance with God's will, but, in human terms, it appears neither a major fault of Moses' leadership skills nor even required to prove the efficacy of those skills. After all, the Israelites did indeed ultimately enter the land of Canaan even without Moses as their leader but instead with Joshua at the helm.

The reason this could happen is that Moses implicitly understood that leadership continuity was the key to what would be regarded today as organizational survival—or to the survival of a movement and a people in biblical and religious terms. Moses ensured leadership continuity under Joshua, who had served a "leadership apprenticeship" under him. Not only did Joshua serve as a military leader under Moses during a defensive war against the Amalekites[132] but Moses also brought Joshua part of the way up Mount Sinai where Moses would receive the Decalogue—Ten Commandments—from God.[133]

Joshua also served as one of the 12 spies dispatched by Moses to report on the feasibility of conquering Canaan.[134] The result was Joshua (and Caleb) providing Moses with a positive report, for which the reward was entrance to the Promised Land.[135] Based on this apprenticeship, therefore, Joshua

---

[131] Deut. 34:8.
[132] Exod. 17: 8–16.
[133] See Exod. 24:13; 32:17.
[134] Num. 13:16–17.
[135] Num. 14:22–24; 30.

was the natural candidate to assume leadership over the Israelites following Moses.[136]

It is interesting to note that just as God changed the names of Abram to Abraham, Sarai to Sarah, and Jacob to Israel, the Bible states that "Moses changed the name of Hosea son of Nun to Joshua."[137] As Jacob Milgrom notes, "Since the priestly tradition maintains that the theophoric element *yeho* (standing for the Tetragrammaton YHVH) was unknown before the Exodus (cf. Exod. 6:2), Joshua, who was born in Egypt, could not have carried this name from birth."[138] In Hebrew, Joshua is Yehoshua. Despite the origin of his name, Joshua was clearly molded and trained by Moses to ensure leadership continuity.

---

[136] Josh. 1:1–2.

[137] Num. 13:16. Joshua would be referred to once again as "Hosea son of Nun" in Deuteronomy 32:44. Cf. Abram (Gen. 17:5), Sarai (Gen. 17:15) and Jacob (Gen. 35:10).

[138] Jacob Milgrom, *The JPS Torah Commentary: Numbers* (Philadelphia, PA: Jewish Publication Society, 1989), 101.

# Chapter 8

# ASSESSING MOSES' LEADERSHIP STYLE

Leadership has very ancient roots, and Moses is arguably among the best biblical prototypes for effective contemporary leaders. The ancient rabbis were certainly convinced as the following Midrash speaks well of Moses' character and leadership qualities:

> [When Moses shepherded the flocks of Jethro,] he used to stop the bigger sheep from grazing before the smaller ones, and let the smaller ones loose first to feed on the tender grass; then he would let the older sheep loose to feed on the grass of average quality; lastly he let the strong ones loose to feed on the toughest. God said, "Let [...] him who knows how to shepherd the flock, each according to its strength, come and lead My people."[1]

Those who carefully analyze the Bible will recognize that the ideas embedded in the Torah are not limited to laws, but through the example of Moses as described in the Torah and subsequent rabbinic literature, among other non-Jewish and secular writings, we can see aspects of Moses' leadership that continue to be advocated today. Hal Lewis asserts, "Being a leader is not the same as being a bureaucrat. A leader must be sufficiently honest to look in the mirror, to *become* that mirror for others, and to inspire candid organizational introspection on an ongoing basis."[2] Jonathan Sacks maintains that "leadership demands two kinds of courage: the strength to take a risk, and the humility to admit when a risk fails."[3]

While Moses' reputation was that of the most humble of men, and he was certainly well chosen as the leader of the Israelites, Lewis notes that the Talmud, citing *Rosh Hashanah* 25 a–b, makes it very clear that "not every

---

[1] *Exodus Rabbah* 2:2. Joseph Telushkin, *Jewish Wisdom: Ethical, Spiritual, and Historical Lessons from the Great Works and Thinkers* (New York, NY: William Morrow, 1994), 99.

[2] Hal M. Lewis, *From Sanctuary to Boardroom: A Jewish Approach to Leadership* (Lanham, MD: Rowman & Littlefield, 2006), 101.

[3] Rabbi Jonathan Sacks, *Lessons in Leadership: A Weekly Reading of the Jewish Bible* (New Milford, CT and Jerusalem, Israel: Maggid Books, 2015), 128.

Jewish leader will be a person of impeccable integrity or one who has been destined for greatness from birth. Far from being an innate trait, leadership involves a set of behaviors and activities, much of which must be taught."[1] This certainly applies to all people who are prospective leaders, regardless of religion or ethnicity.

Just as Moses had an early apprenticeship followed by learning on the job, most aspiring leaders need to be taught specific leadership skills. Warren Bennis agrees with this thinking. According to Bennis and Goldsmith, "Leaders are made, not born, and are created as much by themselves as by the demands of their times. They have talent for continually learning about themselves. They seek to know who they are, what they want, why they want it, and how to gain support to achieve it," and, they assert, "leaders love to learn."[5] However, personality characteristics, whether inborn or developed, are essential for the cultivation of leaders, of which Moses provides an exceptional model.

Indeed, considering modern communal leaders, Lewis suggests, they "do themselves and their followers a disservice by failing to honestly analyze their organization's strengths and weaknesses with regularity," and, Lewis asserts, no true leadership is being exercised by "exaggerating successes, minimizing challenges, and misrepresenting reality all in the name of institutional hype, marketing, or an unwillingness to rock the boat."[6]

* * *

While modern leadership theorists may not ascribe their views to Moses, this does not mean that we cannot see in Moses particular leadership behavioral traits and strategies that continue to be emulated. After all, this book has argued that Moses provides a paradigm or model of leadership that leaders of contemporary organizations largely adhere to, emulate, and advocate—if not always to the same degree of success, so they perhaps ought to focus more on the essential qualities of leadership that Moses reflected.

Regarding the application of management skills to Moses' effective leadership model, he showed that delegation is a very important task and remains so for any effective visionary leader. A leader cannot possibly do everything alone. Other reliable and capable people are needed, who must be held accountable for their actions. Through the delegation of authority or

---

[1]  Hal M. Lewis, "Making Leaders: How the American Jewish Community Prepares Its Lay Leaders," *Journal of Jewish Communal Service* 80, nos. 2/3 (2004): 158.

[5]  Warren Bennis and Joan Goldsmith, *Learning to Lead: A Workbook on Becoming a Leader*, rev. ed. (New York, NY: Basic Books, 2010), 2.

[6]  Lewis, *From Sanctuary to Boardroom*, 101.

the delegating of responsibilities more can be achieved because the leader is relieved of heavy time burdens that prevent the leader from pursuing his or her leadership role. Jethro, Moses' father-in-law, gave wise advice to Moses, who had complained of fatigue at having to adjudicate all disputes among the Israelite people. Jethro advised Moses to appoint judges to carry out this work. Moses could then adjudicate over the most significant disputes. Such words seem self-evident today, but delegation or power sharing has not necessarily been the obvious choice for many leaders in business, yet this was the biblical recommendation expressed so long ago through Moses.

Much has been said about the effectiveness of Moses as a leader, particularly as an influential empathic leader. But does this style lend itself to cultish behavior? Could a leader in a high or influential position become a cult leader whom people regard as virtually divine and never to be questioned? Moses resisted this potential and remained true to his vision.

## Resisting the Cult of Leadership

Moses was successful in resisting what some refer to as the "cult of leadership," or power for its own sake, characterized by self-aggrandizement rather than by helping those being led attain a greater objective. A true leader must inspire those being led to accept the vision, follow the mission statement and achieve the stated goals. Moses accomplished each of these tasks admirably. Hence, Moses proved to be a leader worthy of emulation.

The Pharaoh is an obvious example of poor leadership, particularly at the time Moses returned to lead the Israelites out of Egypt. The Pharaoh lost many among the Egyptian people due to his reckless resistance to avoid releasing the Israelite slaves. He was certainly stubbornly arrogant. Aaron Wildavsky points out the stark differences between Moses and the Pharaoh:

> Pharaoh thinks he does not have to consider the preferences of his followers when deciding whether to give in or to resist, whether to accept or reject a concession; his followership is assured. Not so for Moses, who must persuade his people. Pharaoh has the power to enforce commands; Moses must learn how to formulate an agreement to cover contingencies so he will know whether agreements are kept or broken; this may well call for learning how to detect and deal with duplicity. Moses has to consider carefully what ruses to try, for he must justify the consequences of his actions to his followers. By contrast, until he starts to lose his grip, Pharaoh need not use guile.[7]

---

[7] Aaron Wildavsky, *The Nursing Father: Moses as a Political Leader* (Tuscaloosa: University of Alabama Press, 1984), 71.

Indeed, contrasting the leadership style of Egypt's Pharaoh with that of Moses provides an educational lesson. However, taking the "cult" notion literally, Tikva Frymer-Kensky maintains that "if we look at the situation of the people of Israel immediately after they left Egypt, it is apparent that they shared many of the characteristics recognized in potential converts to the modern cults."[8] Frymer-Kensky outlines the criteria:

> They were totally removed from their old life, for they were no longer slaves and no longer in Egypt. They underwent a complete change of diet, from the "leeks and cucumbers" of Egypt to the manna of the desert. Moreover, they were clustered around a strong leader, and they believed that they were the founders of a new order. Despite this, they did not form a modern "cult;" the new religion did not center around the figure of Moses.[9]

This is key to understanding non-cultish leadership. Moses was never worshipped nor was he a central focus for the functioning of any particular religion. Above all Moses was a political and military leader with abilities that apply to organizational leadership. Moses was a human being who was fallible yet humble. In contrast, the Pharaoh claimed both a political and religious leadership function that Egyptians were expected to follow. He was an oppressive autocrat. Even the Bible quotes God telling Moses, "Pharaoh is stubborn; he refuses to let the [Israelite] people go."[10] As the supreme ruler over Egypt, the Pharaoh was viewed in god-like terms within Egyptian society, and he expected to be treated according to his societal role. This made him an arrogant ruler. Ultimately, as the Bible reports, the Pharaoh led his people to catastrophe when his arrogant pursuit of the Israelites brought about the ten plagues.[11]

Moses was not a leader of a cult, and his leadership was not reflective of a cult. Yet contemporary examples of leadership cults abound. British academic Christopher Bones argues the inherent dangers of leadership cults in his book *The Cult of the Leader*. He focuses on the contemporary business world, and the negative impact on society in general, but such leadership cults are no stranger to history. For Bones, "All leaders are flawed because all human beings are flawed."[12] From a Jewish perspective this might be deemed an

---

[8] Tikva Frymer-Kensky, "Moses and the Cults: The Question of Religious Leadership," *Judaism* 34, no. 4 (1985): 445.

[9] Frymer-Kensky, "Moses and the Cults," 445.

[10] Exod. 7:14.

[11] See Exod. 7:14–10:29; 11:1–12:30.

[12] Christopher Bones, *The Cult of the Leader: A Manifesto for More Effective Business* (San Francisco, CA: Jossey-Bass, 2011), 6.

extreme view as it reflects a Christian outlook that "we are all born with sin and are capable of it"[13] that contrasts with Judaism, which rejects Original Sin in its theology.

According to Alfred J. Kolatch, "St. Augustine (353–430) was the first theologian to teach that man is born into this world in a state of sin. The basis of this belief is the Bible (Genesis 3:17–19) where Adam is described as having disobeyed God by eating the forbidden fruit of the tree of knowledge in the Garden of Eden. This, the first sin of man, became known as original sin [in Christianity]." This doctrine of original sin, notes Kolatch "is totally unacceptable to Jews [who] believe that man enters the world free of sin, with a soul that is pure and innocent and untainted." Despite a few contrary opinions in Talmudic times, "the dominant [Jewish] view by far was that man sins because he is not a perfect being, and not, as Christianity teaches, because he is *inherently* sinful."[14]

Perhaps a reflection of other sins, Bones makes the interesting, if not biting, observation that the "modern leader is egoistic, blind to their own faults, surrounded by people created in their own image and committed to actions driven more by the need to enhance their self-image than by anything else."[15]

Bones asserts that there has been a move away from "ranking *companies* and their performance to personalizing such comparative exercises by focusing on their CEOs, as though the CEO was the defining differentiator without which the organization would not have achieved their success."[16]

As Bones outlines, in contemporary times the "gods of business" include such names as Lee Iacocca, Jack Welch, Niall FitzGerald, Bernard Arnault, Donald Trump, Lord Alan Sugar of Clapton, Sir John Harvey-Jones, Sir Gerry Robinson, Sir Richard Branson, Lord John Browne, Jack Ma and others. They are, according to Bones,

> lionized, attended to with reverence, and placed on pedestals from which they pronounce on the issues of the day. Many have become best-selling authors, chat show guests, and even hosts of their own prime-time television shows. Some even make it, albeit briefly, into government. With all this adoration can you blame them for believing in their own immortality? Can you blame others for working hard to join them in the ranks of

---

[13] Bones, *The Cult of the Leader*, 6.
[14] Alfred Kolatch, *The Second Jewish Book of Why* (Middle Village, NY: Jonathan David, 1985), 63–64.
[15] Bones, *The Cult of the Leader*, 7.
[16] Ibid.

the deified? Once at this level these people (and despite what is said there are women in this group as well as men) see themselves as Titans.[17]

For Bones, there is a crisis of leadership today, and, considering his examples, there is truth in this observation. "In business, just as much as in any other part of society, good men and women are needed to lead their organizations through the challenges they face," Bones asserts, "yet today business leaders are as ill-regarded as politicians. At the heart of this ill-regard is a belief that they are overrated, over-powerful and over-paid."[18] Ultimately, this may simply be due to the cult of celebrity, which focuses primarily on actors and other types of performers or people on television who are idolized simply for being celebrities or pop culture sensations, and then is broadened to include business and political leaders.

* * *

Regarding what modern leaders do wrong, Bones cites his colleague Malcolm Higgs' view for the bad leadership habits associated with many contemporary leaders. Such leaders abuse their power for personal gain; inflict damage on others by bullying subordinates; excessively control in order to satisfy their own needs; break rules for self-serving purposes; and apply inappropriate leadership behaviors to reflect and support positional power.[19] Bones notes that gaps in leadership skills exist. Similarly, Lewis notes skill gaps in the Jewish leadership community.

What is the solution to this leadership problem? Bones does not state it, but it could involve returning to good leadership practices, such as the kind Moses demonstrates. After all, today's leadership crisis is not new. Aside from Egypt's Pharaoh, some well-known figures of the Bible among the Israelites were famous for less-than-stellar leadership. King Saul, while first king of the Israelites, ultimately disobeyed God, for example, by offering burnt offerings rather than wait for a priest to provide sacrifices.[20] Even Solomon's kingship ended badly as his observance of the law waned.[21] As stated in the Tanakh, "In his old age, his wives turned away Solomon's heart after other gods, and he was not as wholeheartedly devoted to the Lord his God as his father David had been."[22] Likewise, after territorial

---

[17]  Ibid., 7–8.
[18]  Ibid., 9.
[19]  Ibid., 39.
[20]  1 Sam. 13:8–13.
[21]  1 Kings 11:1–43.
[22]  1 Kings 11:4.

separation, there were bad endings for many kings of the Northern and Southern kingdoms.

But Moses was different. Moses did not represent the negative side of leadership. Rather, he embodied many of the strategies contemporary leadership theorists ascribe to successful leaders. Moses had a vision, a mission statement, clear objectives and went about achieving them while serving as an empathic, visionary leader for the Israelites who for the most part succeeded. He held subordinates accountable for their responsibilities. At Sinai, when in Moses' absence his brother, Aaron, lost control over the people, Moses revealed a frustrated and angry side of his personality. As related in the Book of Exodus, Moses' anger was clear: "As soon as Moses came near the camp and saw the [golden] calf and the dancing, he became enraged; and he hurled the tablets from his hands and shattered them at the foot of the mountain. He took the calf that they had made and burned it; he ground it to powder and strewed it upon the water and so made the Israelites drink it."[23]

This was a moment of unmitigated anger, though understandable under the circumstances. Yet the Israelites' idolatry of a golden calf nearly derailed the course of Moses' leadership. But it was quickly stopped with violence that was not unknown in biblical times. The drama of Moses' smashing the tablets, grinding the calf into dust, was followed by a request for the support of his fellow Levites, which ended up in the killing of 3,000 people on that day. As Jonathan Sacks observes, "History judges Moses a hero but he might well have been seen by his contemporaries as a brutal autocrat."[24]

Moses is not viewed in such negative terms because we understand the context from the scenario outlined in the Bible. However, the above was certainly an extreme situation of leadership challenge not worthy of emulation. Nonetheless, notes Sacks, "it is easy to be critical of people who fail the leadership test when it involves opposing the crowd, defying the consensus, blocking the path the majority is intent on taking. The truth is that it is hard to oppose the mob. They can ignore you, remove you, even assassinate you. When a crowd gets out of control there is no elegant solution."[25] So, whether this outcome represents a grand failure in leadership or a major success depends on one's perspective.

The reason the calf was built, Aaron maintained, was due to Moses' absence when he went atop Mount Sinai to obtain his mission statement from God.[26] He not only returned with tablets of commandments according to

---

[23] Exod. 32:19–20.
[24] Sacks, *Lessons in Leadership*, 108.
[25] Ibid.
[26] Exod. 32:23–24.

which the Israelites should live but, in line with Jewish traditional teachings, he also returned with an Oral Law to help guide the people. However, Sacks notes that "Aaron blames the people" because they had "made the illegitimate request" to build the calf, for which "Aaron denied responsibility."[27] But Aaron was not a leader of the people like Moses. Not only did Moses lead his people toward the Promised Land but also through his personal example, traits and leadership principles, influenced the behavior of successive generations until this very day.

## Moses as a Timeless Leader

Jewish tradition supports the necessity and importance of appropriate leadership and desired leadership skills and traits that can arguably be cultivated but most certainly emulated. The following Midrash makes this message explicitly clear:

> Samuel bar Nahmani said: "It is natural that people should imitate their leaders. If the Patriarch gives permission to do that which is forbidden by the Torah, the chief of the court says to himself: 'If the Patriarch permits this, why should I forbid it?' The Justices say: 'If the chief of the court has given permission, why should we forbid?' And the people say: 'If the Justices have given permission, shall we consider it forbidden?' It is clear that it is the initial sin of the Patriarch which has caused the entire generation to be sinful."[28]

In other words, the rabbis understood that leadership qualities trickle down to the masses, whether positive or negative, which is why those who find themselves in leadership roles need to ensure they are providing the best leadership example as possible. It also strongly suggests that people are influenced by their leaders. This is applicable to everyone, not just the Jewish people. Leadership is not guided by one single religion or cultural environment.

Nonetheless, observes Lewis, "the lesson of Moses and subsequent Jewish authorities is that leadership cultivation is a comprehensive and pervasive mindset, not a course offering or occasional seminar. Unless leadership development is a goal of the entire enterprise, beginning with the current leaders, then all other efforts are destined to fall short."[29] Again, this is applicable to everyone.

---

[27] Sacks, *Lessons in Leadership*, 107.
[28] *Deuteronomy Rabbah* 2.
[29] Lewis, *From Sanctuary to Boardroom*, 81.

As a model of leadership, therefore, Moses stands out among the many names one could cite from the Bible or from ancient, medieval or modern history because much can be discerned from his leadership example that spanned decades and faced so many tests. "Moses neither got nor offered direct didactic advice on leadership," Wildavsky notes, so "learning how to interrogate experience, past and present, is the essence of the Mosaic method. Leaders must be continual participants in their own education."[30] Indeed Moses provides everyone, regardless of religious or cultural background, an excellent guide for leadership.

\* \* \*

While Moses was ultimately obliged to delegate responsibly, there were limitations on participative decision-making. Moses remained the quintessential leader over the Israelites. Hence, Moses does not fit the essential criteria for Servant Leadership—a subtype of leadership popular among some leaders today depending upon the organization they lead—because, while he shares much of its criteria for leadership that this book discussed at length, such as power sharing, putting the needs of others first and helping people develop and perform, all of which Moses accomplished, he did not meet a particular criterion required by Robert Greenleaf, who first coined the term "servant-leader" and theory of Servant Leadership while an executive at AT&T.

According to Greenleaf, "The servant-leader *is* servant first. [...] It begins with the natural feeling that one wants to serve, to serve *first*. Then conscious choice brings one to aspire to lead. That person is sharply different from one who is *leader* first, perhaps because of the need to assuage an unusual power drive or to acquire material possessions. [...] The leader-first and the servant-first are two extreme types."[31]

Although the nuance is subtle, Moses was a leader first who grew into his servant role. He was called upon by God to lead. Leadership for Moses was therefore neither a conscious choice nor a natural aspiration. However, Moses was a humble and initially reluctant leader whom God felt ought to become a leader of a great nation because he had the inner qualities one requires to be a good leader in the broadest sense of the term. Arguably, his need to intervene is not necessarily reflective of an inner desire or need to serve. This

---

[30] Wildavsky, *The Nursing Father*, 5.
[31] Robert K. Greenleaf, "Servant Leadership," in *The Leader's Companion: Insights on Leadership Through the Ages*, ed. J. Thomas Wren (New York, NY: Free Press, 1995), 22.

was evident in Moses' behavior at the burning bush as well as the stories from early Exodus describing Moses' choice to intervene and help others.

Moses was not an autocratic leader who maintained strict control over the leadership activities and results of those to whom he delegated certain powers. Nor was he an example of laissez-faire or permissive leadership, where subordinates have a full participatory role in the overall leadership of the organization or of society in the case of Moses and the Israelites.

But as a leader—in the general and most common sense of the term—Moses effectively proved to be an example for many of the types of contemporary leadership discussed in this book. Moses exhibited *heroic* and *charismatic* tendencies. He was certainly *empathic* yet his leadership style was also *transactional, transformational,* and *visionary*. As a leader, he accomplished what he needed to accomplish. He ensured leadership continuity and avoided becoming the focus of a cult of leadership because the Israelites and the monotheistic religion they followed did not focus its reverence on the figure of Moses but that of a greater power.

Moses meets the defining criteria of a Great Man, but gender is not the criterion upon which his effective leadership hinged. He possessed qualities of empathy, humility, modesty, integrity, mercy, compassion, trust, wisdom, perseverance and purpose that established his reputation and underscored support for his good character. He embodied the traits of a *mensch*, a Yiddish term far ahead of his time, but he possessed what could be termed the mensch factor as a critical component at the core of his good character, as revealed through his personal qualities and performance as a leader.

Moses did not need to possess every possible talent—such as that of a highly skilled orator—to effectively carry out his leadership role. He had people like his brother, Aaron, to whom he could delegate tasks of this sort. Indeed Moses remains a powerful model for contemporary organizational leadership. Leaders regardless of background who choose to follow Moses' example can continue to emulate an admirable model of exceptional leadership.

Hence, considering biblical precedent, anyone who wishes to learn how to lead, and to learn what characteristics are beneficial for effective leadership, would do well to study the example of Moses.

# GLOSSARY

*Aggadah* (plural, *aggadot*)—Aramaic for "lore" and "tales" derived from the Hebrew for "telling." Rabbinic literature comprising interpretations and discussions on various subjects related to theology, philosophy and ethics, and referring to those aspects of rabbinic literature that are not focused on law (*Halakhah*). While *Halakhah* centers on how a Jew is expected to behave, *Aggadah* is concerned with the issue of what a Jew is to believe, and therefore includes ethical, homiletical, exegetical or even historical statements dealing with Jewish belief. *Aggadah* and *Halakhah* are both reflected in the *Talmud* and *Midrash*.

*Amidah*—Literally, "standing," or the "standing prayer," also known as the *Shemoneh Esrei* (Eighteen Benedictions) or *Ha'Tefillah* (The Prayer). It is a central rubric of Jewish religious services and among the very oldest in the tradition.

*Amoraim* (singular, *Amora*)—Aramaic for "spokesmen," Jewish rabbinic scholars whose discussions on the Oral Law both in Babylonia and the Land of Israel between ca. 200 and 500 CE became known as the *Gemara*, which combined with the Mishnah, became the Talmud, of which there were two versions: the *Talmud Bavli* (Babylonian Talmud) and the *Talmud Yerushalmi* (the Jerusalem or Palestinian Talmud, also known as the Talmud of the Land of Israel), the former regarded in the Jewish tradition as the more authoritative of the two. See *Tannaim*, Jewish scholars whose discussions are contained in the *Mishnah*.

*Aristotle* (ca. fourth century BCE)—Greek philosopher and scientist who, along with Plato and Socrates, remains among the most influential figures in the history of Western philosophy. Among his numerous writings, *Nicomachean Ethics* is perhaps Aristotle's best-known work in the ethical literature.

*Ashkenazi*—The term applies to the Jews of Central and Eastern Europe, many of whose descendants immigrated to North America and the Land of Israel from the nineteenth century onward together with their religious and cultural traditions. The term comes from the Hebrew word *Askhenaz*, associated with Germany and the Slavic regions since medieval times. Various dialects of Yiddish became the vernacular of Ashkenazi Jews. See *Sephardi*.

*Ba'al Ga'avah*—Hebrew for an arrogant person who is boastful and proud.

*Bachya ibn Paquda* (ca. eleventh century CE)—He was a rabbi, moral philosopher and ethicist based in Saragossa, Spain, known particularly for his influential medieval Jewish ethical work, *Duties of the Heart* (originally written in Arabic and later translated into Hebrew entitled, *Chovot ha-Levavot*) that taught the "duties" that Jews should observe in order to reach spiritual perfection.

*Chesed*—Hebrew for "loving-kindness," or simply "kindness" or "love" for one's fellow human being and God. It is a Jewish central value concept that is embraced in Jewish ethics and theology. In the Mishnaic tractate *Avot*, it is stated that the world stands on three legs: the Torah, service of God (prayer), and *gemilut chasadim*—in which *chesed* is present—acts of loving-kindness or caring for others (*Pirkei Avot* 1:2).

*Chumash*—Hebrew word derived from the number "five," Chumash refers to the Torah, or the Five Books of Moses. See *Torah (Written)*.

*Chutzpah*—Hebrew for an impudent, bold or arrogant person. In its modern use, it can sometimes be viewed in a positive way, in Yiddish and English, to express audacity or boldness.

*Decalogue*—A set of ten commandments, or *Mitzvot*, derived from Latin but based on the earlier Greek term for "ten words," though popularly known in English as the "Ten Commandments" (in Hebrew, *Aseret HaDevarim*, or "ten words") found in the Book of Exodus 20:1–17 and in the Book of Deuteronomy 5:4–21. As leader of the Israelites, Moses is described in the Torah as receiving them from God at Mount Sinai. See *Mitzvot*.

*Diaspora*—From the Greek for "dispersion," the word applies to Jews who reside in communities outside of the Land of Israel.

*Exilarch* (in Judaism)—Also known as *Resh Galuta* (Aramaic for "head of the exile"), the title applied to the lay leaders of the Babylonian Jewish diaspora.

*Gemara*—Aramaic for "teaching," the collected Aramaic debates and commentary on the *Mishnah* composed by the *Amoraim* (Aramaic for "spokesmen," who followed the *Tannaim*). The combination of the Hebrew *Mishnah* and the largely Aramaic *Gemara* comprises the *Talmud*. There are two Gemaras, one based on the debates in the Land of Israel and the other from the debates in Babylonia, which became more authoritative. Both were attempts to clarify the *Mishnah* of the *Tannaim*. The *Mishnah* combined with the respective *Gemara* led to the Babylonian Talmud (*Talmud Bavli*) and the Jerusalem Talmud (*Talmud Yerushalmi*).

*Hadith*—Arabic for "report," refers to collections of Islamic literature based on oral reports that circulated following the passing of Muhammad.

*Halakhah*—Hebrew word meaning "a way of going" but translated as "Jewish law," the set of Jewish religious laws derived from the Torah—both Written and Oral—covering the full legal spectrum from religious laws to both criminal and civil law that were further developed in the Talmud and in later rabbinic legal codes and writings. *Halakhah* is focused on how Jews ought to behave.

*Haredi*—Hebrew term that reflects contemporary ultra-Orthodox Judaism that adheres very strongly to all aspects of Jewish religious law.

*Hillel* (ca. 110 BCE–10 CE)—Known as Hillel the Elder, or simply as Hillel, he was both sage and scholar, famous for his humility and legal insights. Born in Babylonia, settling in Jerusalem, Hillel became one of the most influential figures in Jewish history. He often disagreed on basic issues with his colleague Shammai, with Hillel's views generally prevailing, as recorded in the Mishnah and the Talmud.

*Hutzpah*—See *Chutzpah.*

*'ish*—Hebrew, literally "man."

*Jesus*—Jesus of Nazareth, a Jew regarded by Christians (from the Greek) as Jesus Christ, or the messianic figure prophesied in the Hebrew Scriptures. The Christian New Testament focuses on Jesus and his teachings.

*Judah HaNasi* (ca. 135–220 CE)—Literally, "Judah the Prince," he was a Tannaitic rabbi and served as the redactor of the *Mishnah*, a compilation of Tannaitic debates on the Jewish Oral Law, which, after the Bible, is viewed in Judaism as a seminal work of Jewish law that, after further debates on its content, led to the Talmud.

*Kabbala*—Hebrew term for "receiving," it denotes the mystical strand of the Jewish tradition evident in mystical writings and mystical interpretations of the Torah to uncover hidden meanings in the text.

*Kohanim*—Hebrew term for Jewish priests (singular, *kohen*), who descend from Aaron, a member of the tribe of Levi. While Jewish status traditionally passes through the matrilineal line, Jewish priests descend through the patrilineal line.

*Kollel*—Hebrew for "community" or "gathering," the term evolved to represent a higher institute of advanced Talmudic studies.

*Koran* (or *Qur'an*)—Arabic for "the recitation," the central religious text of Islam, believed by Muslims to be God's verbal revelation to Muhammad.

*Maimonides* (ca. 1135–1204 CE)—Rabbi Moses ben Maimon, also known by the Hebrew acronym *Rambam* and the Latin/Greek, Moses Maimonides, was a highly influential medieval Jewish scholar, rabbi, philosopher and physician. He was born in contemporary Spain and later moved to Egypt where he wrote many of his seminal Jewish religious, legal, philosophical and medical works. Besides his role as an influential rabbinic authority, he served as the court physician to the Egyptian sultan Saladin and his royal family. One of his many influential works was his Jewish legal code, the *Mishneh Torah.*

*Mensch*—Yiddish word (derived from the German word *Mensch*, which literally means "person") that refers to an individual who is honorable and decent, someone who possesses qualities that are worthy of admiration and emulation.

*Midrash*—Hebrew for "investigation" or "inquiry," it is the term for a body of Rabbinic literature featuring interpretations of the biblical text from a careful process of examination of each verse or word. During the early Rabbinic period, Jewish sages—the *Tannaim* and the *Amoraim* (the rabbis of the third through the sixth century CE)—illuminated the biblical accounts and interpreted these biblical sources through the lens of the past, their own time and the future, making the Bible a guide of lessons applicable simultaneously to past, present and future. The Hebrew Bible was the source for *Midrash*, serving as a form of commentary on the written text of the Hebrew Bible.

*Mishkan*—"Tent of Meeting," as described in the Book of Exodus, a mobile Tabernacle that served as the dwelling place of God while the Israelites journeyed through the wilderness on their way to the Promised Land. According to tradition, its specifications were dictated by God to Moses at Mount Sinai. It was later superseded by the first Temple in Jerusalem.

*Mishnah*—From the Hebrew for "recitation" or "repetition," a seminal work in the Jewish tradition comprising the discussions of the *Tannaitic* Jewish sages on the Oral Law. It forms the basis for the *Gemara*, which together form the *Talmud*. The *Mishnah* was edited ca. 200 CE by Rabbi Judah HaNasi. See *Judah HaNasi*.

*Mishneh Torah*—Hebrew for "Repetition of the Torah," is a Jewish legal code (*Halakhah*) compiled in the twelfth century by the medieval Jewish religious authority, Maimonides. See *Maimonides*.

*Mitzvot*—Hebrew for "divine commandments" (the singular is *Mitzvah*), rabbinic tradition holds that Moses was given 613 commandments (*Mitzvot*), or various injunctions that are found in the Pentateuch, or first five books of the Bible known as the Torah. Modern streams in Judaism interpret these commandments in various ways, but still recognize the significance of *Mitzvot* found in the Torah even if their interpretations of each might differ.

*Muhammad* (ca. 570–632 CE)—Born in Mecca in present-day Saudi Arabia, he is regarded by Muslims as the last prophet. Non-Muslims recognize Muhammad as the founder of the monotheistic religion of Islam.

*Nasi*—See *Patriarch*.

*New Testament*—The second part of the Christian Bible including works unique to Christianity such as the four Gospels and other writings focused on Jesus as the messianic figure central to the many sects of Christianity.

*Old Testament*—The term Christianity applies to the first part of the Christian Bible, the Hebrew Scriptures, which represent the biblical canon of Judaism.

*Patriarch* (in Judaism)—Also known as *Nasi*, Hebrew for "prince," title for the leader of the religious life of the Jews who remained in Roman-ruled Palestine following the destruction of the Second Temple in Jerusalem in 70 CE. The Patriarch was head of the *Sanhedrin* (Jewish Supreme Court), who held political and economic control by virtue of Roman approval.

*Pentateuch*—Greek for "five books," the term refers to the first five books of the Hebrew Bible. See *Torah*.

*Pharaoh*—Title for a position of power that represented the political and religious ruler of ancient Egypt.

*Pirkei Avot*—The Hebrew title of a tractate in the *Mishnah* known as "Sayings of the Fathers" or "Sages." Together with the accompanying *Gemara*, it is included in the *Talmud*.

*Rabbi*—Hebrew title literally meaning "my master" or "my teacher" was originally applied to the great Talmudic Jewish sages but later was traditionally given to those who were qualified to make decisions on questions of Jewish law and supervise religious institutions, and, often, to heads of Talmudic institutions of higher learning. Today, the rabbi's functions also include giving regular sermons, engaging in pastoral duties and acting as Jewish representatives among other communities. Regardless of their duties over the past two millennia, rabbis have always tended to hold powerful leadership roles within Jewish communities.

*Rashi* (ca. 1040–1105 CE)—Hebrew acronym for Rabbi Shlomo Yitzchaki, an influential rabbinic commentator on the Tanakh and Talmud who was based in medieval France.

*Rebbe*—Literally, a Yiddish form of the Hebrew word "rabbi." As a formal title, the contemporary use of the term applies to the influential religious leaders of various dynasties or sects in Hasidic Judaism whose hierarchical leadership position is above that of the rabbis within their respective Hasidic group. In Israel, the Modern Hebrew version of this title is the acronym *Admor* (from *Adoneinu Moreinu v'Rabeinu*—"our lord or master, our teacher, and our Rabbi"), but outside of Israel, the title *Rebbe* prevails for the heads of Hasidic dynasties.

*Resh Galuta*—See *Exilarch*.

*Sanhedrin*—The Jewish Supreme Court during the Roman period in Judea that was comprised of 71 Jewish judges who served as its legislative body.

*Selichot*—Prayers of repentance and Divine forgiveness from sin traditionally recited in Jewish religious practice on the Saturday evening prior to Rosh Hashanah, the New Year according to the Jewish calendar.

*Sephardi*—Term that refers to the Jews of Spain and Portugal and their descendants, many of whom settled around the Mediterranean lands after the 1492 expulsion from Spain, with strong communities later found in Northern and Western Europe, and elsewhere. The word is derived from the Hebrew *Sepharad*, referring to the Iberian Peninsula and, in Modern Hebrew, means Spain. The language of Sephardi Jews was Ladino, a dialect of Spanish with influence from other languages and written in the Hebrew script. Ashkenazi Jews spoke Yiddish, which was also written using the Hebrew script. See *Ashkenazi*.

*Shabbat*—Derived from the Hebrew for "cessation," it corresponds to the seventh day of the Jewish week, Saturday, which, according to the Torah, is the traditional day of rest from the labors of work.

*Talmud*—From the Hebrew for "study" or "learning," the Talmud is a vast compendium of Jewish literature that consists of the *Mishnah* and the *Gemara*, Since there are two Gemaras—one from the rabbis in the Land of Israel and another by the rabbis in Babylonia—there are two Talmuds. The Talmud refers, therefore, to the Mishnah with either of the two Gemara commentaries on it, the Jerusalem Talmud (*Talmud Yerushalmi*), redacted in ca. 400 CE in Tiberias, and the Babylonian Talmud (*Talmud Bavli*), redacted in ca. 500 CE in Babylonia. The *Bavli* is considered the more authoritative of the two Talmuds and became the most influential source of traditional Jewish study.

*Tanakh*—Acronym for the Hebrew Scriptures, the Jewish canon of biblical texts that consist of the Torah (*Chumash*, or the first five books of the Hebrew Bible—Genesis, Exodus, Leviticus, Numbers and Deuteronomy), the Prophets (*Neviim*), and Writings (*Ketuvim*).

*Tannaim* (singular, *Tanna*)—Hebrew for "repeaters," the Jewish sages who debated the Oral Law between ca. 10 CE and 220 CE whose discussions were redacted into the *Mishnah*. They were followed by the *Amoraim*. See *Amoramim*.

*Tefillin*—Hebrew, also known from the Greek as phylacteries. Jewish boxes containing particular biblical verses (from Exodus 13:1–10; 13:11–16 and Deuteronomy 6:4–9; 11:13–21), the origin for donning them is traditionally associated with the biblical verse Deuteronomy 11:18. The boxes are tied on the left arm and over the head during weekday morning prayers.

*Ten Commandments*—See *Decalogue*.

*Tent of Meeting*—See *Mishkan*.

*Tikkun Olam*—Hebrew for "repair of the world" through good deeds. A Jewish value concept.

*Torah (Oral)*—Refers to laws not recorded in the Written Torah that, according to rabbinic tradition, was given by God to Moses at the same time

as the Written Torah at Mount Sinai and passed down orally until ultimately recorded in written form following the destruction of the Second
Temple in 70 CE in order not be forgotten. Among the major repositories
of the Jewish Oral Law is the *Mishnah* edited by Rabbi Judah HaNasi in
ca. 200 CE.

*Torah (Written)*—Torah in its written form, specifically the Five Books of
Moses, that is, Genesis, Exodus, Leviticus, Numbers and Deuteronomy.

*Yeshiva* (pl. *yeshivot*)—An institution for higher learning in Judaism.

*Yiddish*—Literally, "Jewish" in German, a Jewish secular language based
on medieval German and infused by Hebrew and Slavic vocabulary that
became widespread among Ashkenazi Jews in Central and Eastern Europe
from the Middle Ages through the modern period, developing a rich literature that embodies Jewish sensibilities. In writing, Yiddish uses the
Hebrew script.

# BIBLIOGRAPHY

Adair-Toteff, Christopher. "Max Weber's Charismatic Prophets." *History of the Human Sciences* 27, no. 1 (2014): 3–20.

Amsel, Nachum. *The Jewish Encyclopedia of Moral and Ethical Issues*. Northvale, NJ: Jason Aronson, 1994.

Anderson, Evangeline. "Engendering Leadership: A Christian Feminist Perspective from India." In *Responsible Leadership: Global and Contextual Ethical Perspectives*, edited by Christoph Stückelberger and J. N. K. Mugambi, 13–20. Geneva, Switzerland: WCC Publications, 2007.

Aronson, Robert P. "On Jewish Leadership." *Contact: The Journal of the Steinhardt Foundation for Jewish Life* 11, no. 1 (2008): 7.

Bakan, David. *Sigmund Freud and the Jewish Mystical Tradition*. Mineola, NY: Dover, 2004.

Baron, David, and Lynnette Padwa. *Moses on Management: 50 Leadership Lessons from the Greatest Manager of All Time*. New York, NY: Pocket Books, 1999.

Bass, Bernard M. *Leadership and Performance Beyond Expectations*. New York, NY: Free Press, 1985.

Bass Bernard M., and Ronald E. Riggio. *Transformational Leadership*. 2nd ed. Mahwah, NJ: Lawrence Erlbaum, 2006.

Bennis, Warren. *On Becoming a Leader*. Cambridge, MA: Perseus Books, 1989.

Bennis, Warren, and Joan Goldsmith. *Learning to Lead: A Workbook on Becoming a Leader*. Rev. ed. New York, NY: Basic Books, 2010.

Bennis, Warren, and Patricia Ward Biederman. *Still Surprised: A Memoir of a Life in Leadership*. San Francisco, CA: Jossey-Bass, 2010.

Bennis, Warren G., and Robert J. Thomas. *Geeks and Geezers—How Era, Values, and Defining Moments Shape Leaders*. Boston, MA: Harvard Business School Press, 2002.

Berenbaum, Michael. *Elie Wiesel: God, the Holocaust, and the Children of Israel*. West Orange, NJ: Behrman House, 1994.

Berkson, William. *Pirkei Avot: Timeless Wisdom for Modern Life*. Philadelphia, PA: Jewish Publication Society, 2010.

Berlin, Adele, and Marc Zvi Brettler, eds. *The Jewish Study Bible*. New York, NY: Oxford University Press, 2004.

Bianco, Anthony. *The Reichmanns: Family, Faith, Fortune, and the Empire of Olympia & York*. New York, NY: Random House, 1997.

Bones, Christopher. *The Cult of the Leader: A Manifesto for More Effective Business*. San Francisco, CA: Jossey-Bass, 2011.

Borowitz, Eugene B., and Naomi Patz. *Explaining Reform Judaism*. West Orange, NJ: Behrman House, 1985.

Braude, William G., and Israel J. Kapstein, trans. *Tanna Debe Eliyahu: The Lore of the School of Elijah*. Philadelphia, PA: Jewish Publication Society, 1981.

Brown, Erica. *Inspired Jewish Leadership: Practical Approaches to Building Strong Communities*. Woodstock, VT: Jewish Lights, 2012.

———. *Leadership in the Wilderness: Authority and Anarchy in the Book of Numbers*. Jerusalem, Israel: Maggid Books, 2013.

Burns, James MacGregor. *Leadership*. New York, NY: Harper, 1979.

———. *Transforming Leadership: A New Pursuit of Happiness*. New York, NY: Grove, 2003.

Chemers, Martin M. "Contemporary Leadership Theory." In *The Leader's Companion: Insights on Leadership Through the Ages*, edited by J. Thomas Wren, 83–99. New York, NY: Free Press, 1995.

Cohen, Harry A. *A Basic Jewish Encyclopedia: Jewish Teachings and Practices Listed and Interpreted in the Order of Their Importance Today*. Hartford, CT: Hartmore House, 1965.

Cohen, Norman J. *Moses and the Journey to Leadership: Timeless Lessons of Effective Management from the Bible and Today's Leaders*. Woodstock, VT: Jewish Lights, 2007.

Collins, Jim. *Good to Great: Why Some Companies Make the Leap… and Others Don't*. New York, NY: HarperCollins, 2001.

Cooper, Julie E. *Secular Powers: Humility in Modern Political Thought*. Chicago, IL: University of Chicago Press, 2013.

Couto, Richard A. "The Transformation of Transforming Leadership." In *The Leader's Companion: Insights on Leadership Through the Ages*, edited by J. Thomas Wren, 102–7. New York, NY: Free Press, 1995.

Covey, Stephen R. *Principle-Centered Leadership*. New York, NY: Fireside, 1992.

Crossan, Mary, Jeffrey Gandz and Gerard Seijts. "Developing Leadership Character," *Ivey Business Journal* (January/February 2012). Online: http://iveybusinessjournal.com/publication/developing-leadership-character/ (accessed November 24, 2015).

Donin, Rabbi Hayim Halevy. *To Pray as a Jew: A Guide to the Prayer Book and Synagogue Service*. New York, NY: HarperCollins, 1980.

Drucker, Peter F., and Joseph A. Maciariello. *Management*. Rev. ed. New York, NY: HarperCollins, 2008.

Edmundson, Mark. *The Death of Sigmund Freud: The Legacy of His Last Days*. New York, NY: Bloomsbury, 2007.

Eisenberg, Ronald L. *The JPS Guide to Jewish Traditions*. Philadelphia, PA: Jewish Publication Society, 2008.

Etshalom, Yitzchak. *Between the Lines of the Bible, Exodus: A Study from the New School of Orthodox Torah Commentary*. New York, NY: Orthodox Union Press, 2012.

Federation of Jewish Women's Organizations of Maryland. *Leadership Logic: A Manual of Organizational Know-How*. Rev. ed. Baltimore, MD: Ottenheimer Publishers, 2000.

Feiler, Bruce. *America's Prophet: Moses and the American Story*. New York, NY: William Morrow, 2009.

*Financial Times Lexicon*, s.v. "empathic leadership." Online: http://lexicon.ft.com/Term?term=empathic-leadership (accessed January 25, 2013).

Foster, Peter. *Towers of Debt: The Rise and Fall of the Reichmanns*. Toronto, ON: Key Porter Books, 1993.

Frank, Daniel H. "Humility as a Virtue: A Maimonidean Critique of Aristotle's Ethics." In *Moses Maimonides and His Time*, edited by Eric L. Ormsby, 89–99. Washington, DC: Catholic University of America Press, 1989.

Freud, Sigmund. *Moses and Monotheism*. Translated by Katherine Jones. New York, NY: Vintage Books, 1939.

Frymer-Kensky, Tikva. "Moses and the Cults: The Question of Religious Leadership." *Judaism* 34, no. 4 (1985): 444–52.

Gardner, John W. *On Leadership*. New York, NY: Free Press, 1990.

Gentry, William A., Todd J. Weber and Golnaz Sadri. "Empathy in the Workplace: A Tool for Effective Leadership." Online: http://www.ccl.org/leadership/pdf/research/EmpathyInTheWorkplace.pdf (accessed January 25, 2013).

Gilbert, Martin. *Churchill and the Jews: A Lifelong Friendship.* New York, NY: Henry Holt, 2007.

Glustrom, Simon. *The Language of Judaism,* 2nd rev. ed. New York, NY: Ktav, 1973.

Goffee, Robert, and Gareth Jones. "Why Should Anyone Be Led by You?" *Harvard Business Review* 78, no. 5 (2000): 62–70.

———. *Why Should Anyone Be Led by You? What It Takes to Be an Authentic Leader.* Boston, MA: Harvard Business Review Press, 2015.

Goodman, Nadia. "How to Become a Better Leader." *Entrepreneur,* July 31, 2012. Online: http://www.entrepreneur.com/article/224097 (accessed January 25, 2013).

Greenberg, Irving. *For the Sake of Heaven and Earth: The New Encounter Between Judaism and Christianity.* Philadelphia, PA: Jewish Publication Society, 2004.

Greenleaf, Robert K. "Servant Leadership." In *The Leader's Companion: Insights on Leadership Through the Ages,* edited by J. Thomas Wren, 18–23. New York, NY: Free Press, 1995.

Hersey, Paul, and Kenneth H. Blanchard. "Situational Leadership." In *The Leader's Companion: Insights on Leadership Through the Ages,* edited by J. Thomas Wren, 207–11. New York, NY: Free Press, 1995.

Hertz, J. H., ed. *The Pentateuch and Haftorahs,* 2nd ed. London, UK: Soncino Press, 1960.

"Hillary Clinton Answers a Rabbi's Question on Ambition and Humility." YouTube video, 4:34. Posted by "Hillary Clinton," February 4, 2016, https://www.youtube.com/watch?v=CWS21zYx6J8&feature=youtu.be (accessed March 11, 2016).

Hoenig, Samuel N. *The Essence of Talmudic Law and Thought.* Northvale, NJ: Jason Aronson, 1993.

Hoffman, Brian J., David J. Woehr and Robyn Maldagen-Yongjohn. "Great Man or Great Myth? A Quantitative Review of the Relationship between Individual Differences and Leader Effectiveness." *Journal of Occupational and Organizational Psychology* 84, no. 2 (2011): 347–81.

Hofstede, Geert. *Cultures and Organizations: Intercultural Cooperation and Its Importance for Survival.* London, UK: McGraw-Hill, 1991.

———. *Culture's Consequences: Comparing Values, Behaviors, Institutions, and Organizations Across Nations,* 2nd ed. Thousand Oaks, CA: Sage, 2001.

Holladay, William L., ed. *A Concise Hebrew and Aramaic Lexicon of the Old Testament.* Grand Rapids, MI: Wm. B. Eerdmans, 1988.

Hutton, Rodney R. *Charisma and Authority in Israelite Society.* Minneapolis, MN: Fortress Press, 1994.

ibn Paquda, Bachya ben Joseph. *Duties of the Heart.* Translated by Daniel Haberman. Vol. 2. Nanuet, NY and Jerusalem, Israel: Feldheim, 1996.

Jacobs, Rabbi Jill. "On Charisma and Jewish Leadership." *Contact: The Journal of the Steinhardt Foundation for Jewish Life* 11, no. 1 (Autumn 2008): 5–6.

Kahaner, Larry. *Values, Prosperity, and the Talmud: Business Lessons from the Ancient Rabbis.* Hoboken, NJ: John Wiley & Sons, 2003.

Kamin, Debra. "How Jewish Values Help Ivanka Trump Stay Classy." *Haaretz* August 11, 2015. Online: http://haaretz.com/jewish/news/1.670584 (accessed November 22, 2015).

Kampeas, Ron. "How a US Rabbi Opened Hillary Clinton's Heart—in His Own Words." *Jerusalem Post,* February 5, 2016. Online: http://www.jpost.com/Diaspora/How-a-US-rabbi-opened-Hillary-Clintons-heart-in-his-own-words-443969 (accessed March 11, 2016).

Kaplan, Mordecai M. *Questions Jews Ask: Reconstructionist Answers.* Rev. ed. New York, NY: Reconstructionist Press, 1966.

Kirkpatrick, Shelley, and Edwin Locke. "Leadership: Do Traits Matter?" In *The Leader's Companion: Insights on Leadership Through the Ages,* edited by J. Thomas Wren, 133–43. New York, NY: Free Press, 1995.

Kirsch, Jonathan. *Moses: A Life.* New York, NY: Ballantine Books, 1998.

Kolatch, Alfred J. *The Second Jewish Book of Why.* Middle Village, NY: Jonathan David, 1985.

*The Koran: Interpreted.* Translated by Arthur J. Arberry. Oxford, UK: Oxford University Press, 1983.

Kravitz, Leonard, and Kerry M. Olitzky, eds. and trans. *Pirke Avot: A Modern Commentary on Jewish Ethics.* New York, NY: UAHC Press, 1993.

Kushner, Harold S. *Overcoming Life's Disappointments: Learning from Moses How to Cope with Frustration.* New York, NY: Anchor Books, 2007.

Laufer, Nathan. *The Genesis of Leadership: What the Bible Teaches Us about Vision, Values and Leading Change.* Woodstock, VT: Jewish Lights, 2006.

Lewis, Hal M. *From Sanctuary to Boardroom: A Jewish Approach to Leadership.* Lanham, MD: Rowman & Littlefield, 2006.

———. "Making Leaders: How the American Jewish Community Prepares Its Lay Leaders." *Journal of Jewish Communal Service* 80, nos. 2/3 (2004): 151–9.

———. *Models and Meanings in the History of Jewish Leadership.* Lewiston, NY: Edwin Mellen, 2004.

———. Review of *Moses and the Journey to Leadership: Timeless Lessons of Effective Management from the Bible and Today's Leaders,* by Norman J. Cohen. *Shofar: An Interdisciplinary Journal of Jewish Studies* 27, no. 1 (2008): 111–14.

Lieber, David. L., ed. *Etz Hayim: Torah and Commentary.* New York, NY: Rabbinical Assembly of the United Synagogue of Conservative Judaism, 2004.

Locke, Edwin A. *The Essence of Leadership: The Four Keys to Leading Successfully.* Lanham, MD: Lexington Books, 1999.

Meyer, Michael A. *Response to Modernity: A History of the Reform Movement in Judaism.* New York, NY: Oxford University Press, 1988.

Milgrom, Jacob. *The JPS Torah Commentary: Numbers.* Philadelphia, PA: Jewish Publication Society, 1989.

Minkoff, Harvey. "Moses and Samuel: Israel's Era of Charismatic Leadership." *Jewish Bible Quarterly* 30, no. 4 (2002): 257–61.

Nadler, David A., and Michael L. Tushman, "Beyond the Charismatic Leader: Leadership and Organizational Change." In *The Leader's Companion: Insights on Leadership Through the Ages,* edited by J. Thomas Wren, 108–13. New York, NY: Free Press, 1995.

Neusner, Jacob. *There We Sat Down: Talmudic Judaism in the Making.* Eugene, OR: Wipf & Stock Publishers, 1977.

Nielsen, Rob, Jennifer A. Marrone and Holly S. Slay. "A New Look at Humility: Exploring the Humility Concept and Its Role in Socialized Charismatic Leadership." *Journal of Leadership & Organizational Studies* 17, no. 1 (2010): 33–43.

Owens, Bradley P., and David R. Hekman. "Modeling How to Grow: An Inductive Examination of Humble Leader Behaviors, Contingencies, and Outcomes." *Academy of Management Journal* 55, no. 4 (2012): 787–818.

"Paul Reichman." Online: http://www.shemayisrael.com/ozerhatorah/reichman.htm (accessed February 8, 2013).

Pope, Alexander. *An Essay on Criticism.* Online: http://www.gutenberg.org/dirs/etext05/esycr10h.htm (accessed January 11, 2013).

Rosen, Robert H. *Leading People: The 8 Proven Principles for Success in Business*. New York, NY: Penguin, 1997.

Rosten, Leo. *The New Joys of Yiddish*. New York, NY: Three Rivers Press, 2001.

Roth, Cecil, ed. *The Concise Jewish Encyclopedia*. New York, NY: New American Library, 1980.

Sacks, Rabbi Jonathan. *Lessons in Leadership: A Weekly Reading of the Jewish Bible*. New Milford, CT and Jerusalem, Israel: Maggid Books, 2015.

Sarna, Nahum M. *Exploring Exodus: The Origins of Biblical Israel*. New York, NY: Schocken, 1996.

———. *The JPS Torah Commentary: Exodus*. Philadelphia, PA: Jewish Publication Society, 1991.

Schein, Virginia. "Would Women Lead Differently?" In *The Leader's Companion: Insights on Leadership Through the Ages*, edited by J. Thomas Wren, 161–7. New York, NY: Free Press, 1995.

Scherman, Rabbi Nosson, ed. *The Stone Edition Tanach*. Brooklyn, NY: Mesorah, 1998.

Schiffman, Lawrence H. *From Text to Tradition: A History of Second Temple & Rabbinic Judaism*. Hoboken, NJ: Ktav, 1991.

Senge, Peter. *The Fifth Discipline: The Art & Practice of the Learning Organization*. Rev. ed. New York, NY: Random House, 2006.

Shapiro, Joanna. "How Do Physicians Teach Empathy in the Primary Care Setting?" *Academic Medicine* 77, no. 4 (2002): 323–29.

Smith, Houston. *Why Religion Matters: The Fate of the Human Spirit in an Age of Disbelief*. New York, NY: HarperCollins, 2001.

———. *The World's Religions: Our Great Wisdom Traditions*. New York, NY: HarperCollins, 1991.

Steinsaltz, Adin. *Biblical Images*. Oxford, UK: Rowman & Littlefield, 2004.

Tamari, Meir. *Jewish Values in Our Open Society: A Weekly Torah Commentary*. Northvale, NJ: Jason Aronson, 2000.

Telushkin, Joseph. *Hillel: If Not Now, When?* New York, NY: Schocken, 2010.

———. *Jewish Wisdom: Ethical, Spiritual, and Historical Lessons from the Great Works and Thinkers*. New York, NY: William Morrow, 1994.

Tigay, Jeffrey H. *The JPS Torah Commentary: Deuteronomy*. Philadelphia, PA: Jewish Publication Society, 1996.

Trompenaars, Fons, and Charles Hampden-Turner. *The Seven Cultures of Capitalism*. London, UK: Judy Piatkus, 1993.

Trump, Donald J., and Tony Schwartz. *Trump: The Art of the Deal*. New York, NY: Random House, 1987.

Twersky, Isadore, ed. *A Maimonides Reader*. Springfield, NJ: Berman House, 1972.

Visotzky, Burton L. *The Road to Redemption: Lessons from Exodus on Leadership and Community*. New York, NY: Crown, 1998.

Weber, Max. *Ancient Judaism*. Translated and edited by Hans H. Gerth and Don Martindale. New York, NY: Free Press, 1952.

Wiesel, Elie. *Messengers of God: Biblical Portraits and Legends*. New York, NY: Touchstone, 1994.

Wildavsky, Aaron. *The Nursing Father: Moses as a Political Leader*. Tuscaloosa: University of Alabama Press, 1984.

Wolak, Arthur J. "Alcohol and the Fate of Nadab and Abihu: A Biblical Cautionary Tale against Inebriation." *Jewish Bible Quarterly* 41, no. 4 (2013): 219–26.

————. "Australian and Canadian Managerial Values: A Review." *International Journal of Organizational Analysis* 17, no. 2 (2009): 139–59.

————. "Australia's 'Irish Factor' as a Source of Cultural Difference from Canada." *Australasian-Canadian Studies Journal* 25, no. 1 (2007): 85–116.

————. *The Development of Managerial Culture: A Comparative Study of Australia and Canada.* New York, NY and London, UK: Palgrave Macmillan, 2015.

Woolfe, Lorin. *The Bible on Leadership: From Moses to Matthew—Management Lessons for Contemporary Leaders.* New York, NY: AMACOM, 2002.

Wren, J. Thomas, ed. *The Leader's Companion: Insights on Leadership Through the Ages.* New York, NY: Free Press, 1995.

Zivotofsky, Ari Z. "The Leadership Qualities of Moses." *Judaism* 43, no. 3 (1994): 258–69.

# INDEX

Aaron 5, 17, 30, 61, 92
  delegation to 41, 103–4, 128
  envy and criticism of Moses 40–41, 65
  Golden Calf incident 81, 82, 111,
    112, 115–16, 125–26
  as high priest 113–14
  leadership skills and roles
    of 59, 112–16
  power sharing with 108, 109
  sons of 43
Abihu 43, 113n113
Abraham 16, 30, 90, 111, 118
Adair-Toteff, Christopher 42
Adenauer, Konrad 46
Agag 7
*aggadot* (singular, *aggadah*) 25, 129
Alexander the Great 48
Alexandri (rabbi) 102
Amalekites 7, 70, 107–8, 117
American Progressive movement 56
*America's Prophet
  Moses and the American Story*
    (Feiler) 47
Amidah 8, 129
*Amoraim* (singular, *Amora*) 64–65, 129
*Amos* (book of) 55
Amos (prophet) 42
Amram 5
Amsel, Nachum 54, 71–72
*anav* (humble) 70–71
*anavah* (humility), 72n52
*Ancient Judaism* (Weber) 42
Anderson, Evangeline 18, 41
Aristotle 71, 129
Arnault, Bernard 123–24
Aronson, Robert 57
arrogance
  as impeding delegation 101–3

in contrast to humility 63, 64–65,
    67–69, 85
*Aseret Ha'Devarim. See* Decalogue
Ashkenazi 65, 73, 88, 129
Attlee, Clement 29
Augustine (saint) 123
Augustinian 68

*Ba'al Ga'avah* 101–2, 129
Babylonia 23, 64–65
Baron, David 32–33, 97
Bass, Bernard 28
Behavioral Theory of
    Leadership 20
Ben Zvi, Ehud 66–67
Bennis, Warren 34–35, 38, 69–70,
    89, 120
Berenbaum, Michael 17
Berkson, William 13, 63–64, 106
Bhutto, Benazir 19
Bianco, Anthony 72–78
Boards of Directors, God as metaphorical
    embodiment of 7n13, 33, 85,
    101, 109
Bones, Christopher 27, 122–24
Borowitz, Eugene 55
Branson, Richard 123–24
Brown, Erica 49–50, 90, 91–92, 98
Browne, John 123–24
Buber, Martin 45
burning bush, Moses' encounter at
    90–92, 94, 98, 127–28
Burns, James MacGregor 17,
    27, 28–29, 37, 45, 46, 48,
    109–10

Caleb 41, 111–12, 117
Catherine the Great 18

charismatic leadership 1–2, 40–48, 79, 128
  genetics as secondary to ability to
    lead 42–43
  imperfection and 44
  limitations of 48
  misuse of 44
  Moses as charismatic leader 41, 44,
    45–46, 47–48
  romanticization of 43–44
  as unnecessary to effective
    leadership 46
checks and balances 48
*chesed* 54–55, 130
Christianity
  Christian Social Gospel 56
  Moses and Ten Commandments 93
  original sin 123
  significance of Moses to 14–15
*Chumash* 15, 130
Churchill, Winston 8–9, 13, 29, 46, 48
*chutzpah* 102, 130
Clinton, Hillary 79–80
Cohen, Norman 35–36, 94, 95,
    96, 103
Collins, Jim 70
compassion ix, x, 35, 50, 59, 63,
    80–86, 128
conflict resolution 110–17
Conservative Judaism 56, 75–76
consistency 21, 35, 89
contingency theories 20
Cooper, Julie E. 67–68
Covey, Stephen 50, 69, 94, 108, 112–13
Crossan, Mary 86–87
cultural differences, leadership
    and 1

*Daniel* (book of) 16
David (king) 19, 23, 59, 124
de Gaulle, Charles 29
Deborah (judge and prophet) 17, 18–19
Decalogue (*Aseret Ha'Devarim*; Ten
    Commandments) 96, 109, 117
  as articulation of values 97–98, 99
  defined 130
  as mission statement 92–94, 100
delegation 1–2, 6, 101–3, 107–9, 112,
    113, 117

Jethro's advice regarding 32, 103,
    104–5, 120–21
  making most of employee
    differences 2–3
  as source of strength fueling
    leadership 41
*Deuteronomy* (book of) 6, 55–56, 105–7
diaspora 21, 24, 88, 130
direct effects of leadership xiii
distributed leadership 103, 108. *See also*
    delegation; empowerment
Donin, Hayim 8, 16
Drucker, Peter F. 33, 44, 46, 48, 60, 89
Durkheim, Émile 43–44
*Duties of the Heart* (ibn Paquda) 63–64

*Ecclesiastes* (book of) 5, 7, 106
Edmundson, Mark 36
Eisenberg, Ronald 83
Eisenhower, Dwight 46, 48
Elazar (rabbi) 53
Eliezer (rabbi) 91
Eliezer (son of Moses) 5, 113n113
Elijah (prophet) 15
Elizabeth I 18
Elizabeth II 18
empathic leadership xii, xiii, 2–3, 86,
    125, 128
  defining empathy 49, 61
  developing empathy 61–62
  importance of empathy 50–61
  Moses as empathic leader 50–61
  Moses' defense of Jethro's
    daughters 58–59
  Moses' killing of Egyptian oppressor
    51–54, 57–58
  social justice movement 55–57
empowerment 1–2, 6, 28, 89, 103, 107–8.
    *See also* delegation; power sharing
Etshalom, Yitzchak 41, 45
Exilarch (*Resh Galuta*) 23, 130
*Exodus* (book of) 6, 18, 30, 53, 83, 95, 97,
    106, 107, 128
Ezekiel (prophet) 42
Ezra (the Scribe) 15

faith 29, 35, 47, 79, 81, 96, 100
Feiler, Bruce 47

female leadership 36
  examples of effective 17–19
  leadership as character-based instead of
    gender-based 18–19
FitzGerald, Niall 123–24
focus, maintaining and renewing
    leaders' 32–33
forgiveness 7–8, 82, 87–88
Foster, Peter 76–77
Fox, Nili S. 65
Frank, Daniel H. 71
Freud, Sigmund 16–17, 19–20, 31, 36,
    37, 100
Frymer-Kensky, Tikva 122

Gandhi, Indira 19
Gandhi, Mohandas 99
Gandz, Jeffrey 86–87
Gardner, John 21, 29, 31–32, 99–100, 117
Gates, Bill 40
*Geeks and Geezers* (Bennis and
    Thomas) 69–70
Gemara 13, 45–46, 130
gender 36, 41–42, 88, 128
  examples of effective female
    leadership 17–19
  leadership as character-based instead of
    gender-based 18–19
*Genesis* (book of) 14n7, 16
Gentry, William 61
Gershom 5
Gideon (prophet) 47
Gilbert, Martin 8–9
Glustrom, Simon 67, 72, 92, 101–2
Goffee, Rob 2–3, 39, 52
Golden Calf incident 50, 60, 70, 81–84,
    86, 110–11, 112, 115–16, 125–26
Goldsmith, Joan 120
*Good to Great: Why Some Companies
    Make the Leap…and Others Don't*
    (Collins) 70
Goodman, Nadia 60
Gorbachev, Mikhail 29
Great Man Theory 19–20, 28, 31, 36, 37,
    40, 100, 128
  dispositional-based component 40
  inspiring allegiance 40
  interpersonal skills 39

  Moses as heroic leader 40
  as obsolete or declining 37–38
  traits and qualities 38–39, 40
Greenberg, Irving 57
Greenleaf, Robert 127
Gurwitz, Leib 74

*hadith* 15, 16, 130
*Halakhah* 130–31
haredi communities 75–76, 78, 131
Harvey-Jones, John 123–24
*Ha'Tefillah* 8
Hekman, David R. 79
hereditary leadership 23, 42–43, 101
heroic leadership 37–40, 115, 128
  dispositional-based component 40
  inspiring allegiance 40
  interpersonal skills 39
  Moses as heroic leader 40
  traits and qualities 38–39, 40
Heschel, Abraham Joshua 56
Higgs, Malcolm 124
Hillel (the Elder) 116, 131
Hitler, Adolf 35, 44, 48
Hiyya bar Ashi (rabbi) 102
Hoffman, Brian J. 38, 39, 40
holiness 68–69, 72, 78, 80, 114
honesty 39, 69, 78, 80
Hosea (prophet) 55
Huldah (prophet) 17
humility ix, 1–3, 21, 49, 101, 103,
    106–7, 119, 128
  arrogance in contrast to 64–65, 67–69
  bad kind of 63–64
  Clinton, Hillary (on ambition and
    humility) 79–80
  defining 70–72
  holiness and 72, 78, 80
  meekness versus 70–71
  *mensch* and good character 85–88
  mercy and compassion 80–83
  modern rejection of 63
  modesty and 72–80
  Moses as humble leader 65, 70–71
  prophetic statements regarding 66–67
  Reichmann contrasted with
    Trump 72–79
  secular 67–68

Huna (rav) 102
Hur 108
Hutton, Rodney 43–44, 45–46

Iacocca, Lee 123–24
ibn Paquda, Bahya (rabbi) 63–64, 130
imperfection and flaws
    of Moses 6–8, 85
    revealing 2–3
indirect effects of leadership xiii
inspiring others 2–3, 30–31
    heroic leadership 40
    leadership vs. management 34
integrity xi, 39, 59, 76, 78, 80, 87, 89,
    120, 128
intuitive sensors, leaders as 2–3
Isaac (patriarch) 16, 30, 81, 90, 111
Isaac (rabbi) 91
Isaiah (prophet) 42, 47
'ish (man) 53–54, 58, 86, 88, 131
Islam
    Moses and Ten Commandments 93–94
    significance of Moses to 13, 15, 16,
        47, 48, 56
Ithamar (son of Aaron) 113n113

Jacob (patriarch) 16, 30, 90, 111, 118
Jacobs, Jill 41, 44
Jeremiah (prophet) 42, 47, 67
Jesus 15, 131
Jethro 119
    advice to delegate 32, 103, 104–5, 121
    Moses' defense of daughters of 58, 87
Job (book of) 106
Jobs, Steve 40, 60–61
Jochebed 5, 51
Johnson, Lyndon 21, 29
Jonah (prophet) 47
Jones, Gareth 2–3, 39, 52
Joshua 13, 111–12
    delegation to 41, 42, 70, 107–8
    leadership continuity and 117–18
    leadership succession and 101
    name change 118
    reticence of 47
    transmission of values to 108–10
Joshua (book of) 6, 6n7
Judah (tribe of) 16, 67–68

Judah HaNasi 13, 14, 106, 131
Judaism x, 10–11, 21–22
    charismatic leadership 41
    Conservatism and Orthodoxy in North
        America 75–76
    effects of Jewish education
        and upbringing on view of
        leadership 34–35
    haredi 75–76, 78, 131
    humanization of Moses 6
    Jews as humblest of all nations 66
    key features of great Jewish
        leadership 57
    Modern Orthodoxy 55–57
    original sin 123
    Reform movement 55–56
    Reconstructionist movement 56–57
    Renewal movement 56
    resistance to concentration of power 23
    significance of Moses to 4, 13–14, 16
    three daily worship services 15–16
    views of defense of Jethro's
        daughters 58–59
    views of Moses' killing of Egyptian
        oppressor 53–54, 57–58
Judges (book of) 18

Kabbala 59, 83, 131
Kahaner, Larry 78
Kaplan, Mordecai 56–57
Kennedy, John F. 29
Kerr, Steve xiii
Khrushchev, Nikita 29
Kirkpatrick, Shelley 38–39
Kirsch, Jonathan 6n7, 15, 16
kohanim (singular, kohen) 43, 104, 131
Kolatch, Alfred J. 123
kollel 78, 131
Koran (Qur'an) 15, 93–94, 131
Kravitz, Leonard 55
Kushner, Harold 15, 47, 83–84, 96n33

Lakish, Simeon ben (rabbi) 90
Laufer, Nathan 96–99
leadership
    as character-based instead of
        gender-based 18–19
    conflict resolution 110–17

context and 2
continuity of 117–18, 128
cult of 121–24, 128
cultural differences and 1
delegation 101–3, 104–5, 107–8
direct and indirect effects of xiii
effective female leaders 17–19
empowerment 103, 107–8
expectations of xii
four essential qualities of 2–4
lack of definitive listing of behaviors of
    effective 20–21
lack of effective training in Jewish
    organizations 9–10
with management skills 99–101
management versus 1, 10, 30, 31–36
mission statements 94–99
Moses as prototype for 22–26
need for principled xi
resisting cult of 121–24, 128
return to good practices 124
theories of 19–21
values 18–19, 109–10
visionary leadership 90–94
wisdom 108–10
*Leadership Logic: A Manual of Organizational
    Know-How* 10
leadership continuity 117–18. *See also*
    leadership succession
leadership succession 61, 101, 108, 109
Levinson, Bernard 105, 110
*Leviticus* (book of) 6, 43
Lewis, Hal 9–10, 20–21, 23, 31, 35,
    37–38, 41, 63, 64, 66, 67, 69, 70,
    103, 104, 107, 112, 119–20,
    124, 126
Lincoln, Abraham 46
Locke, Edwin A. 38–39
long-term thinking 32, 34, 96

Ma, Jack 123–24
Maimonides (Moses ben Maimon;
    *Rambam*) 13, 69, 71, 76, 131, 107n84
Malachi (prophet) 67
Maldagen-Yongjohn, Robyn 38, 39, 40
management and managers 31
    leadership and leaders versus 1, 10, 29,
        30, 31–36

leadership with management
    skills 99–101
Moses as leader/manager 30–31
trust vs. control 89
management theories 20
Mao Tse-tung 29, 44, 48
Marrone, Jennifer A. 79
Marshall, George 46
meekness 70–71
Meir, Golda 19
Men of the Great Assembly (*Anshei Knesset
    Ha'Gedolah*) 13, 14, 15
*mensch* 11, 85–88, 108, 128, 132
mercy 83, 85, 86, 127, 128
Merkel, Angela 19
Meyer, Michael 56
*Micah* (book of) 66–67
Micah (prophet) 17, 66–67
Midrash 4
    defined 132
    embellishments made to biblical
        accounts 87
    on burning bush, Moses' encounter
        at 90–91
    on gender and leadership 18–19
    on importance of good leadership 126
    on Moses and Jethro's flock 58–59
    on Moses' killing of Egyptian oppressor
        53–54, 57–58
    on Moses' leadership qualities 119
    on Oral Law 25
Milgrom, Jacob 8, 65, 70, 118
Minkoff, Harvey 42, 43
Miriam (prophet) 5, 17–18, 40–41, 51, 65
*Mishkan* (Tent of Meeting; Tabernacle) 33,
    104, 112, 132
Mishnah 13, 14, 22, 25, 45–46, 54
    on *chesed* 54
    defined 132
    link to Moses 13–14
    rabbinic authority and 22
    on wisdom 106
*Mishneh Torah* (Maimonides) 71, 76, 132
mission statements 6, 80–81, 89, 94–99,
    100, 121, 125
Mitzvot (singular, Mitzvah) 63–64, 66,
    130, 132
Modern Orthodox Judaism 55–57

modesty 66–68, 72–80, 85, 86, 128
Moses ix–xiii, 3–4
    absence of burial place 16
    age at beginning of public leadership 36
    anger of ix, 60, 69, 84–85, 125
    burning bush, Moses' encounter
        at 90–92, 94, 98, 127–28
    as charismatic leader 41, 44,
        45–46, 47–48
    childhood of 51
    Churchill on 8–9, 13
    defense of Jethro's daughters 58–59
    development of rabbinic tradition
        22, 23, 25
    dissuading people from emulating less
        attractive actions 87
    as empathic leader 50–61
    family life of 5–6, 51
    Freud on 17, 31, 36, 37, 100
    God's view of as leadership
        material 40–41
    goodness of 7
    as heroic leader 40
    historicity of 16
    as humble leader 65, 70–71
    imperfection and flaws of 6–8, 44
    influence on social justice
        movement 55–57
    killing of Egyptian oppressor 51–54,
        57–58, 87
    as leader driven solely by right
        motivation 87, 88
    as leader/manager 30–31
    as leader par excellence 6
    leadership of compared to Aaron 115, 116
    leadership of compared to
        Pharaoh 121–22
    meaning of name 51
    as mensch 86–87, 88
    as merciful and compassionate 80, 81
    as prototype for leadership 22–26
    resisting cult of leadership 121–22
    shaping of American identity 47
    significance to Christianity 14–15
    significance to Islam 15, 16
    significance to Judaism 4, 13–14, 16
    striking rock to produce water 7–8, 45,
        61, 85, 96
    study of, and one's personal
        background 4
    as timeless leader 126–28
    as transformational leader 28, 29
    using leadership theories to examine
        example of 21
    as visionary leader 30–31, 90, 91–92,
        96, 120–21
Moses and Monotheism (Freud) 16
Moses and the Journey to Leadership
    (Cohen) 103
Moses on Management (Baron) 32
Muhammad 15, 16, 132

Nadab 43, 113n113
Nadler, David 46
Nahman bar Isaac (rabbi) 102
Neusner, Jacob 23–24
New Testament 15, 93, 132
Nicomachean Ethics (Aristotle) 71, 129
Nielsen, Rob 79
Nightingale, Florence 99
Noadiah (prophet) 17
Noah 58
Numbers (book of) 6, 65, 67

Old Testament 133
Olitzky, Kerry M. 55
On Becoming a Leader (Bennis) 34
Oral Law 14, 25, 125–26, 129, 132,
    134–35. See also Mishnah
original sin (Christianity vs.
    Judaism) 123
organizational change and
    development 28
Orthodox Judaism 56, 57, 75–76. See
    also Modern Orthodox Judaism
    and Haredi
Overcoming Life's Disappointments
    (Kushner) 47
Owens, Bradley P. 79

Passover 83
patience 35, 50, 67, 81, 84
Patriarchs (biblical) 16, 36, 90
Patriarchs (Nasi) 17, 23, 126, 133
Patz, Naomi 55
Paul 15

Pentateuch 9, 15, 133
perseverance ix, 83–86, 128
personal values 1–2
Pharaohs 14, 18, 29, 30, 34, 45, 47, 50,
    51, 52, 66, 70, 84, 92, 100, 103, 110,
    121–22, 124, 133
*Pirkei Avot* 13, 14, 16, 22, 54, 106, 133
Pope, Alexander 7
power sharing ix, 2–3, 28, 41, 101, 103,
    107–8, 121, 127. *See also* delegation;
    empowerment
*Principle-Centered Leadership* (Covey) 50, 94
*Proverbs* (book of) 102, 106
*Psalms* (book of) 16, 69, 102, 106
purpose, sense of 60–61
pushing people beyond their
    boundaries 33

Qur'an (Koran) 15, 93–94, 131

rabbis 13–14
    burning bush, Moses' encounter
        at 90–91
    competing human drives 106
    defined 133
    humility and arrogance 63–65,
        67, 68–69
    Moses' killing of Egyptian oppressor 53
    Moses' motivation for action 87–88
    transmission of leadership from Moses
        to 22, 24–25
*Rambam* (Maimonides; Moses ben
    Maimon) 13, 69, 71, 76, 131
Rashi (Shlomo Yitzchaki) 95–96, 106, 133
Rebbes 41, 133
Reconstructionist Judaism 56–57
Red Sea 31
Reform Judaism 55–56
Reichmann, Albert 75
Reichmann, Henry 74
Reichmann, Paul 72–75, 76–79
    contrasted with Trump 72–79
    study of Talmud 73–74, 77–78
    study of Torah 73–74, 78
Reichmann, Ralph 75
Reichmann, Renée 77
relationship theories 20
reluctance and reticence 47

Renewal Judaism 56
*Resh Galuta* (Exilarch) 23, 130
resilience 47
Robinson, Gerry 123–24
Romans 64–65
Rosen, Robert 89–90
Rosh Hashanah 82
Rosten, Leo 86
Russell, Robert xii–xiii

Sacks, Jonathan 88, 110, 116, 119,
    125, 126
Samuel (prophet) 7, 42–43
Samuel bar Nahmani 126
Sanders, Bernie 79
*Sanhedrin* 23, 133
Sarah 118
Sarna, Nahum 51, 52, 82, 90,
    93, 105
Saul (king) 7, 19, 42, 124
Schein, Virginia 19
Schiffman, Lawrence 64–65
*Secular Powers: Humility in Modern Political
    Thought* (Cooper) 67–68
self-esteem 64
self-reflection 32–33
*Selichot* 82, 83, 133
Senge, Peter 103
Sephardi 88, 134
Servant Leadership xii–xiii, 127
Shabbat 77, 100, 134
Shachter-Shalomi, Zalman 56
Shapiro, Joanna 62
Shavuot 83
*Shemoneh Esrei* 8, 129. *See* Amidah
Shlomo Yitzchaki (Rashi) 95–96,
    106, 133
Simlai (rabbi) 66–67, 98n45
Simon the Righteous 54
Sisera 18–19
Situational Leadership Theory 20
Smith, Huston 15, 16, 24–25
social justice movement 55–57
sociopathic leadership 49
solitary reflection 33
Solomon (king) 124
Soloveitchik, Joseph 56, 57
*Song of Songs* (book of) 106

speaking truth to power 100
Spira-Savett, Jonathan 79
Stalin, Joseph 29, 44, 48
Steinsaltz, Adin 114, 115–16
Stone, A. Gregory xii–xiii
Sugar, Alan 123–24
Sukkot 83
sympathy 49, 50–51, 65

Tabernacle. *See Mishkan*
Talmud 4, 13, 21, 22, 23–24,
    67–68, 92, 95
    defined 134
    on arrogance 63, 102–3
    on humility 63
    on Jewish activity in Babylon 64–65
    on leadership qualities as
        learned 119–20
    on meaning of 'man' ('*ish*) 54
    on modesty 66, 67–68
    Oral Law transmitted by Moses 25
    Reichmann and study of 73–74,
        77–78
    on three daily worship services 16
Tamari, Meir 80, 82, 87–88,
    100–1, 107
Tanakh 4, 6, 14–15, 116n129, 124, 134
*Tannaim* (singular, *Tanna*) 134
*tefillin* 68, 134
Telushkin, Joseph 5–6
Ten Commandments. *See* Decalogue
tenacity ix, 21, 35
Tent of Meeting. *See Mishkan*
Thatcher, Margaret 19, 29
*The Cult of the Leader* (Bones) 122–24
*The Essence of Leadership*
    *The Four Keys to Leading Successfully*
        (Locke) 39
*The Fifth Discipline*
    *The Art & Practice of the Learning*
        *Organization* (Senge) 103
*The World's Religions* (Smith) 15
*Thirteen Attributes of Mercy* 82, 83
*Thirteen Principles of Faith* (Maimonides) 13
Thomas, Robert 38, 69–70
Tigay, Jeffrey 81, 83, 92, 105–6, 107n84,
    107n85, 113

*Tikkun Olam* 57, 134
timing, of actions 2–3
Torah 22, 66, 67, 82–83, 87, 93, 99,
    100, 119
    authorship of 9
    chronology of 52
    defined 4, 134–35
    on hereditary leadership 43
    on modesty 72
    on Moses as humble 67, 70n40
    on Moses' life and career as a leader 6
    Moses' role in transmission of 13–14,
        23–24, 25
    on Moses' tribe 16
    on mourning for Moses and
        Aaron 116–17
    rabbinic authority and 22
    Reichmann and study of 73–74, 78
    traditional number of
        commandments in 98
Trait Theory of Leadership 20, 38–39
transactional leadership 20, 27, 28, 128
transformational leadership 20, 27–29, 61,
    89, 128
Truman, Harry 29, 46
Trump, Donald 72, 73, 75, 76–77,
    78–79, 123–24
Trump, Ivanka 73n58
trust ix, 2, 28, 34, 89–90, 105, 128
Tushman, Michael 46
Tzipporah 5
*Tzniut* 72n52

values 1, 10, 11, 16, 18–19, 24, 32,
    45, 56, 57, 69, 76, 78, 94, 97, 98,
    99, 108–10
Victoria (queen) 18
vision ix, 6, 30–31, 32, 121, 125. *See also*
    mission statements
    articulation of 2–3, 89
    creating 89–90
    leadership vs. management 34
    lifting to higher sights 33
visionary leadership 28, 30–31, 57, 89,
    90–94, 96, 120–21, 125, 128. *See also*
    mission statements
Visotzky, Burton 107–8

Weber, Max 42, 43–44
Weber, Tod 61
Welch, Jack 123–24
Wiesel, Elie 6, 8, 56, 59, 84, 85
Wildavsky, Aaron 112, 121, 127
wisdom ix, 1–2, 22, 54, 67, 69, 86, 105–10, 113, 128
Woehr, David J. 38, 39, 40
Woolfe, Lorin 60–61

Yael 18
Yehudah (rabbi) 54

Yehudah ben Teima 106
yeshivot (singular, yeshiva) 73–75, 76, 78, 135
*yetzer ha-ra* 106
*yetzer ha-tov* 106
Yiddish 11, 73, 85–86, 88, 102, 128, 129, 135
Yochanan bar Nafcha (rabbi) 41
Yom Kippur 7

Zevit, Ziony 17–18
Zivotofsky, Ari 53–54, 58–59, 85–86, 87, 88, 91

Lightning Source UK Ltd.
Milton Keynes UK
UKOW01n2214210217
294964UK00001B/4/P